PHAKAMA

Making Participatory Performance

Caoimhe McAvinchey, Lucy Richardson and Fabio Santos

Illustrations by Andrew Siddall

Bloomsbury Methuen Drama
An imprint of Bloomsbury Publishing Plc

B L O O M S B U R Y

LONDON · OXFORD · NEW YORK · NEW DELHI · SYDNEY

Bloomsbury Methuen Drama
An imprint of Bloomsbury Publishing Plc

Imprint previously known as Methuen Drama

50 Bedford Square	1385 Broadway
London	New York
WC1B 3DP	NY 10018
UK	USA

www.bloomsbury.com

BLOOMSBURY, METHUEN DRAMA and the Diana logo are trademarks of Bloomsbury Publishing Plc

First published 2018

British Library Cataloguing-in-Publication Data
A catalogue record for this book is available from the British Library.

ISBN: HB: 978-1-4742-2361-4
PB: 978-1-3500-4445-6
ePDF: 978-1-4742-2363-8
eBook: 978-1-4742-2364-5

Library of Congress Cataloging-in-Publication Data
A catalog record for this book is available from the Library of Congress.

Cover design: Louise Dudgale and Holly Bell
Cover image © Hadrian Howarth/Contributor/Getty Images

Typeset by Deanta Global Publishing Services, Chennai, India
Printed and bound in Great Britain

To find out more about our authors and books visit www.bloomsbury.com. Here you will find extracts, author interviews, details of forthcoming events and the option to sign up for our newsletters.

For everyone who was, is and will be part of the collaborative act of Phakama.

CONTENTS

PART THREE CELEBRATION 195

LIST OF FIGURES

CONTRIBUTORS

Ananda Breed is reader of Performing Arts at the University of East London (UEL) and author of *Performing the Nation: Genocide, Justice, Reconciliation* (2014) in addition to several publications that address transitional systems of governance and the arts. She has conducted applied performance workshops in the Democratic Republic of Congo (DRC), Indonesia, Japan, Kyrgyzstan, Nepal, Palestine, Rwanda and Turkey. Breed is co-director of the Centre for Performing Arts Development (CPAD) at UEL and former research fellow at the International Research Centre Interweaving Performance Cultures at Freie Universität (2013–14).

Shirley Brice Heath is an American linguistic anthropologist, and Professor Emerita, Margery Bailey Professorship in English, at Stanford University. She has led groundbreaking research on rehearsal zones and studios of all the arts. She is the author of a dozen books and more than 100 articles and book chapters. She has taught at universities throughout the world, most notably Stanford University and King's College of the University of London.

Caroline Calburn, director of the Theatre Arts Admin Collective, Cape Town, initiated the organization in 2009 after a long history in theatre in which she has been a performer, theatre director, educator and facilitator. She has worked in both universities and communities, using theatre to forge a democratic and non-racial society. She lectured at the Drama Department at the University of Cape Town, and set up Iindiza, the Mielie Stalks Theatre Co. Caroline is a founder member of Project Phakama and has been involved since 1996.

Tony Fegan is a theatre director and arts learning practitioner. He was head of drama at Holland Park School, London (1977–85) before becoming artistic director of Battersea Arts Centre, London (1985–8) and pioneering the establishment of a Performing Arts Faculty at Queen's Park Community School London (1989–91). Tony was Director of Learning at London International Festival of Theatre (LIFT) (1992–2007) where he developed a wide-ranging and highly influential arts learning programme with national and international artists working with youth, community groups, schools and universities. He is a founder member of Project Phakama and has extensive experience in creating multilingual performance through artist in residence projects in intercultural and international settings. Since 2007, Tony is director at Tallaght Community Arts in Dublin, a participatory arts organization working closely with communities in Tallaght and across South Dublin County.

Charlotte Higgins is the chief culture writer of *The Guardian* newspaper, based in London.

Sara Matchett is a senior lecturer in the Department of Drama at the University of Cape Town and cofounder and artistic director of The Mothertongue Project women's arts collective. She is also an associate teacher of Fitzmaurice Voicework®. Her teaching profile centres around practical and academic courses and her research explores the body as a site for generating images for performance making.

Caoimhe McAvinchey is Reader in Socially Engaged and Contemporary Performance at Queen Mary University of London. Prior to this, she established the MA Applied Drama programme at Goldsmiths, University of London (2005–9). Publications include *Theatre & Prison* (2011), *Performance and Community: Case Studies and Commentary* (2013) and, forthcoming, *Applied Theatre: Women and the Criminal Justice System* and a monograph about Clean Break theatre company.

Corinne Micallef is a director specializing in making theatre with young people and communities. She created international exchanges in Germany, South Africa, Indonesia and Japan and has worked with the National Theatre, LIFT, ETT, Tate, Unicorn, MakeBelieve Arts, LYT and Theatre Peckham. She is currently Artistic Director/Joint CEO of Pegasus Theatre in Oxford. She worked with Phakama for thirteen years and was artistic director from 2014 to 2016.

Selloane Mokuku is an experienced theatre maker and a storyteller who has worked with and for young people at a local and international level. She is a Drama for Life Alumni, ShakeXperience Programmes Manager and a D Tech student at Tshwane University of Technology, South Africa. Her research area is in arts education. She is a cofounder of Winter Summer Institute and coproducer of the award winning African adaptation of *Animal Farm*.

Lucy Neal is a theatre maker and community activist, interested in how celebratory events act as a catalyst for change. Cofounder director of the London International Festival of Theatre (1981–2005), she is an active player in the global grassroots Transition movement and a Creative Associate of Encounters. Her recent handbook, *Playing for Time – Making Art As If the World Mattered* (2015) maps collaborative arts practices emerging in response to planetary challenges.

Lucy Richardson is senior lecturer and teaching fellow in Theatre and Performance Practice at London Metropolitan University. She has been involved with Phakama as coordinator, facilitator and documenter since 1997. Her research and practice in theatre explores the ethics and politics of participation and gives a platform to marginalized voices.

Fabio Santos joined Phakama in 1999 and was artistic director/CEO of Project Phakama UK (2005–14), for which he was awarded an MBE for Services to Participatory Arts. Previously he worked as an actor in Brazil with Bando de Teatro Olodum and trained as a dancer with the Joffrey Ballet School (New York), the Conservatoire of Dance (Holland), the London Contemporary Dance School and Circus Space (London). Performance credits include *4D* at London Contemporary Dance School, *Ovo* (The Millennium Dome, 2000), *The Lion King* (Lyceum, London, 2001) and *The Birds* (National Theatre, London, 2002). Fabio was interim artistic director/CEO of LIFT and an artist facilitator for Contacting the World International Festival and has contributed to *Playing for Time – Making Art as If the World Mattered* (2015).

Andrew Siddall, known as Sid, is an artist, teacher and project director working internationally in theatre, education and community settings. He has a particular interest in youth-oriented, site-specific events involving space transformation, installation and procession. He is a founder member of Phakama, Youth Engagement coordinator of Platform Shift+, Associate Artist with Tallaght Community Arts and guest tutor at London Metropolitan University.

Vidyanidhee Vanarase, known as Prasad, is a theatre practitioner from Pune, India. He has gained proficiency in three interrelated areas – direction, administration and management of Arts and Applied Arts. His versatility has enabled him to work with children, young adults, amateurs as well as seasoned professionals. He is a founder director of International Association for Performing Arts and Research (IAPAR).

FOREWORD

Mandla Mbothwe

When I first encountered Project Phakama, I had just graduated from the University of Cape Town as an actor. Since my inception at the university, my motive for being an artist had always been a sociopolitical one: it was not to be a superstar in television soapies or to be famous, but to go back to my community and use the creative arts as a transformative tool for the people. This seed was planted long before my professional encounters with theatre and my formal university training. It had been planted in me at high school where arts and culture activities and political activities were intertwined – arts were used simply for the mobilization, conscientizing and politicizing of the students and the community at large.

On graduating from an actor-based training that had focused entirely on the individual, joining Project Phakama resuscitated that motive. Project Phakama's motive of engaging with young people using the creative arts revitalized my spirit and understanding of an artist with a holistic purpose. Its approach of interdisciplinary work opened my mind to the true African aesthetic of performance. Its process of inclusive creation ensured the transferring of skills to all those who participated: this was exactly how the African tradition of storytelling and other forms of performances shifted from one generation to the next. Its approach and philosophy of Give and Gain in training, teaching and performance represented what still is central to my work and my leadership practices. Its emphasis on the maximum participation of the participants in creation; its interdisciplinary embrace in the making of the performance; its site-specific and public art aesthetics; its processional and mass community engagement spirit; its ritualistic engagement with the Elements of Life (fire, water, air and earth) in the performance; its dealing of 'The Now' through the fresh voices of the participants was a total reclamation of a stolen memory in African performance, both traditional and contemporary. Project Phakama's approach is one that heals, that develops through telling the stories that matter the most to those who tell them. It is a total resuscitation of an African spirit in the creative arts.

Now, twenty years later, most of these elements can be seen in my work and the way in which I approach processes of working with various people from a wide variety of backgrounds, skills levels, age groups, cultures and religions. It is engaging with the community at hand: a spirit of 'nothing about us without us'. The Phakama approach stimulated for me the notion that all are participants (facilitators and young people/community) and it is from this village spirit that healing in each and everyone of us is ignited.

Phakama: Making Participatory Performance acknowledges this experience and the experience and expertise of many who have and will contribute in making a Phakama project. But in addition to acknowledging it, it gives insight and access to this approach so that others may test and adapt it in their own particular contexts, for their own specific needs. There are many publications that document specific theatre histories or particular artists' approaches to making work. This book acts as testimony to the possibility of collaborative theatre practice with people from a wide range of backgrounds and experiences. It acts as a call to action. Phakama: rise up, elevate, empower yourself!

Mandla Mbothwe is a leading South African theatre director, producer, writer, researcher, teacher and curator. Previous positions include creative manager for Artscape Theatre Centre, Cape Town, artistic director of The Steve Biko Centre, Eastern Cape and of Magnet Theatre, Cape Town. Mandla has facilitated many participatory projects in a variety of educational and community setting. His multi-award winning theatre practice is highly collaborative, includes site-specific work and often involves many performers.

ACKNOWLEDGEMENTS

This book reflects the many voices of Phakama. We are indebted to all those who generously contributed to the development of this book.

Yorie Akiba
Olivia Barron-Beukman
Jake Boston
Danny Braverman
Caroline Calburn
Maylene Catchpole
Rose de Wend Fenton
Vunda Demula
Tony Fegan
Charlie Folorunsho
Tracey-Lee Gates
Juancho Gonzalez
Regis Gnaly
James Hadley
Liesl Hartman
Barbara Heinzen
Abu Jafor
Cedoux Kadima
Phyllis Klotz
Lance Kirby
Craig Koopman
Andrienne Kossa
Lora Krasteva
Salwa Lalaoui
Anna Ledgard
Jessica Lejowa
Luvuyo Mabuto

Jenny Macdonald
Kaori Matsui
Charlotte McCabe
Angela McSherry
Corinne Micallef
Rachael Mullally
Lucy Neal
Tabitha Neal
Kelvin O'Mard
Clinton Osbourn
Sam Quinn
Amitabh Rai
Beverley Randall
Julia Rowntree
Almudena Segura
Jean September
Mpotseng Shuping
Andrew 'Sid' Siddall
Katrina Smith-Jackson
Mildrett Stevens
Sumiko Tamuro
Ines Tercio
Alpha Thiam
Lineo Tsikoane
Nozuko Tsetsane
Stephanie White
Gemma Emmanuel-Waterton
Sharon Waverley
Benjamin Victor
Ali Zaidi

The board members – past and present – of Project Phakama UK and Project Phakama SA.

Ines Tercio who, in her role as Executive Producer, with Fabio Santos, grew Project Phakama UK into a pioneering participatory arts organization.

Bibi Francis (Operations and Project Coordinator) and Corinne Micallef (Artistic Director 2014–16) and Keiko Higashi (Director 2016–) who have continued to develop the work of Phakama in the UK.

Caroline Calburn and Theatre Arts Admin Collective for hosting the book research in Cape Town, South Africa in May 2015.

The South African practitioners, including Luvuyo Mabuto and the young people from Project Playground, who took part in our workshops to frame and articulate the exercises detailed in this book in Cape Town, South Africa in May 2015.

Accademia Dell' Arte and artists at the CrisisART Festival, Arezzo, Italy for hosting and participating in workshops to further test and share these ideas in July 2016.

We have been unable to contact every participant and collaborator who has, since 1996, contributed their time, commitment and creativity to this collaborative approach to performance making. This book is testimony to a collective understanding of Phakama.

Thank you to Susan Nicholls for transcription and to Harprit Sekkon, Kemi Aofolaju and Rachel Dolan for research support in the early stages of this project.

Thank you to Charlotte Higgins and *The Guardian* for kind permission to include Charlotte's feature on *The Street Is My Backyard* (2006).

We would especially like to thank Anna Brewer, Commissioning Editor at Bloomsbury Methuen Drama for her enthusiastic and considered commitment for this project; Queen Mary University of London (QMUL) for hosting Phakama as a company in residence since 2009 and Drama at QMUL for providing financial support for aspects of the research process; London Metropolitan University for part funding research in South Africa; Julia Rowntree for her insight, care and digital interventions; to our readers – the known (David Annen, Tony Fegan, Sue Mayo, Sara Matchett, Paul McAvinchey and Ines Tercio) and the anonymous – thank you for your rigor, insight and care.

To our families: Stuart Wilsdon; David, Charlie and Marian Annen; David, Finn and Molly McFetridge – thank you for your support and patience as we prepared this book.

To the founder members of Phakama, thank you for your vision, care and commitment. From South Africa, Gauteng – Raphael Mchunu, Benedict Mashiyane, Shirley Mzizi, Manya Gittel; from Limpopo – Donald Legodi; from North West – Pogiso Mogwera; from Mpumalanga – Jabu Masilela, Pandora Ngubane and Ephraim Hlophe; from Western Cape – Trevor Engel, Martin Ngwenyana and Caroline Calburn; from the United Kingdom – Tony Fegan, Beverley Randall, Andrew Siddall and Ali Zaidi.

INTRODUCTION

Phakama is an approach to making participatory performance that has been practised, for more than two decades, by a network of artists and arts educational practitioners from countries including South Africa, Lesotho, the UK, India, Ireland, Brazil and Argentina. The crucible for this practice was a month-long 'experimental residency' between artists and educators from South Africa and the UK, facilitated by Sibikwa Community Theatre and the London International Festival of Theatre (LIFT) in Benoni, a suburb of Johannesburg in July 1996.[1] Sibikwa Community Theatre Project was established in 1988 by Phyllis Klotz and Smal Ndaba. Over the past three decades it has played a fundamental role in supporting communities navigate the social, political and economic landscape of South Africa through training in the arts and developing indigenous South African work, committed to reaching new audiences locally, nationally and internationally (Roberts 2015: 17–42).[2] LIFT was established in 1979 by Lucy Neal and Rose de Wend Fenton and pioneered new territory in international co-production, site-specific performance and collaborations in and with communities (de Wend Fenton and Neal 2005). Two years after the end of apartheid and the first free elections in South Africa, this residency modelled a practical political commitment to international collaboration and the sharing of theatre-making skills that could be adapted and employed across South Africa. 'Phakama', a Xhosa and Zulu word for 'rise up, elevate, empower yourself', was both an articulation of the imperative for this work and what could be achieved together: it was a statement of intent, of *why* this approach to participatory performance-making matters.

During apartheid the cultural boycott meant limited opportunity for artists or educators to engage in sustained collaboration with international networks of practitioners. The Sibikwa/LIFT residency was a response to this: four British artists from diverse backgrounds with different disciplinary skills worked

---

[1] This was a phrase used by Caroline Calburn during a symposium, 'Making Tracks: Participation, Performance and Heritage', Pearse Museum, Dublin, 8 July 2016.
[2] For further information on contemporary South African Theatre and Performance see Middeke, Schnierer and Homann (2015); Anders and Krouse (2010); Hauptfleisch (1997); Fuchs (1990).

intensively with eight arts educators from across South Africa, engaged in a range of educational environments, from secondary schools to young offender centres. This group included, from South Africa, Caroline Calburn, Trevor Engel, Manya Gittel, Donald Legodi, Benedict Mashiyane, Pogiso Mogwera, Martin Ngwenyana, Raphael Mchunu, Jabu Masilela, Ephraim Hlophe, Pandora Ngubane and Shirley Mzizi and, from the UK, Tony Fegan, Beverley Randall, Andrew Siddall and Ali Zaidi. All involved were alert to the extraordinary circumstances they were navigating – a context where people were raw with the trauma of generations of violence, abuse and inequality while hopeful for the possibilities of a new political future.

Throughout the first two weeks of the residency, the group shared their practices and debated differing ideologies on education – particularly the relationship between the teacher and learner and how knowledge is shared and developed – as well as the role of the director and writer in the staging of new performance texts. Colonial histories, race and both deference and resistance to the authority of expertise 'brought' by the British artists infused every transaction. However, this residency was not a theatre training programme with an established methodology to disseminate from one group of 'experts' to another group of apprentices: it was a commitment to forge a new approach to working together where everyone's experience and expertise were acknowledged, where the hierarchical role of teacher and pupil was usurped by a practice of active learning from one another and where responsibility for leading and creating work was shared by all. Through this, a new approach to devising theatre was kneaded into being through experiment, dialogue, reflection and leaps of faith: an approach informed by a playful attention to site, honouring the stories of individuals and the principles of person-centred learning. During the third week of the residency, the original team of artists and arts educators – now facilitators – was joined by over fifty young people, from schools and townships around Benoni. Together, they experimented with this particular approach to making theatre to stage a promenade, site-specific performance, *Bulang Dikgoro/Open the Gates* (1996), that explicitly engaged with the hopes and concerns of the young people for South Africa at this moment in time. The project had become something different to the expectations of either Sibikwa or LIFT. It was raw, local and participatory. Both Phylis Klotz and Smal Ndaba from Sibikwa saw the potential for it to be led organically by an international group of facilitators. Recognizing the project's success Klotz said, 'We withdrew from Phakama because we saw that it had been taken on by you all. You didn't need us' (Klotz 2016).

Six months later, in January 1997, many of the original group of facilitators met in Cape Town to reflect on the learning from the initial exchange, to map adaptations of this approach in their local practice and to plan further opportunities to bring young people from across South Africa and the UK to work together.

Caroline Calburn's (2016) reflections on this meeting illustrate the ambition and determination shared by the newly formed collective of practitioners.

> We did detailed lesson planning and how to write up and think about lesson planning. We also worked on thinking about what Project Phakama was – we wrote up aims, objectives, mission statement etc and finally we each had to dream up and present project proposals. These became the projects we then did between 1997 and 2001.

Over twenty years later, the reverberations of this experimental residency continue to reach across time and continents, bringing an ethos of non-hierarchical collaboration into dialogue with local performance traditions. The cultural practice of Phakama has brought together young people in India to examine the inequities of the caste system in *The Phakama Way* (2002); more than sixty young people from six different European countries addressed issues of climate justice and water democracy in *Message in a Bottle* (2012); in *Tripwires* (2012), international considerations of the legal and cultural practices of censorship and freedom of expression were explored by a multicultural group of young Londoners; the experience of immigration, exile, the search for sanctuary and the negotiation of identity informed *Strange Familiars* (2003); in *The Street Is My Backyard* (2006) young people from Argentina addressed social inequality, pollution and the environment through a *murga* street carnival. Across this diverse range of subjects and contexts, all of the work shares a common commitment to attend to the 'processes, relations and happenings' (Schechner 2002: 1–2) that are in play when creating spaces where people feel equipped and compelled to make and share work with public audiences.

At various times, there have been formal administrative structures that have supported the network of practitioners engaged in the Phakama approach to making participatory performance. Some of these have been funded; some of these have been organized without financial support. In the late 1990s Caroline Calburn led Phakama South Africa with the support of Andrew Siddall. In the UK, LIFT hosted Phakama as a strand of its work between 1996 and 2007. In 2008 under the leadership of Fabio Santos and Ines Tercio, Phakama UK became an independent arts organization and charity and has been arts organization in residence at Queen Mary University of London since 2009. Beyond this, Phakama exists as a network of affiliated practitioners that come together to work on specific projects either locally or, occasionally, with international Phakama partners. Phakama in India, for example, was initiated in 2002 on an informal basis with its activities coordinated by Sanjna Kapoor, Prasad Vanarase, Meera Oke and Divya Bhatia. Later it was hosted for a short while by FLAME School of Liberal Education in Pune.

The formality of the infrastructure offered by both South Africa and the UK reflects something of the arts and education policy landscapes in both contexts where, particularly in the UK in the late 1990s and early 2000s, investment in participatory arts practices by funding bodies, both state and grant-giving, allowed for the development of an organizational infrastructure. In the UK, Phakama has been a recipient of core funding from the Arts Council England since 1998 with specific programmes of work supported by funders, including Youth in Action and the National Institute of Adult Continuing Education (NIACE) who supported *Strange Familiars* (2003–4). The European Union's Lifelong Learning Programme, Grundtvig, supported collaborations across four European countries (2002–4) and, with support from Youth in Action, another six European countries collaborated on *Message in a Bottle* (2011–13). The British Council has supported work in India, Lesotho and South Africa. Other major funders include Save the Children and the Esmée Fairbairn Foundation and many projects have been made possible because of grants from smaller, local organizations as well as sponsorship and in-kind support from businesses, universities and partners in each location.

A Phakama Book – Why This One?

The story of Phakama is one of the people who have committed to a very particular approach to making participatory performance. This book bears witness to them – to the thousands of people who have shared a political commitment to making work that is person-centred rather than autobiographical; that prioritizes a process of unfolding shared discovery rather than something pre-authored and directed; that promotes critical reflection on the inequities that shape daily life; and that demands an audience's engagement to complete the making of the performance.

Often histories of theatre and performance focus on people and practices associated with cultural institutions with an established international profile.[3] Phakama is different: it operates in a cultural economy that prioritizes the collective that makes the most of the opportunities of circumstance – the people, site and materials present – and culminates in performances, usually staged in non-traditional theatre venues with a limited run, often between one and three performances. This book seeks to further extend areas of theatre practice that are considered to be significant and the characteristics of the work that makes it so. Over the past two decades, Phakama participants, facilitators and partners have articulated, with clarity and conviction, the particular and considerable impact of this work on their personal lives and professional practice: of the intertwined relationship between making performance through collaboration and making sense of how to navigate a world fractured through unequal power relations. But what is it about Phakama that is so affective? And how can this distinctive

---

[3] For example, Rosenthal (2014); Turan and Papp (2010); Trowbridge (2013); Melvin (2006).

approach to participatory performance making be articulated and shared in ways that not only *accounts* for it but which *extends* the politics of this practice? This is the imperative for *Phakama: Making Participatory Performance.*

Until now, the Phakama approach has been disseminated through encounters between people when they make performances together: it has been a practical, cultural and social practice. There have also been a small number of reviews in national newspapers (Higgins 2006; Gardner 2009; Sichel 1996) along with chapters or articles which attend to aspects of this work written by facilitators and academics (Banning 2002; Banning et al. 2006; Richardson 2007a,b; Beswick 2016). Over the past two decades, ongoing conversation across the Phakama network considered potential appropriate forms to articulate and share practice. In 2009, Phakama UK hosted a week-long 'book residency' in London with international facilitators: Caroline Calburn (South Africa), Vidyanidhee Vanarase (India), Lucy Richardson (UK), Tony Fegan (UK and Ireland), Fabio Santos (UK), Ines Tercio (UK), Andrew Siddall (UK and South Africa). This was facilitated by Sue Mayo (Goldsmiths University of London) and Caoimhe McAvinchey (Queen Mary University of London). Throughout this week of reflection and debate a fundamental condition was reiterated – Phakama is a collaborative, participant-centred and intercultural approach to making performance and therefore the structure of the book and its range of contributors must reflect the principles of this practice.

In his essay, 'The Politics of Historiography: Towards an Ethics of Representation' (2005), Bill McDonnell prompts an attention to the

> ethics of representation as it might apply to the historiography of those theatres which claim to be radical, or to intervene on the side of the 'marginalised and oppressed' for which 'there is often a dearth of texts or other written sources' (128).

He asks: How are the histories of these practices researched and articulated? By who? And for what audiences? In short, what are the systems of power iterated in the acts of writing about theatre practices *with* and *about* participants? How are they represented? What role do they play in the co-creation of new understandings about specific theatre practices and the contexts they operate within? In the meeting with Phakama collaborators in 2009, these questions resonated throughout conversations about the as-yet-to-be-defined Phakama book. McDonnell offers some practical considerations in response to these provocations, drawing on the work of anthropologist Clifford Geertz and, particularly, social researcher Norman Denzin who argues for a 'thick description' of practices that 'reveals or permits the uncovering of underlying knowledge and relational structures... [it] goes beyond fact to detail, context, emotion, and webs of affiliation and micro power' (130). McDonnell extends this by considering sociologist Himani Bannerji's appeal for critical writing informed by 'taking sides, believing that things can change, fighting for it, an activist epistemology grounded in commitment' (136).

Phakama – whether in performance-making or book-making practice – commits to collectively authoring the 'underlying knowledge and relational structures' that shape our world and our experiences of it. Questions of authority, authorship, representation, knowledge, access and audience have continually informed the ways in which this book has developed – the research methodologies employed, its structure and tone – in order to reflect the international, poly-vocal, dialogic characteristics of the work. At various points in every Phakama performance process, different people take responsibility to lead aspects of it. This has also been the case in the development of this book. It has been a collaborative commitment, bringing together the experiences of a diverse range of people who are part of the wider Phakama network: participants, facilitators, producers, funders, academics and audience members from many different countries. Fabio Santos, Lucy Richardson and Caoimhe McAvinchey, as the authors who have taken on responsibility to shape this collective knowledge of Phakama, have strived to curate an ethical politics of representation which, as McDonnell (137) argues,

> might ensure that those who are the subjects of these histories do not remain silent extras in a tale told for others, but become collaborators in a respectful dialogue: one which sees the making of theatre, and the making of its history, as a unitary political praxis.

The practice of developing a performance or book project is, necessarily, always informed by the knowledge and relationships that individuals have with the material. For Santos, Richardson and McAvinchey, their very different relationships with Phakama over the past two decades have shaped their particular engagement with and commitment to the realization of this book.

Fabio Santos first worked with Phakama in 1999 as a guest movement/ drumming facilitator for *Be Yourself* produced for the LIFT festival that year. But, he said,

> my relationship with Phakama began before this. In 1992 I was a young actor back home in Brazil working with Bando de Teatro Olodum. Lucy Neal, one of LIFT's directors, was traveling the country seeing Brazilian companies and exploring the possibility of presenting their work. She came to see a rehearsal by Bando de Teatro Olodum and a relationship with LIFT was established. It was not until a few years later that Lucy reminded me of that initial encounter.
>
> In 1994 I left Brazil to study dance in New York. After a year, I moved to San Antonio, Texas to teach dance to children. Around the same time, and unknown to me, Bando de Teatro Olodum's artistic director, music director and choreographer started to prepare an original Brazilian play, *Zumbi*, for the

LIFT festival in partnership with Black Theatre Co-op with an entirely British cast. One evening in 1995 I got a call from Bando de Teatro Olodum's artistic director asking me if I would like to travel to London to choreograph a piece with homeless teenagers as Tony Fegan (Director of Learning for LIFT) was producing a parallel play, *Rush*, directed by Cyril Nri with homeless British teenagers based on the Brazilian book *Capitaes de Areia*. I said yes, travelled to London and met the LIFT team: Tony Fegan, Beverley Randall and, of course, Lucy Neal.

I remember being struck by the vibrancy of LIFT, how one was hosted, fed and looked after and, perhaps more importantly, how incredibly diverse the work they presented was – how much work by and with young people was at the centre of what was happening. This, combined with pertinent social-political issues being explored throughout the festival, took me right back to the earlier years working in Brazil with Bando de Teatro Olodum. Equally, working with *Rush*, took me right back to my time working with street kids back home in Brazil.

When the festival was over, I made my way to Holland to continue my dance studies there. A year later I got a call from Beverley Randall saying that Bando de Teatro Olodum (this time the entire company) was coming back to London to present *Ere* (their play based on the Candelária massacre where eight street children were killed by members of the police force in Rio de Janeiro's Candelária Church) as part of Out of LIFT '96. Beverley asked me if I would work as company manager and again I said yes and made my way back to London.

After Out of LIFT I decided to stay in London and as well as working as a performer, I also took part in a number of LIFT projects as an arts facilitator. Then in 1999 Tony Fegan invited me to be part of Phakama's *Be Yourself*.

My background working in Brazil with Bando de Teatro Olodum and consequently my involvement with LIFT and Phakama helped me decide to stop performing and focus on my growing passion for participatory performance with young people – to teach, direct, choreograph and facilitate projects where all I have learned from these three organisations informed everything I did.

In 2004, I took the directorship of Phakama UK and, for ten years, had the privilege of working with the most talented, ingenious, inspiring, resilient and socially committed people of all backgrounds and cultures. People genuinely committed to practice better ways of living together in the world.

Lucy Richardson joined Phakama in 1997. She was then artistic director of Lewisham Youth Theatre (LYT), a group that provides free participatory theatre projects to a diverse group of young people in south-east London. The newly formed Phakama invited her to bring a group of young people on a cultural exchange arts project that was to take place in London and South Africa.

I was doing the 'get out' for an LYT show at The Albany Theatre in Deptford, South East London with the production manager of The Albany, Sid. As we de-rigged the last light he turned to me and said: 'How do you fancy spending winter in Cape Town with a group of your young people.' Of course I said yes – but with little idea that the project I had committed to would extend into twenty years' involvement with Phakama and change the way I work forever.

The first project I worked on was terrifying. Whilst I had made several experimental promenade productions with Lewisham Youth Theatre, the work had always been director led and we mostly worked from existing theatre texts. With Phakama it appeared that no-one was in charge and no-one really knew what we were doing. However, the joyful spirit of the work, made palpable by the constant singing and dancing led by the South African young people, was infectious. As we worked I began to identify underlying processes that accessed the young people and their lives in a way that was new to me. It allowed them a voice and a platform for their ideas, experiences and hopes. It generated images and material that spoke powerfully of their shared experience and lent a depth to the final performance. It insisted that the work was made together in a true collaboration. It also, for the first time, made me realise that we were all – facilitators and participants – part of the work: I could not set myself apart but rather my experience, story, identity and talent needed to be shared alongside those of the young people. I had not to lead the room, but put myself in the room – I found this very empowering.

Since 1997 I have co-ordinated several of the big international projects and worked as a facilitator on others. I have also documented the work and been an audience member at many performances. I continue to work as a teacher and director elsewhere, but Phakama has altered my practice. The methodology can and should be used with any group of people engaged in a common endeavour. I try now to always remember, whoever I am working with or whatever work I am making, that the process needs to allow all participants ownership, equity and collaboration. In order for this to happen the ground always needs to be prepared, in the ways described in this book, before real creativity can flourish.

Caoimhe McAvinchey first encountered Phakama in 2001 while working at LIFT, where Phakama UK was based.

My first memories of Phakama are of walking into the LIFT offices one morning and the air was rich with the lingering smell of delicious food from a Phakama meeting the day before; of seeing Fabio – who always seemed to be standing – in the Phakama corner of the LIFT office, surrounded by young people who were all talking animatedly with one another. There was a great sense of people wanting to be together, of shared focus, of something-about-to-happen-ness. When I first saw a Phakama performance I then truly understood that all of these elements that seemed to be on the periphery – food, spending time together, being available to each other outside of rehearsals – were central to Phakama. After I moved from working as a cultural producer into academia, I continued to follow Phakama's work. In 2008, Phakama UK was making the transition from being a project housed within LIFT to becoming an independent arts organisation and charity. Fabio and Ines Tercio, the Executive Producer at the time, invited me to consider how Phakama could collaborate within a university context – how we could develop both practical support as well as structures for critical reflection about Phakama's practice and how, in turn, Phakama could contribute to the life of the university.

Phakama has been Company in Residence at QMUL since 2009 and during that time I've worked with Phakama to think about how it articulates its work and the extraordinary web of influence it has had not just on individuals across the world but on the organisational practices of partners, locally and internationally, from a residential care home in East London to the British Council in Cape Town. My research addresses the cultural politics of participatory arts practices, how these are documented and represented in different media (films, critical writing, evaluation materials, company websites). Working on this book has brought these interests together.

I am struck by the work of Miriam Jakel, who wrote her PhD thesis on the Guatemalan Community Arts Network and Caja Lúdica. In this, Jakel boldly declared herself a 'fan' of these practices and, rather than considering this a problem of objectivity, reframed this as a critical opportunity. She draws on the work of Fiske (1992) who declares that a fan is an 'excessive reader' who is 'able to move beyond simple fascination or adoration, and to develop a critical and in depth account despite emerging criticism, frustrations and antagonisms' (Jakel 2016: 24). So, I declare, I too am a fan – I am fan of Phakama: of the story of how it grew into being; of the people who continue to commit to this politics of collaboration; of a generous and demanding performance making practice that acknowledges and tackles the inequities that shape our world; of a cultural and social practice that creates new public spaces in which people gather to acknowledge and celebrate one another.

The social scientist Michael Pickering argues that experience 'is not simply equivalent to what happened to us. Experience is just as much about what we make out of what happened to us' (2008: 19). For us – Richardson, Santos and McAvinchey – these reflections on encounters with Phakama are not only descriptions of events but articulations of what we made of and from them: how these experiences have shaped our practices as theatre makers, teachers and academics which, in turn, informs the imperative for this book.

Over the four years of researching and writing this book, we have carried out archival research in the LIFT archive and with materials from both Phakama UK and South Africa offices. We have observed practice in the UK, South Africa and Japan. But the most important methodological approach has been the gathering of stories from over one hundred Phakama collaborators internationally. Pickering proposes that stories are fundamental organizing strategies through which we select, consider and articulate our knowledge:

> Stories are central to the ways in which people make sense of their experience and interpret the social world. In everyday life and popular culture, we are continually engaged in narratives of one kind or another. They fill our days and form our lives. They link us socially and allow us to bring past and present into relative coherence. (2008: 6)

Every Phakama participant, facilitator, project partner or audience member has a story about what Phakama is, informed by their experience. These stories are partial, skewed by perspective, relationships, time and memory. However, they are also richly textured, revealing insights into the Phakama process and, particularly, how people articulate their understandings of it, themselves and the world, through it. In addition to interviewing individuals based around the globe, our process has been shaped by the need to create spaces where people reflect on their experience of Phakama together: where understandings are articulated and shared with others who contribute and extend them through listening and responding to one another – they are generative rather than solely 'fact finding'. We held research conversations in London (December 2014, April 2015) and Cape Town (April to May 2015) and these, echoing Denzin's earlier comment, reached 'beyond fact to detail, context, emotion, and webs of affiliation and micro power' (McDonnell 2005: 130).

Phakama resists a linear articulation of processes and prescribed outcomes, of hierarchies of knowledge, skill and experience – it is about clearing ground for people to meet each other with different terms of engagement. In reflecting on this process, we bring together the voices of people who participated as teenagers in Phakama projects more than fifteen years ago alongside academics in Linguistic Anthropology and Theatre and Performance; supporters from the British Council South Africa are in dialogue with young people who have participated in the Spotlight cultural leadership programme in London. This book seeks to formalize and share testimony of an international network of people who have contributed to Phakama – to identify (but not limit) aspects of the *it-ness* of Phakama. It is poly-vocal, with layers of voices that engage in this work in different tones and registers – from reflection to critical enquiry; from the exposition of exercises to critical consideration on these in the context of a particular project.

Two decades of international practice offers an invitation to reflect on the reach and implications of Phakama. At a time when government and grant-giving bodies are increasingly requiring organizations to declare and account for the social and economic impacts of projects, this collaborative enquiry recognizes this but defines its own terms of enquiry within it: it reflects a longitudinal consideration of the slow, enduring, contemplative reach of influence of an approach to collaboration that is carried beyond a project into people's personal and professional practice. It is also a call to consider the detailed, negotiated demands of democracy – where spaces are created for people's voices to be heard, where consensus is not something given into but rather something worked towards by everyone.

Phakama Projects (1996–2016)

We have identified and detailed the range of Phakama's practices across the past two decades in different international contexts. While we have attempted to include all the work carried out under the Phakama banner, there may be other, smaller projects for which we have no formal record.

Project name	Year(s)	Summary
Bulang Dikgoro/Open the Gates – Sibikwa Community Theatre, Johannesburg, South Africa.	1996	This month-long 'experimental residency' for artists, arts educators and young people was the genesis of Phakama. The site-specific promenade performance, *Bulang Dikgoro/Open the Gates,* was inspired by the stories offered by the participants about surviving the day-to-day realities of life as a teenager in Benoni and their aspirations for life in post-apartheid South Africa.
		Funders and supporters included the British Council, Gauteng Arts Council, Cape Tercentenary Foundation and Mmabana Cultural Centre.
		Following this residency, each of the South African facilitators returned to their respective provinces and explored how they could implement and adapt these experiences in their places of work. Over the next six months a range of local projects took place in Gauteng, the Northern Province, the North West and the Western Cape. These projects and the young people involved became the backbone of the SA Phakama group for the next five years.
If I were in your shoes/ Izimbadada – Albany Theatre, Deptford, London, UK.	1997	Twenty young South Africans came to London to work with twenty young Londoners from LYT in a three-week 'experience and skills' workshop culminating in a performance as part of LIFT '97.

Project name	Year(s)	Summary
Ka Morwalo Ka Seatleng/ With a Suitcase in my Hand – Warehouse 61, Seshego, Northern Province (now Limpopo) South Africa.	1997	This week-long residential in Seshego brought together British and South African teams working with seventy young people from the North West, Western Cape, Gauteng and the Northern Provinces. The show was performed in a vast warehouse, home to BAAGI Arts under the leadership of Donald Legodi, to audiences of 250 each night. *Ka Morwalo Ka Seatleng* is the Pedi translation of 'a suitcase in my hand'.
Met'n Sak Onner die Blad/With a Suitcase in My Hand – Gilray Scout Camp, Grassy Park, Cape Town South Africa.	1998	One hundred young people from across South Africa and London joined Western Cape participants to explore their stories and responses to a series of cultural visits made in Cape Town including Robben Island, District Six and Cape Point.
		The artist tutor team consisted of twenty-four people from diverse cultural backgrounds with skills in a range of arts disciplines and experience in arts education in the formal and informal sector.
		Met'n Sak Onner die Blad, a large-scale, site-specific performance featuring fire, dance, theatre and song, focused upon memory and reconciliation.
		Following this residency all participants returned to their own communities to organize and facilitate short projects, informed by the Phakama approach.
		Met'n Sak Onner die Blad is the Afrikaans translation of 'with a suitcase in my hand'.
Be Yourself – Tricycle Theatre, London, UK.	1999	Ten young Londoners and twenty young South Africans from Gauteng, the North West and Northern Provinces and the Western Cape came together to explore London over an intensive three-week period.
		At the heart of *Be Yourself* lay the idea of looking at London through the eyes of another. A series of cultural tours provoked a debate about institutions and the imaginary cultural maps people hold in their heads of cities in foreign countries. Through discussions, drawings, soundscapes and choreography, the South Africans examined their preconceptions of London, while the Londoners used the same methods to imagine how their city might appear to a newcomer. The show was performed as part of LIFT '99.

Project name	Year(s)	Summary
Wololo! Y2K Kom Verby (Battswood Arts Centre, Cape Town, South Africa)		A local project of forty young Cape Town Phakama participants that explored critical moments in their lives which fundamentally changed them – attended by an audience of one hundred; funded by the British Council.
Call me Not a Woman Phase 1 – local projects including two houses and a road in Genadendal, a Moravian village in Western Cape, South Africa. Phase 2 – international project in two homes in Mmabatho, North West, South Africa.	2000	The aim of the project was to explore the role women have played in South African society and the part they have played in shaping their communities in the new South Africa. Facilitators from South Africa, Great Britain, Namibia, Mozambique, Mauritius and Lesotho took part in a residential training programme at Mmabana Cultural Centre, Mmabatho, in the North West Province of South Africa. The international project culminated in a ninety-minute performance by sixty young people set in two homes on either side of a highway. This project was funded by LIFT and the British Council.
The Robben Island Freedom Project – Robben Island Museum, Cape Town, Western Cape, South Africa.	2001	Commissioned by the Robben Island Museum, this was the first public performance by young people to take place on the infamous prison island off the coast of Cape Town. Thirty young people and their tutors from Phakama groups all over South Africa came to stay on Robben Island where they worked closely with an ex-prisoner and staff of the Robben Island Museum. A group of young people living on the Island also joined the project. The young people came from different regions and spoke ten of South Africa's national languages. Four months of devising between artists and young people from around the country culminated in performances on the island for Freedom Day and explored the understanding of Freedom and Responsibility.
The Phakama Way – Garware Bal Bhavan, a children's recreation centre, Pune, India.	2002	*The Phakama Way* was a month-long training course held in Pune, India, and hosted by the Prithvi Theatre, Mumbai. Artists from Prithvi joined *The Robben Island Freedom Project* and collaborated on other South African projects throughout 2002. As a result of their experiences they set up this course to help arts workers in addressing some of the barriers between the different Indian castes.

Project name	Year(s)	Summary
		Over thirty community leaders, theatre makers, university lecturers and school teachers gathered to share ideas, exchange processes and develop a locally based methodology for implementing Phakama philosophies in India, with the guidance of experienced facilitators from South Africa and the UK. This project culminated in a site-specific performance with young people from Mumbai.
Grundtvig: Agüime Centre for Culture, Agüime, Gran Canaria, 2002; Olsen Centre for Theatre Research, Olsen, Poland, 2003; Amadora Social Centre for Learning, Lisbon, Portugal, 2003; The Horniman Museum and Gardens and Dulwich College, London, UK, 2004.	2002–4	In 2002, Project Phakama UK embarked on a two-year research project with cultural and community organizations in Germany, Gran Canaria, Northern Ireland, Poland and Portugal to explore, 'How can art act as a catalyst for social inclusion and shared inter-cultural learning?' Funded by the EU Grundtvig programme, it had four phases of enquiry: in Gran Canaria, exploring the similarities and differences between work undertaken in each country; in Poland, focusing on work undertaken in rural communities; the third phase in Portugal enabled participants to experience working in different community contexts; and finally, Phakama participants hosted learners from each country in London.
The Child I Curry – Morija Morija Museum, Lesotho; Maitisong Festival, Gaborone, Botswana.	2003–4	This three-phase project involved young people and practitioners from Botswana, Lesotho, the UK, Mauritius, Mozambique, Namibia and South Africa. Phase 1 was hosted by Project Phakama Lesotho and involved seventy young people and twelve facilitators. In phase 2, each country established local initiatives designed to develop Phakama projects throughout the community. Phase 3, hosted by Project Phakama Botswana, brought all the groups back together to deliver a performance at the Gaborone International Festival. Four hundred young people took part in this creative, critical exploration of social justice, good governance and human rights.

Project name	Year(s)	Summary
Strange Familiars – National Children's Home, London, UK. *Breaking the Glass Box –* Horniman Museum and Gardens, Forest Hill, London, UK, 2004.	2003–4	*Strange Familiars* involved young refugees and unaccompanied asylum seekers in an exploration of the strange and the familiar of the city of London. The project was developed in response to the increasing numbers of isolated young asylum seekers in the city. Working in collaboration with local refugee organizations and the Refugee Council, the project assisted young refugees and asylum seekers in building confidence and life skills. It was funded by NIACE. The first phase of the project included ten months of weekly workshops, drawing on both traditional ethnic and contemporary art forms and culminated in a week-long residency at The National Children's Home in North London and a performance as part of LIFT's Family Friendly Season, 2003. In the second phase, the *Strange Familiars* group worked with LYT to create a performance *Breaking the Glass Box*, at the Horniman Museum and Gardens in south-east London.
Creative Skills for Life *Postcards from Here* – the steps of St Paul's Cathedral, parks, cemeteries, markets, alleys and streets of the eastern central London, UK.	2005–6	The *Creative Skills for Life* programme built upon the foundations and network of social support developed during *Strange Familiars,* enhancing young refugees and asylum seekers' interpersonal and practical skills. The programme culminated in a promenade performance, *Postcards from Here*. The Arts Council England and Trinity College Arts Awards accredited the programme.
Well... Whose Coin Is It, Anyway? (!) – Foundation for Liberal and Management Education Pune, India and Contact Theatre, Manchester, UK, 2006.	2005–6	Project Phakama India was one of the twelve international companies selected for the Contacting the World Festival (CTW) 2006. This international exchange project for young theatre makers is produced by Contact Theatre in Manchester, UK. CTW brings together young people from across geographical, cultural and social divides and unites them through the common aim of devising new performance work born out of conversation and sharing of cultural perspectives and experiences.

Project name	Year(s)	Summary
		Project Phakama India collaborated with Nine, a young people's theatre company from Manchester.
		Well… Whose Coin Is It, Anyway? (!) examined globalization from an Indian perspective by considering two polemic experiences: the boom of the Business Process Outsourcing industry that provides jobs and fast-cash to mainly young people employed in call centres and agencies that facilitate global capitalism; and the despair of mainly older agricultural workers who were unable to pay off their debts and committed suicide. The play set these two distinct and disparate economies side by side.
South America/UK exchange. *The Street Is My Backyard* – Fundación Defensores del Chaco, Buenos Aires, Argentina. *Connections beyond Frontiers* – Vila Velha theatre, Salvador, Brazil.	2006–8	This training programme featured international exchanges with emerging and established artists, community leaders and young participants from Fundación Defensores del Chaco (Argentina), Cia Novos Novos (Brazil) and Project Phakama (UK). The project supported the development of arts skills in different community settings, and culminated in two large-scale site-specific performances.
		The first phase of the South America/UK partnership took place over three weeks in Argentina, involving fifty young people and professional artists from the three countries. This culminated in a public performance, *The Street Is My Backyard*, presented to an audience of four hundred.
		The second phase of the project, staged in Salvador, Brazil, involved young people from the participating organizations and from Phakama South Africa. After a two-week process exploring differences and similarities, links and barriers, a promenade performance, *Connections Beyond Frontiers* was presented at the Vila Velha theatre.
Eat London – Trafalgar Square, London, UK.	2007	Project Phakama UK was one of the thirteen groups that took part in *Eat London*, an edible installation created by London communities with food artist, Alicia Rios and architect, Barbara Ortiz. Over three months, artists, designers and cooks, worked with community groups and local organizations to design and build a

Project name	Year(s)	Summary
		three-dimensional representation of central London out of food. Each group was responsible for one square of the map and, through observation, discussion and experiment, they turned their food into bricks, glass, steel and tarmac. *Eat London* culminated in a feast in Trafalgar Square, where the city was built, devoured and digested by London's citizens and visitors.
When Time Is Not – The Liverpool Institute of Performing Arts (LIPA), UK.	2008	Project Phakama UK was one of the twelve international youth arts organizations taking part in Contacting the World 2008. Over a period of twelve months, Phakama collaborated with its twin company CAT (the Creative Arts Team, New York) and produced *When Time Is Not* as part of Liverpool's Capital of Culture celebrations. Funded by Contact, ACE and the British Council.
The Trashcatchers Ball – Stratford Park, Stratford, London, UK.	2008	*The Trashcatchers Ball* was devised in collaboration with twenty young participants, creating beauty from rubbish through the design, fabrication and animation of sculptures and costumes from discarded materials. Through public workshops and the project's finale, the ball, audiences were encouraged to reassess the beauty and use of the things that get thrown away and imagine a world where the lack of resources makes this an imperative. The event was part of LIFT 2008.
Move – Cape Town Central Station, Observatory Station and surrounding streets, Theatre Arts Admin Collective, Cape Town, South Africa.	2009	*Move* explored the reasons for people moving – homes, cities, countries – and involved moving the audience by train, taxi and bus with a stop off for a cup of soup in a pop-up soup kitchen under a bridge. The performance which began on Platform 24 of the central Cape Town Station, culminated in an interactive performance in the Methodist Church Hall. It was performed by Cape Town – based Phakama facilitators who had been involved in Project Phakama between 1996 and 2009. *Move* was funded and presented by Cape 09.

Project name	Year(s)	Summary
Mutu – a high school in Maitland, Cape Town, South Africa.		*Mutu* was a reflection by the young people in Phakama South Africa on the material and political conditions of life. The project took place in Maitland, a semi-industrial, racially mixed suburb which houses a large percentage of the African refugees in Cape Town. *Mutu* is a Setswana Word meaning 'human', referencing ubuntu, a Bantu expression of 'personhood', humanity or humanness.
Work in Progress – FLAME School of Liberal Education, Pune, India; Contact Theatre, Manchester, UK; Queen Mary University of London, UK.	2010	Hosted by FLAME School of Liberal Education, this on campus project was a three-month process wherein participants looked at their own experiences of life. The idea of 'Life in Progress' culminated into a devised performance of 'Work in Progress'. Expressing oneself was an inevitable part of this work. Participants worked with real-life situations and real-life stories. They played with their own stories and looked at them as dramatic texts. The devised piece was performed at Pune, CTW in 2010 and Queen Mary University of London.
Trashcatchers Carnival – Tooting High Street, London, UK.	2010	*The Trashcatchers Carnival* was a stunning procession bringing together schools and community groups from across Tooting in south-west London and featured mechanical sculptures and costumes created out of trash! Project Phakama UK, Emergency Exit Arts and Transition Town Tooting worked with community groups for over a year exploring humans' relationship to Earth, creating beauty from rubbish and looking at change in how we live, where we live. Over one thousand people took part. This project was a Tipping Point Commission, supported by a range of partners including Arts Council England, Wandsworth Council, the Big Give/Reed Foundation, Tooting Town Centre, Tooting Schools Cluster and Tooting Parents Teachers Association.
The World At My Feet – British International School, Jakarta, Indonesia.	2010	*The World At My Feet* was a collaboration between Project Phakama UK, Teater Tetas and the British International School (BIS) Jakarta. For two months both Project Phakama and Teater

Project name	Year(s)	Summary
		Tetas independently explored ideas about recycled worlds, stories and dreams and joined together for a fourteen-day residency at the BIS Jakarta to create a performance at BIS, Gedung Kesenian Jakarta and Trento Free School. The project was supported by the BIS, World Theatre and Gedung Kesenian Jakarta.
From Somewhere to Nowhere – Orpheus Centre, Godstone, Surrey, UK.	2010	The Orpheus Centre is a residential arts and training centre for young disabled artists. During a two-week residency, Phakama's and Orpheus's young artists and facilitators brought together shared experiences and stories that became a short exploratory performance about journeys and dreams full of puppetry, music and audience interaction.
Tripwires – The Pavilion, Mile End Park, London, UK.	2011	*Tripwires* was a training programme, developed in collaboration with Index on Censorship, using the arts to explore and express ideas of freedom of expression, self-censorship and offence. Each week there was a different theme – music, satire, acrobatics, banned plays, film, photography. Guest artists included Belarus Free Theatre, the Burmese artist Htein Lin and young artists from Georgia, Abkhazia and Afghanistan.
		Tripwires explored physically and intellectually what freedom of expression means to young Londoners today. The project culminated in an interactive multimedia performance about censorship and freedom of expression where participants asked the question: Where do you draw the line?
Message in a Bottle and *Tributaries* – Queen Mary University of London and local primary schools, UK.	2011–13	*Message in a Bottle* was an international exchange project bringing together young people from six European countries to investigate, creatively and practically, how water (or the lack of it) has an impact on their lives. Water was used as a metaphor for cultural exchange, creative dialogues and environmental learning.
		In 2011, young people from the UK, The Basque Country, Poland, Portugal, Turkey and Ireland collaborated through virtual dialogue, exchange visits and local small-scale performances. In 2012 Phakama UK hosted sixty-four young people

Project name	Year(s)	Summary
		from all the six countries over two weeks to create a site-specific performance inspired by all the learning that took place.
		After two international exchanges in London, Phakama embarked on a third phase of the project entitled *Tributaries*. In 2013 Phakama worked with archaeologist Mike Webber and a team of young artists investigating artefacts, stories and histories of the river Thames and its tributaries. The young artists then turned the findings into music, poems, drama, painting, etc. This format was implemented through science and arts workshops at Guardian Angels Primary School in East London.
		Project funders include Youth in Action and Natwest Community Fund.
Velela! Pop Up Festival – Queen Mary University of London, UK.	2012	*Velela!* was a two-week creative residency in London for young artists and involved voices, talents, expertise and contributions from almost one hundred young people from around the world.
		Funders include ACE, Youth in Action, Natwest Community Fund, QMUL.
The Edible Garden – Mile End Park, London, UK. *The Edible Garden: Recipes for Romance* – Hawthorn Green Care Home, London, UK. *The Edible Garden: Tasty Trilogy.* *The Edible Garden: Bitesize* – The Rosary, Bridgewater; The Winsor Nursing Home, Minehead; Ivydene Residential and Nursing Home, Plymouth;	2011–16	In 2011, in partnership with the East End Women's Institute and Mile End Park, Growing Zone and in collaboration with local daughters, mothers and grandmothers, Phakama grew an edible garden with and for the whole community through growing, cooking, storytelling and performance events.
		In 2013 Phakama embarked on another phase of the project and working with students at Newham Sixth Form College, residents at Hawthorn Green Care Home and Stepney City Farm to grow a garden and share stories with one another from their lives to create *Recipes for Romance*.
		In 2014 Phakama was commissioned by Sanctuary Housing to deliver *The Edible Garden* project in three care homes as part of Sanctuary's Shine! programme – an initiative which promotes the use of arts in residential care homes, highlighting residents' talents, rather than their limitations.

Project name	Year(s)	Summary
Fernihurst Nursing Home, Exmouth; Greenslades Nursing Home, Exeter; Forest Dene Residential Care Home, London; Rowanweald Nursing Home, London.		In 2015 Phakama was commissioned to run *The Edible Garden* in eight different care homes, six in the south-west of England and two in London as part of Sanctuary Housing programme, Shine! This meant that the project had to run in Bitesize chunks, working in each home over two days, with local schools that the home had been paired with. In intergenerational pairs, participants worked collaboratively and creatively through story and with music.
Trashcatchers at Morley – Morley College, London, UK.	2013	Phakama UK teamed up with Morley College to work with an intergenerational group of twenty participants to stage a version of *The Trashcatchers Ball*. Through workshops, a creative residency during Morley's Summer School and the project's finale, participants and audiences were encouraged to reassess the beauty and use of the things that get thrown away and imagine a world where the lack of resources make this an imperative. This was supported by Youth in Action.
Spotlight – Queen Mary University of London, UK.	2013–15	*Spotlight* was a major training and employment programme for young people in the arts, supported during various phases by Esmée Fairbairn, Youth in Action, CCSkills Creative Employment Programme and QMUL.
		Spotlight was borne out of Phakama UK's desire to equip the next generation of artists and producers with the practical and social skills needed to access the industry with knowledge, confidence and experience.
		In 2014 Phakama offered fifteen young people who were not in employment, education or training, and who had been claiming benefits, the opportunity to take part in the Spotlight programme – a combination of extensive training in the behind the scenes of the arts and professional work placements in one of our partner organizations including Rich Mix, Graeae Theatre Company, Magic Me, Iniva, Theatre Centre, Morley College, Newham Archives, Hawthorn Green Care Home, Oval House, East London Dance, Apples and Snakes, Emergency Exit Arts and Campaign for Drawing. The final year of the Spotlight programme culminated in the Sankofa festival curated, performed and produced by the trainees.

Project name	Year(s)	Summary
Three Percent – Mosaic Rooms, London, UK.	2014	*Three Percent* was a collaboration with The Mosaic Rooms inviting young women aged 16–25 to engage with the work of Tunisian artist Nadia Kaabi-Linke and her exhibition, *The Future Rewound & The Cabinet of Souls*. The project considered themes in the artist's work including restriction, confinement and freedom, creatively exploring ideologies of capitalism and colonialism and the unseen systems that control our daily lives. Two months of weekly workshops culminated in a public sharing of work at The Mosaic Rooms gallery.
Ten in a Bed – Zander Court Community Centre, London; Mowlem Primary School, London and William Davis Primary School, London, UK.	2015–16	*Ten in a Bed* was a workshop and performance project, made with and for small children and their families to develop storytelling, creativity and language skills. It engaged directly with families to enhance literacy and family learning opportunities. Phase 1 of the project was run in partnership with Well London Old Bethnal Green and took place at Zander Court Community Centre. It was funded by Awards for All, Big Lottery fund and QMUL. Phase 2 of the project was funded by Tower Hamlets Public Health.
Rise Up – Rich Mix, London, UK.	2015–16	Phakama's young company of emerging artists was selected to perform their new piece at the Rich Mix Youth Takeover Festival, August 2015. Led by Phakama's youth board, and supported by associate artists, *Rise Up* was a space to make, create and collaborate. Phakama's young company explored the city, venturing into its hidden depths to reveal personal treasures, asking questions along the way: What if you could make up your own rules? What would you say if you could make your voice heard? What would you do if you could change the way we live in the city? The work was funded by Esmée Fairbairn.
Landmarks of the Unknown – Tokyo Metropolitan Theatre, Tokyo; Toyohashi Arts Theatre, Toyohashi; Asahi University, Gifu, Japan.	2015	Phakama was funded by the Daiwa Anglo-Japanese Foundation to develop a three-week residency with partners in the Tokyo Metropolitan Theatre, Toyohaski Arts Theatre and Asahi University, Gifu. The residency culminated in a site-specific performance with young people from the Satsuki Class of Kani City International Exchange Association and Asahi University, based on themes of language, home and belonging.

Project name	Year(s)	Summary
Of All People – The Gate Darkroom and Deptford X, London, UK.	2016	*Of All People* is the first project to come out of the Phakama Artist Bursary, a bursary offered to Associate Artists giving them a chance to explore and create their own ideas.
		Using a mixture of storytelling techniques and pinhole photography participants shared moments of their lives, creating images that reflected these stories. The project was intergenerational and set about to find the commonalities between people.

Methodological Challenges

In this book, when we refer to Phakama, we are discussing it as an approach to participatory performance practice rather than a single organization. While the practice is reflective and we have placed it within theoretical frameworks, the methodology is based in doing, making, being together. Phakama is a collaborative practice in which everyone's story is valued. There are, necessarily, structures and processes in place which facilitate decision-making about the materials used in the final performances that also give individuals particular responsibilities and roles (but not status). In the book we refer to coordinators/leading artists who might oversee the whole project; facilitators who have responsibility for structuring the practice and framing the discussions; trainee facilitators – who are supported in this role; and participants. The book tries to include all their voices. We have written the full name of anyone who has worked directly with Phakama or contributed during the research process. At other times, we give first names to protect the identity of vulnerable children, young people or adults.

Throughout the development of this book we have been keenly aware of the particular methodological challenges of shaping unfolding narratives from so many contributing voices, of seeking ways to curate resonances rather than repetition. *Phakama: Making Participatory Performance* cannot tell all the stories about Phakama or people's experience of it. We were not able to contact each of the many hundreds of participants and collaborators from across the past two decades but they have, in their contribution to each Phakama project, informed the context and understandings of it. While some voices and experiences are explicitly referred to in the book through case studies or interviews, it is imperative to acknowledge that every conversation has informed the structure, content and tone of it.

We are also mindful of the politics of epistemology at play in any project that aims to frame and share new understandings, particularly in a practice that is as collaborative and far reaching as Phakama. Postcolonial histories and legacies have been live issues throughout this process. This book proposes one form of distilling and articulating new understandings and sharing practice through words, in English, in a publication that speaks to an academic as well as arts, youth and social work professional audience: this may seem far removed from the embodied knowledge that is iterated in each moment of making participatory performance with a group of sixty people in a rehearsal process.

Over the past two decades there have been over forty Phakama projects and performances. In the context of this book, we can't attend to each one with the same weight of consideration and some projects are given greater attention than others. There are some pragmatic reasons for this: some projects had a large number of people involved in their realization so there is a greater body of knowledge to draw upon; some, particularly the early projects as part of the LIFT and South African collaboration, are well documented (reports, faxes, images) that are kept in the LIFT archive; as technology progressed the materiality of documentation that once filled archive boxes and shelf-space has reduced to a hard drive, emails between people, Facebook messages, Flickr albums online; there isn't one repository of information so often we have pursued a particular line of enquiry through a trail of leads from one individual to another in order to access people's personal archives rather than organizational ones. By attending to this process of performance making, across two decades of practice, in a range of contexts, we are unable to attend to the fuller picture of each context's very different social, cultural, political and economic influences. Phakama is not a one-size-fits-all approach, but one that allows for reflexivity and responsiveness to cultural contexts and their specificity.

A book about a particular approach to performance making, engaging a wide range of voices that advocate for the significant influence of this on their professional and personal life runs the risk of hagiography. Throughout the development of the book we have encouraged our collaborators to be bold in identifying the challenges of the Phakama approach to participatory performance making, to identify, as Caroline Calburn so clearly describes, as 'the pleasure and the pain' of intercultural participatory practice – the conflict, challenge and limits of collaboration.

The Structure of the Book

The book is divided into three parts: 'Preparing the Ground'; 'Making the Performance' and 'Celebration'. This structure reflects the Phakama process. Each part addresses particular principles of Phakama's approach and is contextualized through narrative reflections and theoretical engagement with a range of disciplines, including education, sociology and care ethics. We have also detailed a step-by-step outline of particular exercises used in many different projects to give further access to the practical iteration of this work. A wide range of international partners give detailed consideration of a particular project as a case study of these principles in action, including Tony Fegan, Selloane Mokuku, Caroline Calburn, Vidyanidhee Vanarase and Corinne Micallef. Interviews with collaborators from across the past two decades – participants, funders, project partners and participants – give additional insight into the experience of Phakama and how this informed their own professional practice and sense of self. In addition, we have invited cultural commentators and academics, Ananda Breed, Sara Matchett, Lucy Neal and Shirley Brice Heath, who are part of the wider Phakama network of collaborators to contextualize and analyse aspects of this practice as part of a wider body of cultural and social practices that directly engage with young people. At the beginning of each of the three parts of the book we give a detailed introduction surveying the range of voices, materials and ideas you will encounter within it.

Many of the exercises that act as catalysts for generating performance material across the last two decades have originated beyond Phakama: they have been brought into a workshop by people at different times based on their own experience as artists and arts educators working in a range of contexts on different continents. Like so many games or exercises in the repertoire of resources that a theatre practitioner may draw on, they may know when *they* first experienced it, who first introduced them to it, but they won't know the genealogy of the exercise before they encountered it. Ideas are transmitted through practice, adapted and subsumed into a working body of knowledge. While some of the starting points of the examples we explore in this section may be familiar, the approach to how they are then adapted, edited and scored within a performance is distinctive, informed by Phakama's structured invitation to continued participation.

Amid the various organizational and personal archives we have accessed there are many photographs. Some, from earlier international collaborations, before widespread access to digital photography, are printed snapshots smudged with fingerprints from when images were passed around a group of people such as the image of bodies draped over each other and tiny tin-covered London landmarks from *Be Yourself* (UK, South Africa, 1999). Other, digital images from recent projects such as *The World At My Feet* (Indonesia, 2010) show silhouetted bodies clambering over a scaffolding stage set. These photographs offer a moment from a project rather than insight into the particular approach. As the book foregrounds Phakama's approach to making participatory performance rather than a specific project, we were keen that any images reflected this ethos. Andrew 'Sid' Siddall's illustrations offer us a visual distillation of specific principles or exercises as they are in process. Sid is a founder member of Phakama who has continued to work on various international projects over the past two decades. During the process he often articulates concepts being discussed through drawing. Sid's illustrations, in their apparent simplicity, give deep and direct access to ideas that have taken many hundreds of words to articulate. We have chosen to include this form of documentation, illustrations based on sketches from his notebook, to reflect this approach.

And finally, there are many possible books that could be written about Phakama. This practice resonates across a wide range of areas within the academic study of theatre and performance – applied and socially engaged practices; theatre for development; community performance; devised performance. It offers a rich invitation to consider issues of youth protagonism, cultural citizenship, cultural leadership, arts management, international co-production and activism in a wider context of neoliberalism, globalization and social inequity. There is potential for a collection of essays or books that explicitly focuses and examines each of these issues. However, *this* book makes a very particular contribution to this terrain of possible knowledge – it sets out to give access to the particularity of Phakama, the practical politics of this and why it matters to make work in this way.

References

Anders, P. and M. Krouse (eds) (2010), *Positions: Contemporary Artists in South Africa*, Johannesburg: Jacana Media Ltd.

Banning, Y. (2002), 'Footprints on the Shore: Documenting Site-Specific Community Performance. The Freedom Project, Robben Island, April 27, 2001', *South African Theatre Journal* 16: 137–56.

Banning, Y., C. Calburn and L. Richardson (2006), 'Project Phakama: Stories from South Africa, London and Lesotho. Landscapes of the Heart', in Michael Etherton (ed.), *African Theatre: Youth*, Oxford: James Currey, 151–65.

Beswick, K. (2016), 'Ten in a Bed: Literacy, Intermediality and the Potentials of Low-tech', *Research in Drama Education* 21 (3): 337–48.

Calburn, C. (2016) Correspondence with Lucy Richardson, 21 July.

Fiske, J. (1992), 'The Cultural Economy of Fandom', in Lisa A. Lewis (ed.), *The Adoring Audience: Fan Culture and Poplar Media*, London: Routledge, 30–49.

Fleishman, M. (2016), 'Applied Theatre and Participation in the "new" South Africa: A Possible Politics', in J. Hughes and H. Nicholson (eds), *Critical Perspectives on Applied Theatre*, Cambridge and New York: Cambridge University Press.

Fuchs, A. (1990), *Playing the Market: The Market Theatre Johannesburg 1976–1986*, Chur: Harwood Academic Publishers.

Hauptfleisch, H. (1997), *Theatre and Society in South Africa: Reflections in a Fractured Mirror*, Pretoria: J. L. Van Schaik Publishers.

Jakel, M. (2016), 'Youth Weaving Networks Beyond Community Borders: Lessons Learned from Caja Lúdica, a Community Arts Process and Networking Initiative in Guatemala', Unpublished PhD Thesis, University of Manchester.

Klotz, P. (2016), Interview with Caroline Calburn, Cape Town, South Africa.

McDonnell, B. (2005), 'The Politics of Historiography – Towards an Ethics of Representation', *Research in Drama Education* 10 (2): 127–38.

Melvin, M. (2006), *The Art of the Theatre Workshop*, London: Oberon.

Middeke, M., P. Schnierer and G. Homann (2015), *The Methuen Drama Guide to Contemporary South African Theatre*, London: Bloomsbury.

Pickering, M. (ed.) (2008), *Research Methods for Cultural Studies*, Edinburgh: Edinburgh University Press.

Richardson, L. (2007a), 'Project Phakama, Lesotho, 2004: "follow the bird" (birds that Flock are Birds that Learn)', in Martin Banham, James Gibbs and Femi Osofisan (eds), *African Theatre: Companies*, Oxford: James Currey, 54–61.

Richardson, L. (2007b), 'Phakama: A Place of Refuge', *Research in Drama Education* 12 (1): 108–11.

Roberts, S. (2015), 'The Pioneers', in M. Middeke, P. Schnierer and G. Homann (eds), *The Methuen Drama Guide to Contemporary South African Theatre*, London: Bloomsbury, 17–42.

Rosenthal, D. (2014), *The National Theatre Story*, London: Oberon.

Sichel, A. (1996), 'This Landmark Event', *The Star*, 5 September (LIFT Archive, LIFT/1997/CE/023/004).

Trowbridge, S. (2013), *The Rise and Fall of the Royal Shakespeare Company*, Oxford: Editions Albert Creed.

Turan, K. and J. Papp (2010), *Free for All: Joe Papp, The Public and the Greatest Theater Story Ever Told*, New York: Anchor.

PART ONE

PREPARING THE GROUND

INTRODUCTION

Phakama is an approach to making participatory performance. Part One of this book, however, recognizes that this work is embedded in a practice which extends beyond the workshop space and continues after the performance. The ideas and practices in Part One explore how Phakama prepares the ground for individuals to contribute, for creativity to flourish and performance to develop. It is divided into three sections: **Hosting, Give and Gain** and **Cultural Sharing.** In Phakama, these things are not just preparation for or outcomes of the devising process but are a practice in and of themselves. This part of the book hopes to demonstrate the depth of this practice and the intensity of its impact on those involved with Phakama.

In the first section, which is built around the Phakama practice of Cultural Tours, the concept of **Hosting** is explored in relation to the work. This is framed by the feminist political scientist Joan Tronto's 'ethic of care' and includes a case study of *The Child I Curry* (Lesotho, 2003) by Selloane Mokuku.

The second section focuses on one of the most important tenets of Phakama's practice, **Give and Gain**, examining its pedagogical influences and placing it in its historical and cultural context. It includes a case study of *Bulang Dikgoro/Open the Gates* (Johannesburg, South Africa 1996) by Tony Fegan, then director of Learning for London International Festival of Theatre (LIFT), and an interview with Mildrett Stevens, Tracey-Lee Gates and Sharon Waverley, participants in a number of early Phakama projects in South Africa.

The third section introduces *Map of the World* as an example of **Cultural Sharing** drawing upon the sociologist Richard Sennett's provocations on difficult cooperation to articulate this in practice. It includes a case study of *Be Yourself* (Phakama SA and Phakama UK, Tricycle Theatre, London, 1999) by Caroline Calburn and an interview with Maylene Catchpole (participant/facilitator Phakama UK).

Part One concludes with an essay by academic and theatre facilitator Ananda Breed in which she reflects on a particular collaboration between Phakama and The Creative Arts Team (New York City) which was part of Contacting the World (CTW) international festival of theatre with young people.

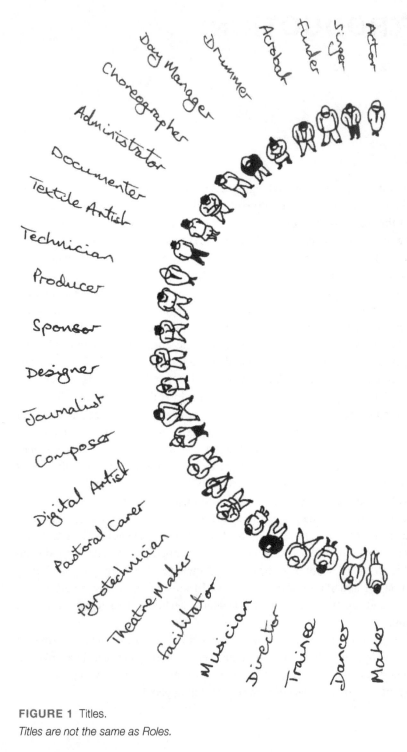

FIGURE 1 Titles.

Titles are not the same as Roles.

HOSTING

Introduction

LIFT, the parent company from which Phakama originated, has, since 1981, invited theatre companies from all over the world to London for extraordinary biannual festivals. LIFT's commitment to bringing high-quality and ground breaking theatre to London is always in the context of understanding that 'a festival's social interactions and the shifts of perception that they engender prove time and again ultimately to become its real subject matter' (de Wend Fenton and Neal 2005: 117). For these interactions to be meaningful they need to be handled with care and given space to unfold. Part of LIFT's success came from the conviction of the founding directors, Lucy Neal and Rose Fenton, that the artists and the work must be hosted carefully in London. To facilitate this, they appointed Group Hosts responsible for each group performing at the festival. With a small budget, they welcomed visiting companies at the airport and looked after them throughout their stay – taking them to BBC interviews, organizing picnics for them, taking them sightseeing or waking them up when they fell asleep on the tube home. Lucy Neal (2014) contextualizes this commitment to hosting when she says:

> Hospitality, honesty, generosity and respect were our four touchstones for LIFT, and Rose and I always considered hospitality the key to all the rest. How you invite people; how you host people; how you say, 'you are welcome'; how you open up the opportunities and hold them – this is really the key to what could happen as a result.

Phakama models this approach. It understands that how you welcome and how you host is crucial to the foundation of relationships built during a project.

The first Phakama projects were international exchanges, with individuals and groups travelling across the world, living communally and working together. There was an emphasis on hosting visitors who arrived in unfamiliar places. Since then, some projects have continued to build upon this model of international exchange but many have developed in a local context. Some have been intensive residencies and others a series of weekly sessions over a period of months. However differently the project is constructed, the concept of hosting has continued to frame all the work.

This section demonstrates, in dialogue with feminist political theorist Joan Tronto's ethics of care (1994), how the attitude and practice of hosting is central to the creative work Phakama does. It includes testimony from Phakama facilitators and participants who speak of the 'guest-friendships' they have developed through the social interactions afforded them during projects. Finally, Phakama facilitator, Selloane Mokuku, who hosted a project in Lesotho in 2003, talks about the impact of that project on the local community and the participants' sense of place.

Phakama Practice: Cultural Tours

One of the practices which emerged from this notion of 'hosting' was the Cultural Tours. Lucy Richardson describes this practice in London and in Cape Town. These examples are referred to by both Caroline Calburn and Maylene Catchople a little later in this section.

These Cultural Tours allow the young people to step up as hosts and to take responsibility for the experience of others. They also let them see their own locality differently and understand it more deeply. Crucially, in both of these examples of UK/South African exchange, some of the places visited were new to both hosts and visitors – explored together with fresh eyes.

Be Yourself (London, UK 1999)

LIFT invited Phakama to produce a show at the Tricycle Theatre as part of the LIFT 1999 festival. A group of twenty South African young people and artists came to London for three weeks to work with a group of young people and artists from the UK.

It was decided that the young people should host the visit to London by scheduling a series of Cultural Tours that represented and responded to their environment. The young people had to decide on places to visit and work out how to get us all there. Our visitors, rather than just seeing the inside of a workshop space, got to visit a series of diverse London sites including Brick Lane – an east London street in the Bangladeshi-Sylheti community renowned for its curry houses – and Harrods – an upmarket department store in one of London's most exclusive neighbourhoods, Knightsbridge. Part of the experience of getting to know the city was travelling with a group of forty young people through London. The South Africans were very taken by the tube, and in particular how serious and silent everyone was. We'd walk down onto the platform and, to the young UK hosts' surprise and joy, Vusi, a South African participant, would sing *Shosholoza*, a popular folk song, in his bass voice and everybody would join in. The young people would spread themselves across the platform and start singing. People on the opposite platform would watch, applaud and sometimes join in. It became a moment of cultural sharing.

The cultural tour I remember most vividly was our visit to Stephen Lawrence's memorial – not least because it was very difficult to get to. The Tricycle Theatre, where we were performing, is in north London and Stephen Lawrence's memorial is in Charlton, south-east London. It took several song-filled tube and bus journeys to get there. In 1993 Stephen Lawrence, a schoolboy from Eltham, was murdered in an unprovoked, racially motivated attack whilst he waited at a bus stop. His death provoked a public enquiry headed by Sir William Macpherson into the Metropolitan Police Service, which found it 'institutionally racist'. This resulted in explicit dialogue about attitudes to race and cultural changes to elements of police practice and the law. The UK young people were from a group based in south-east London who had grown up knowing about Stephen Lawrence, but none of them had been to his memorial before.

The memorial was a simple plaque in a paving stone in a residential street of no other particular note. We stood around the memorial and Robert, a UK participant, told the South Africans the story of Stephen Lawrence. They were visibly shocked and confused. With only the integrated and confident group from Phakama UK as examples, they had not expected racist violence here in the UK. Initially they were completely silenced and then they began to talk, question and worry about it. It was a coming together of the young people in a common understanding that violence and corrupt legal systems exist everywhere and this results in people losing loved ones. One of the South Africans began to sing a funeral song and we stood there in respectful silence. Then we all went on the two-hour journey home.

As with all powerful group experiences, the group's visit to Stephen Lawrence's memorial re-emerged throughout the devising process and production of *Be Yourself.* Personal stories of loss and violence in the workshops unlocked political discussion about multiculturalism and immigration. These ideas became core to the performance. The show opened with the young people lying over each other, as if dead, in the shape of the River Thames – an image which evoked the Conservative minister Enoch Powell's 'Rivers of Blood' speech from 1968 in which he projected the violent outcome of mass migration to Britain. A young woman sang 'Maybe It's Because I'm a Londoner' very slowly, as a lament, singing to the moment when we stood around Stephen Lawrence's memorial. Other young people carried bowls filled with water, with lights underneath and invited the audiences to wash their hands whilst they whispered stories of loss to them.

At the end of the performance – a signature of a Phakama show – the participants went to the audiences and asked them to dance. One night, Stephen Lawrence's father was in the audience and, when invited to dance, he said he vowed never to dance until his son's murderers were brought to justice. His words added another layer to a show which was about cultural exchange, community and personal experience.

Ka Mor Walo Ka Seatleng/With a Suitcase in My Hand (Cape Town, South Africa, 1996)

Everyone we interviewed about *Ka Mor Walo Ka Seatleng/With a Suitcase in My Hand* tells the story of a real event with baboons which featured so prominently in the show. It was a comical scene that asked: who is sillier, baboon or human? One of our Cultural Tours for this show was to Cape Point, the most southerly point of Africa where, allegedly, the Indian and Atlantic oceans meet. When you stand on the cliff and look down you see the waves crashing together. At the time, many black British people wore key rings or badges or T-shirts featuring a map of Africa, identifying a connection with their African heritage. Standing there, on this point of that map, felt very significant to many of them. I remember specifically Anthony, a UK participant, who has now emigrated to Johannesburg, saying 'this feels like home.'

We decided to have lunch on the beach. There were signs saying 'Danger! Baboons!' but nobody took them very seriously – there were no baboons to be seen. We climbed down a very steep set of stairs to the beach and the young people began running about, playing on the sand. Many of the South Africans had never been to this beach because of the legacy of apartheid: people stayed in their own areas. Some of the young people from London had not left the UK before. Then a few people noticed the baboons – some looking over the top of the cliff, some coming down the steps slowly, others approaching across the beach. Everybody had just left their bags lying around. A baboon opened a rucksack, got a book out and appeared to be reading it. Another opened a packed lunch and ate a snack. Another leant over Timmy's (UK participant) shoulder and took a sandwich from his hand. Gradually more people began to notice but we didn't dare do anything – if a baboon stood up it would be as big as most of us. It was frightening but also very funny. All the baboons came down to the beach and then Honza, Robert and Kenny – three of the tallest UK male participants – suddenly looked up from what they were doing, saw the baboons, turned around and started running into the sea: they were fully dressed and up to their waists in water. Everyone was cheering! We got our rucksacks, ran up the steps and got on the bus. Sitting on the back seat of the bus was a baboon and right in the passageway was a big baboon poo. The story of the baboons – our unfriendly hosts – became a central scene in the show.

This practice of Cultural Tours is a very direct form of hosting, welcoming visitors and giving them experience of and insight into the place they are visiting. It helps the visitors to acclimatize, feel comfortable and cared for. It creates shared experiences and relationships between people. Within Phakama, it is also the beginning of the devising process and impacts upon the performance.

For Phakama everything – be it planned or incidental, serious or joyous, profound or superficial – contributes to the process of group making and generates potential material for the show. There is trust that something will emerge from these events, communally experienced by a diverse group of hosts and visitors, which will be worth sharing with an audience. Phakama says to the participants: whatever you consider to be important experiences – even something as playful as the baboon incident – can and should be framed as part of the performance.

The inclusion of moments in and responses to these Cultural Tours within the show is also an important part of the experience for the audiences, who are often people who live locally to where the performance is staged. The nature of Phakama's work is that narrative is not linear or immediately coherent – the action unfolds through a series of curated moments and scenes developed through the devising process. The references to place, for example to London and Stephen Lawrence, or Cape Town and the baboons, are important because they help to anchor the audience's experience when watching the show. Place is recognized. This in turn helps to welcome the audience to witness the show and the audience, who are local to the place referred to, feel a sense of ownership – a responsibility as hosts of the project. Selloane Mokuku expands on this idea in her case study later in this section.

CULTURAL TOURS

Prepare in advance:
- The hosting group of project participants, supported by facilitators, plan a series of Cultural Tours. The tours must reflect the participants' sense of what they think best represents their place.
- The tours can include places they have been to and places they want to visit but have not done so yet. They can include tourist attractions, sites of local or personal interest. They might have an educational (e.g., a museum) or leisure bias (e.g., shopping or swimming).
- The same participants then have responsibility for working out a schedule and planning the routes for these Cultural Tours.
- The journeying to and from the chosen place is considered as important as the visit to the place itself and should be planned carefully.

The Practical Politics of Care

Caring

Good hosting is an element of caring – an idea and value that informs Phakama. In her book *Moral Boundaries: A Political Argument for an Ethic of Care* (1994), Joan Tronto places caring as central to our lived experience and argues that it 'be viewed as a species activity that includes everything we do to maintain, continue and repair our "world" so that we can live in it as well as possible' (103). She, like Phakama, sees care as a practice (a process you do) rather than a disposition (a way you feel), upon which we are all interdependent. She gives the practice of care four phases, caring about, taking care of, care-giving, care-receiving (106–8). From this practice she draws respectively four complimentary ethical elements of care: attentiveness, responsibility, competence, responsiveness (127–35).

Care, in the form in which Tronto describes, permeates the way in which Phakama relationships are formed and maintained. It runs beneath the early conversations between participating groups, the welcome of individuals, the quality of the creative practice, the hosting and the evaluation of projects. Corinne Micallef (artistic director of Phakama UK 2014–16) describes how she first encountered Phakama (2014):

I was doing my placement with LIFT but went round the corner of the open plan office and found Fabio Santos (Artistic Director of Phakama 2002–14) and Phakama. Fabio invited me to come to the Saturday sessions for *Strange Familiars*: this is the moment that my relationship with Phakama began. There was a great sense of welcome: 'Come along and get involved. We don't know how. We don't have to put a name on it yet. Just join us.' It was an invitation of willingness – to find out together.

The first time I went to a Phakama session I didn't know what to expect, except that it was a Saturday project with young refugees. I opened the door and was welcomed, first by one of the participants, Osman Bah. I felt straightaway that this is a great space to be in. There were beanbags, tea and coffee – it was a social space more than anything. Then later in the day-long session we got into the creative content, but in a relaxed way. People were joyful just to be in that room, to share experience with one another and try things out together.

From that very first moment I loved Phakama and wanted to keep coming back each week. That is why participants continue to come to our projects: that feeling of 'Yes, I just like going to this place'. I think it's because of that welcome – it frames and holds everything.

In the feedback at the end of *Three Percent* (London, 2015) – a project that explored ideas of freedom with young women, they said they valued being able to come to that place on a Saturday afternoon and feel welcomed, to be relaxed, have a cup of tea and connect with people. Their experience reflects my 'yes' moment in my first encounter with Phakama.

This approach is typical of the way many participants and facilitators are welcomed to the group – initially and repeatedly. Space is created and time given to each interaction. This allows for attentiveness to individuals' needs. It also gives space for, in this case, Corinne to be responsive to the care offered her: her moment of 'yes'. Ultimately, Tronto argues that care is relational – it is about interdependent beings, in relation to one another. Phakama's work – being participant centred – is built upon the interdependent relationships across all aspects of its practice. This model of responsive care-giving and care-receiving allows people to more explicitly recognize their interdependence through the experience of welcome, hosting and being hosted.

Caring With

In *Caring Democracy: Markets, Equality and Justice* (2013a), Tronto expands on her earlier work on care ethics arguing that the practice of care and the practice of democracy are interrelated. She argues:

> care and democracy don't seem to go together at all. Democracy is about fitness to live together as equals. Almost always when we speak of care we imagine a relationship of asymmetry: of someone who is in need and someone else who is helping them. So how can these two things [democracy and care] ever be put together?

She proposes that in a democratic setting there is a need for an additional fifth element of care which she describes as 'caring with'. This has the ethical element of solidarity and trust (2013b). The Phakama process aims to be democratic, foregrounding 'caring with', where relationships are mutual and dependent: solidarity and trust are essential to, and a by-product of, all of Phakama's work.

This mutual caring is very evident in Corinnne's interview which describes, on a small scale, the ethos that permeates Phakama exchange. In this example, the care-giving participant is a young refugee and the cared for is a trainee facilitator who went on to become the artistic director of the organization. In Phakama the varying degrees of dependence and interdependence between facilitators and facilitators, facilitators and participants and participants and facilitators are acknowledged as always shifting. Of course there are differing roles within each project. Someone may coordinate the whole project, others facilitate the creative practice, others are participants. However, the responsibility of care rests with everyone: this principle is the spine that runs through all areas of the practice.

Similarly, in the conversations which precede the setting up of any Phakama project there is an attentiveness to the needs of all participating organizations and individuals. Phakama breaks with the framework applied in some community arts work and learning environments where the artist/arts organization is likened to a guest arriving in a community and making an intervention, the care giver to a vulnerable group (Thompson 2003; Nicholson 2005). With Phakama, the emphasis is on interdependence – what the communities, including Phakama, can bring to each other. This empowers and demands that all participating organizations are put into the role of caring for and caring with – all have to agree to take responsibility for the project and for each other.

If all parties are to be attentive (to care about each other) and take responsibility (care for each other), it is important that competence (the ability to do the caring) is sought and valued in any groups planning to work together in a Phakama project. There is not a hierarchy of competence and there is an understanding that it can be found in many ways. One group might have competence in working with particular individuals, as was the case both with the refugee organizations partnering on *Strange Familiars* (2003) and the care homes collaborating on *The Edible Garden* (2012–16) Phakama worked with. Others may have competence in providing particular skills for the project – the scientists on *Message in a Bottle* (2012) – or an expertise related to a particular place – the young people of Chaco Chico in Argentina, who knew their polluted river on *The Street Is My Back Yard* (2006). Others may have particular artistic skills. This redefinition of competence is something which is made much more explicit in the practice of *Give and Gain*, outlined in the next chapter.

Opening Your Home

The etymology of 'host', in many languages, includes both the word for 'the person who receives a guest' and the 'stranger'. The implications of this are particularly important in Greek mythology and culture. *Xenos* refers to a stranger, while *Xenia* or 'guest-friendship' refers to hospitality – the welcome and generosity shown to those who are far from home. This relationship – held within it the notion of 'caring with' – was a mutual, reciprocal one. Hospitality – protection, shelter or companionship – was repaid with gifts. No one comes empty handed. In Greek mythology, deities often disguised themselves as mortals and lived among humans. *Theoxeny* is when human beings demonstrate their virtue or piety by extending hospitality to a humble stranger *(xenos)*, who turns out to be a disguised deity *(theos)* with the capacity to bestow rewards. It is wise therefore, in ancient Greek culture, to welcome a stranger into your home – because while it is possible she brings a knife to kill you with, it is just as likely that she will be a deity. With the possibility of *theoxeny* the logic of guest-friendship is firmly established in Greek culture and hospitality valued as a sensible and laudable custom (Louden 2011). Phakama is accessible not because it believes it can bestow 'help' upon or 'transform' those who join but because it values each person who comes through its doors for the gifts and potential rewards they bring: it gives all who participate the status of deities.

In many Phakama residencies, hosting became more personal and people would open their homes to their visitors – sometimes to live with them for the whole residency, sometimes for a night and sometimes just to visit. The residency for *The Child I Curry* (2003) in Lesotho began with facilitators and trainee facilitators hosted in people's home around the village of Morija. In various projects in Cape Town, the British guests were welcomed into the homes of facilitators who lived in townships – to share their food and their sleeping spaces. These interactions helped form guest-friendships that have lasted ever since. Providing hospitality is not always easy. Attitudes towards it are culturally specific and sometimes it is more difficult to invite people into your home for complex reasons. In London, during *Be Yourself* (1999) some of the South African facilitators complained that staying in university accommodation had not allowed them an experience of UK domesticity and they were offended that they had not been invited into the homes of the UK facilitators and participants.

There is slippage between the role of host and guest. On *Ka Mor Walo Ka Seatleng/ With a Suitcase in My Hand* (1997), Craig Koopman travelled as a participant to his first Phakama project from Genadendal to central Cape Town and so was a 'guest'. But he was also 'hosting' people from outside his country, South Africa. Here he talks of his experience of sharing living space and of cultural tours.

When we got to the first day of the project I was impressed because I'd never been out of the province of Cape Town and I had opportunities to meet people from other provinces, from overseas. You got to know different cultures and I believe when people come together from different backgrounds it's always chaos. But you learn from each other. You see people from different cultures working together, living together. There are people using the toilet differently and eating differently. You learn from this, understand the culture behind it, the reasons behind it. So, at first, we were looking around and judging, but everything changed. The two weeks of the project had a huge effect on us. We didn't look down on each other. We were like family. We came and created our own happy place.

I took Honza and Kenny, participants from the UK, home. My pocket money was little at that time, I only received 200 rand for the two weeks. The friendship that I had with the UK participants was important. If I wanted to buy a chocolate, Kenny, for example, would say, 'it's alright, I'll buy it for you'. And that's how we became like brothers. We had a weekend free in the middle of the project. I could have gone home alone but I was thinking, what are the UK participants going to do? I wanted to introduce some of them to my family and my background. We lived in a suburb called Mitchells Plain, Rocklands, so my father came to fetch us whilst my mother was preparing food. We were walking up the road and people could see us. There were gangs there. Honza had a thing about gold, and one local guy was going to run down to his house and get all his cheap gold gleaming: he was going to sell it to Honza. But my other friend said 'you can't do that to him, he's part of us now and if you sell something, you sell something decent'. Some of the guys connected with Kenny and Honza then. They wanted to know more about where they came from. All the guys were sports fans. I'm a diehard Liverpool supporter. I took them to a sports pub near to us to watch a Liverpool game at West Ham. It wasn't like they were looking down at our situation in the house. My mother took them as her sons and my brothers took them as brothers and friends. (Koopman 2015)

Craig's experience is rooted in and articulates a sense of 'caring with' fostered by and celebrated in Phakama's work. The detail with which he recalls that weekend, many years later, evidences the positive impact being the host can have – the care, attentiveness, responsibility and competence with which he and his family undertook this hosting endures.

Hosting as Structured Activity

Beyond the binary exchange model of South Africa/UK that shaped early Phakama projects, the importance of hosting and ethical questions of care were brought into sharp definition in relation to humanitarian crises of refugees fleeing their home countries in search of safety elsewhere. This required a particular attentiveness throughout the Phakama project *Strange Familiars* (2003), where participants were all unaccompanied minors seeking asylum in the UK. In 2006 the UK was the 'third largest asylum seeker-receiving country' in the industrialized world 'with just over 9 per cent of all requests lodged' (Kidd, Zahir and Hybrid 2007: 15). *Strange Familiars* responded to the changes in UK policy on refugees and asylum seekers, including a dispersal policy where 'asylum seekers were dispersed to areas of low housing demand, in order to lessen the burden on local authorities in the South East and London, where most asylum seekers arrive' (Kidd, Zahir and Hybrid 2007: 14). The project attended to the increasing isolation and hostility they faced. *Strange Familiars* was funded by the National Institute for Adult Continuing Education and Arts Council England and was developed in collaboration with the Refugee Council. Stephanie White, a volunteer teacher of English at the Refugee Council, considers the particular benefits of Phakama's hosting for each unaccompanied minor at this point in their lives:

> What I felt they gained from the experience, most importantly, is the sense of belonging. This is something that they really miss in an alien culture. They felt they had a new family – and the family was both the young people and the adults that they worked with. They had a sense of purpose. So much of their lives is outside their own control: they can't choose where they live, they don't know whether they'll be allowed to stay here, they find it very difficult to get into education. The projects Phakama did were a chance for them to be in control. The young people valued the opportunity to create and plan for a future that they knew would take place. Working with Phakama, where something was planned, and you had a timespan, and it happened, was really important.
>
> The trust invested in them by the adults that they worked with was really important because an essential premise of the asylum process is that your story can't be trusted. The young people were used to people always criticising them, querying what they put forward. In Phakama there was a sense that people were absolutely delighted to meet with them, to interact with them. It was a trust that did not involve demanding their backstory. It was just: here we are, we're here to enjoy ourselves together.

Partnership between Phakama and the young people was really important. The activities that they undertook and the things they planned were something they planned themselves. It was not something that was done to them. Lack of control over your life space is particularly hard for a refugee. So the experience that you could decide on something for yourself and make it happen was good. There are other organisations that provided opportunities for teenagers to meet, but Phakama provided an opportunity for responsible teenagers. Many of the social events that are organised for unaccompanied minors were too unstructured and too wild for these youngsters to enjoy. We all have a tendency to feel terribly sorry for the people we encounter and what's happened to them. Sometimes that converts into people not being sufficiently demanding of the people themselves. (White 2015)

Stephanie speaks here of attentiveness, responsiveness and of the importance of trust. However, her emphasis on hosting in a structured and productive setting, to being part of something, is important. Phakama offered something unique to these young people because the participants were involved in a very concrete task – the making of a performance. In Tronto's terms, the process both required them to take responsibility and allowed them to see and use their own competence. It allowed them the opportunity to 'care with' others, for something – the creative practice, the performance. Care and creative practice are always intertwined in Phakama. Phakama hosts in a caring way in order to make a performance. Phakama practices creatively together as a way of practising care. Both are equally important and neither works without the other – it is a symmetrical relationship.

Place as Host

Hosting a Phakama project is an act of generosity. It takes responsibility, time, energy, money and space. Often it involves liaising with people in several different countries or continents. Communication systems, particularly in earlier projects, could be unreliable, organized via faxes written during the day in one part of the world, arriving late at night in another. Given the scale of partnerships at play, there is a risk that basic elements of organization may not work out: in Lesotho participants waited twenty-six hours in an airport before being collected; a facilitator had to drive the length of South Africa twice to get all the participants to a project in Cape Town because the minibus was too small; and in Indonesia the private school Phakama was working in would not allow local 'participants' to sit at the same dinner table as those from the school.

Phakama projects have a tendency to take over a place – to spread outside of the workshop space both physically and metaphorically. In the following case study Selloane Mokuku reflects on how Morija in Lesotho hosted *The Child I Curry*

(2003) and the lasting impact of this particular project. She alludes to the cultural tension between theatre-based and site-specific performance making. She argues that the Phakama approach demands a responsibility by all involved for the place and space inhabited for the brief period of a residency.

References

de Wend Fenton, R. and L. Neal (2005), *The Turning World: Stories from the London International Festival of Theatre*, London: Calouste Gulbenkian.

Kidd, B., S. Zahir and S. K. Hybrid (2007), *Arts and Refugees: History, Impact and Future*, London: Paul Hamlyn Foundation, Arts Council England and the Baring Foundation.

Koopman, C. (2015), Interview at Theatre Arts Admin Collective, Cape Town, SA.

Louden, B. (2011), *Homer's Odyssey and the Near East*, Cambridge: Cambridge University Press.

Micallef, C. (2014), Interview at Queen Mary University, London.

Neal, L. (2015), Interview at Queen Mary University, London.

Nicholson, H. (2005), *Applied Drama: The Gift of Theatre*, Basingstoke: Palgrave Macmillan.

Thompson, J. (2003), *Applied Drama: Bewilderment and Beyond*, Oxford: Peter Lang.

Tronto, J. (1994), *Moral Boundaries: A Political Argument for an Ethic of Care*, London and New York: Routledge.

Tronto, J. (2013a), *Caring Democracy: Markets, Equality and Justice*, New York: New York University Press.

Tronto, J. (2013b), 'The Challenges of Medical Care in a Caring Democracy', *Ethos – Plateforme interdisciplinaire d'éthique*, University of Lausanne, France, 6 June. Available online: http://ethicsofcare.org/joan-tronto/ (accessed 16 May 2016).

White, S. (2015), Interview at London Metropolitan University, London.

CASE STUDY
THE CHILD I CURRY
(LESOTHO, 2003)

Selloane Mokuku

Description: *The Child I Curry* was a Phakama training residency involving facilitators from the UK and six South African Development Countries (SADC) – Botswana, Lesotho, Mauritius, Mozambique, Namibia and South Africa. This led to a site-specific performance involving sixty young Basotho in Morija Museum and Mophato oa Morija Conference Centre and its environs. It explored issues of social justice, good governance, human rights, HIV and AIDS.

Place: Morija, Lesotho.

Date/Duration: 4–26 January 2003.

Partnerships: Morija Museum, Project Phakama.

Facilitators: Clinton Osbourn and Mpotseng Shuping (South Africa); Selloane Mokuku and Phomolo Mosaase (Lesotho); Jessica Lejowa and Boipelo Moagaesi (Botswana); Lucky Peters (Namibia); Christophe St Lambert and Sylvain Polydor (Mauritius); Atanasio Nhussi and Rosa Domingos Chauque (Mozambique); Lucy Richardson and Fabio Santos (UK).

Participants: Sixty young Basotho people from Morija and its environs.

Funders: Save the Children UK, The British Council.

Introduction

I feel nostalgic writing this case study but the sentiment is unavoidable. Not long ago, in an effort to spring clean my wardrobe, I came across a light green apron with traces of yellow and black paint spelling out 'Project Phakama 2003'. The font was faded, along with the memory of that 2003 experience, but the moment I unearthed my apron two words came immediately and vividly to mind: Give and Gain. Along with those two words came a flood of images of the place in which it all transpired – Morija. These memories unlike the words printed on cloth were written within me in indelible ink. I decided to keep the apron, carefully folded it and put it away.

A few weeks later, by chance, at the border crossing between South Africa and Lesotho, I met another Phakama 2003 participant who is now an immigration officer. '*U se ke ua re lahla 'Mè!*' he exclaims when he sees me. '*Phakama ke letheba!*' ('Please do not abandon us mother, Phakama is a mark'). It was, he says, 'such an amazing experience'. I am keen to find out what he means by 'amazing', but we have all been in a snails' queue to enter Lesotho for more than two hours and I can feel the piercing eyes of my fellow snails holding their passports, yearning for their entry stamp, willing me to shut my mouth. I understand, feel embarrassed, so exchange contacts with him and move on – all the while recalling my own sense of how amazing it was to be part of Phakama 2003 and eager to hear from other Phakama participants about their experiences. Since finding my apron I have been talking to participants, facilitators and audience members about the experience of Phakama and *The Child I Curry*. Our conversations have informed the reflections that follow.

Beginnings

I first learnt about Phakama in 2000. At the time, I was a Child Participation Consultant for Save the Children UK, tasked with ensuring that Basotho children made a meaningful contribution towards the international declaration, A World Fit for Children. I was deeply involved with the United Nations General Assembly Special Session on Children (UNGASSoC), travelling extensively, nationally and internationally. For those many trips, I took on different roles – a civil society representative, a facilitator, at times a chaperone – and often with children from diverse backgrounds, as well as government representatives. It was Caroline Calburn (facilitator, South Africa) who invited Phomolo Mosaase (facilitator, Lesotho) and myself to attend *Call Me Not a Woman* (2000), Phakama's international residency at Mmabana Cultural Centre in Mahikeng, North West province, South Africa. We were to be part of the SADC, invited as theatre practitioners to observe and engage with the project.

The energy of the young people and facilitators from South Africa and the UK we witnessed in *Call Me Not a Woman* was infectious: there were thirty facilitators from Britain, India, Lesotho, Mauritius, Mozambique and Namibia as well as sixty young people from across South Africa. The project culminated into a thought-provoking, site-specific performance around issues of gender, violence and social justice. The performances took place in houses within the community as well as the streets. The experience of the creative process was extraordinary. Facilitators met to plan and discuss processes prior to meeting the participants who, in turn, were introduced to concepts and allowed to work on their own, and then came back to share with the group. Daily reflections formed an integral part of the process. As a facilitator, the fundamental principle to remember was not to impose, but to constantly invite an attitude of 'let's find out'. Anthropologist Marimba Ani (1994) asserts that if culture is imposed, one could limit creativity and vision, destroying people's will and intent. My stance therefore was to be an enabler.

Exposure to the work of Zakes Mda (1993), Peter Brook (1968), Bertolt Brecht (1964), Paulo Freire (1996) and Augusto Boal (2002) inspired me. And so the principles of enabling, community engagement, transforming spaces, testing, exploration and collaboration in Phakama resonated well with me. I had previously been involved in participatory approaches to theatre making: in Phakama I felt 'at home'. I had been an active member of Marotholi Travelling Theatre where we had performed in villages and sang with communities. However, after I furthered my studies at the University of Cape Town, training as an actor, I was highly challenged when I came back to Lesotho. I had grown to appreciate theatre as an occasion that takes place in enclosed settings; I yearned for a theatre to take place in a building; I wanted lights, sound, floor plans. In my mind, I had 'progressed'. Rather than taking theatre to the people, travelling to them, I wanted the audience to come to the theatre. In Lesotho, there were no theatres except for one in an international school, Machabeng, in the capital city, Maseru. Perhaps it is Mandla Mbothwe's words that best echo my frustration about 'where' theatre takes place when he said: 'I was trained as an actor. I was introduced to the proscenium arch, to the western ways of telling stories, where I am being locked in one space. Phakama stripped those things and affirmed a lot of my previous experiences' (2015). With my previous Theatre for Development experience and readings of Peter Brook's empty space and Poor Theatre I had been conflicted. In Mahikeng, in *Call Me Not a Woman* (2000), Phakama abandoned the theatre as I had grown to appreciate and transformed spaces into magical places. I told myself that, should the idea of hosting Phakama in Lesotho germinate, choosing a place for a residency would be fundamental.

In Mahikeng, SADC representatives expressed an interest to develop an SADC collaboration informed by the Phakama's philosophy. We agreed that the theme would address the need to involve the participation of children and young people in all matters that concerned them. The application form to Save the Children UK, the result of intensive discussions on how to frame the project, detailed the main idea behind *The Child I Curry*. Often adults talk *about* young people and not *with* them. This denies young people an opportunity to find answers by themselves. Information about young people, their desires and concerns is often flawed with bias and misconceptions, rather like a hurriedly made curry, which may lose its subtle flavour. This idea of currying, of slowly attending to the making of a child and how they navigate the world, became the central metaphor for *The Child I Curry*. The project also intended to look critically at the policies and documentations of countries and international communities and, through such processes, enhance their broader aspiration for social justice for children and young people.

Phakama Lesotho

Lesotho, a constitutional monarchy and a former protectorate of Britain, gained political independence on 4 October 1966. The mountainous terrain covers over 50 per cent of the country, which is completely surrounded by South Africa. According to the latest statistics, 2.1 million people live in this land and over 40 per cent are children below the age of eighteen. Party politics are a thorny rose that continue to unsettle Lesotho's 2020 vision of 'being at peace with itself and its neighbours' (*Lesotho National Vision 2020* 2014: i). In March 2001, facilitators from each of the SADC countries, including South Africa, met in Maseru, Lesotho to plan, while in Lesotho the group met with cultural leaders, policy makers, funders, media and arts organizations. They gave a workshop on theatre techniques for working with children to members of an NGO Coalition on the rights of a Child. They also went for Cultural Tours that included Morija Museum and Archives. At the museum they met its director, Steven Gill, who engaged in discussions about Phakama taking place during the Morija Arts and Cultural Festival. Phakama's relationship with the place, Morija, had begun. Morija, popularly known as *selibeng sa thuto* (loosely translated to mean 'a wellspring of learning or education') is a small town situated in Maseru. When you enter Morija, you are led through patches of a tarred and gravel road with trees along the way to different homesteads and buildings within the town itself. The place's physical location is historically and culturally important. It became a home for participants who unfailingly walked from near and far, to the residency.

The Sites of *The Child I Curry*

At the Mophato oa Morija Conference Centre, where the residency took place, there was a kitchen with a dining hall linked to the main hall. There are a number of modern huts used as dormitories. The place is surrounded by both indigenous and foreign shrubs and trees. In summer the grass grows high and needs constant cutting to preserve the landscape. Clinton Osbourn (facilitator, South Africa) and Christophe St Lambert (facilitator, Mauritius) offered exercises that enabled participants to explore their environment (Drawing the Body and Bird Making).

In the former, participants were asked to outline someone's body, cut, write words, decorate and find a spot for display. (A full description and reflection of this exercise is detailed in Part 2, *Drawing the Body*.) In the latter, participants were introduced to bird making through a paper crafting process. Jessica Lejowa (facilitator, Botswana) notes that 'working outdoors freed the imagination of the young people. There were some brilliant designs' that were incorporated into the performance. Every little activity in Phakama is preserved for use at some point in the process leading to a particular product.

The Morija Museum, where the performance took place, was established in 1956, and holds an invaluable collection giving insight into Lesotho's history and heritage. The Morija Arts and Cultural Festival, which programmed the Phakama performance, is one of the museum's important cultural projects. In the yard of the museum there are tables made of cement attached to immovable chairs. The downward slope forms an amphitheatre, where many musicians perform during the festival. During the Phakama performance we lit fires at the bottom of the slope, among which performers and audience danced. Lineo Tsikoane, now a human rights lawyer, was one of the participants during the residency. She remembered, 'what is engraved in my mind is the performance night. I have a vivid memory of some of the audience being very wowed by us passing them white paper birds. I remember how amazing it was to have the audience as part of the performance' (2015). A flash of an amused face comes to my mind: Vunda Demula, a Save the Children UK staff member. When I ask her if she remembers the performance, she says, 'Very well .... Remember, in those days there was a notion that children were being schooled or made to do things that they did not understand' (2015). Vunda reminds me about the challenges of effecting programmes that were meant to enable children to voice their concerns. One of the things that drew her to Phakama was 'that you mobilised children. All you did was to give them a platform to express themselves. You were not feeding them what to say, but you were guiding them' (2015).

Part of the Phakama philosophy is also to learn about local settings. The places we visited were carefully chosen, exposing the facilitators to the environment that the participants had grown up, and in some cases to allow participants to see their place through different eyes. Some of the excursions we took included going to Thaba Bosiu, Basotho's stronghold at a plateau not far from Maseru and on a walk up to the top of a mountain.

Nozuko Tsetsane (participant, South Africa) asserts that her most enjoyable part in the Phakama process was looking for spaces: 'I liked when we had to go look for a space. I always looked to bad spaces so that I could make them home' (2015). Sara Matchett (facilitator, South Africa) considers the relationship between place and space, 'in Phakama I observed that every project offered a very specific encounter with a space that led to the creation of place, and within every space there were different layers, a palimpsest if you will, of stories that existed in that space prior to our arrival' (2015). The space interacted with us in this way as we created a place for the duration of the project. For two weeks, young people from Morija transformed the space and added other layers. To explore the topic, we engaged in discussions, excursions and at times asked participants to create things out of the environment. There was a young boy who used to come to the residency with his guitar, made out of recycled planks, strings and tin. He had a learning disability and had moments of drifting in and out of sessions. There was a particular tree that became his home; he would just move to the tree and play his guitar. One day, a few people visited him at his 'home' and a scene came out of that. I will never forget the glee on the boy's face. A sense of confidence developed within him. Phakama affirms many things that individuals or spaces may have had, that may have been eroded along one's growth path.

Reflections

When I reflected on the Phakama creative process with Fabio Santos, he used a metaphor: Phakama is like 'a strong elastic band, holding everyone together, but it can move, it can change, it's flexible, but it's strong as it holds a frame together' (2015). Jessica Lejowa confirms this: 'I found myself looking back at that time, and realizing that my experience there forms some of the foundation of my teaching practice, which is a large part of my identity. January 26 2003 was my nineteenth birthday. I left my teenage years in Morija and went home to Botswana with something powerful in my heart' (2015). I add another metaphor to describe Phakama: water. It takes the shape of any container it is placed in, it respects whatever it finds on the ground, and lets itself flow, even be absorbed. Because you constantly have to negotiate, you need to observe the water fitting into a particular shape. Mandla Mbothwe recalls that what he admired most about the methodology was the 'multiple voices and stories that emerge in the process, no individual script, author, director' [an affirmation of] 'pluralism, and the notion of we, the spirit of ubuntu' (2015).

Given the African Union Agenda 2063, a manifesto for 'The Africa we want' (2014), I believe projects like Phakama are invaluable to initiate discourse on pedagogy. When I think about hosting this Phakama residency in Morija, Lesotho, I realise that we have, in our own way, made history at this place.

References

Ani, M. (1994), *Yurugu - An African-Centered Critique of European Cultural Thoughts and Behavior*, Trenton: Africa Research and Publications.
Boal, A. (2002), *Theatre of the Oppressed*, London: Pluto Press.
Brook P. (1996), *The Empty Space*, New York: Touchstone Book.
Demula, V. (2015), Interview, RSA.

Freire, P. (1996), *Pedagogy of the Oppressed*, London: Penguin Books.

Lejowa, J. (2003), Residency Journal. Personal archives.

Lejowa, J. (2015), Email correspondence with the author.

Lesotho Bureau of Statistics (n.d.). Available online: www.bos.gov.ls (accessed 16 May 2014).

Lesotho National Vision 2020 (2014). Available online: www.gov.ls/.documents/.National_Vision_Document_Final (accessed 12 December 2015).

Mbothwe, M. (2015), Interview, Cape Town, South Africa.

Mda, Z. (1993), *When People Play People*, London: Zed Books

Morija Museum (n.d.). Available online: www.morija.co.ls/museum (accessed 16 May 2014).

Tsetsane, N. (2015), Interview with the author, Cape Town.

Tsikoane, L. (2015), Interview with the author, Lesotho.

Willett, J. (1964), *Brecht on Theatre: The Development of an Aesthetic*, New York: Hill and Wang.

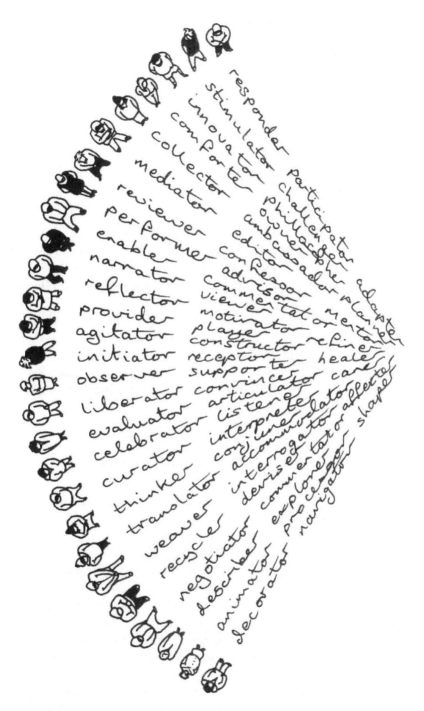

FIGURE 2 Roles.
Roles are not the same as Titles.

GIVE AND GAIN

Introduction

'Give and Gain' is the philosophy which underpins all Phakama's practice, giving structure to the devising process and performances. It values individuals and community, cultural equity and shared responsibility. As with Joan Tronto's notion of 'caring with' (1994), it relies on and builds solidarity and trust. It is the principle from which all the practice outlined in this book grows.

This section describes the practice of Give and Gain, outlines its underlying principles rooted in the specific sociocultural context of South Africa's commitment to full participation in democracy and demonstrates the impact it has had on the work and the people involved. Tony Fegan's case study, *Bulang Dikgoro/Open the Gates* (1996), details the genesis of this principle through the very first Phakama project.

Phakama Practice: Give and Gain

Lucy Richardson describes the first time she encountered Give and Gain in *Ka Mor Walo Ka Seatleng/With a Suitcase in My Hand* (1997).

> The project took place in the hall and gardens of Gilray Scout Camp on the outskirts of Cape Town with six different groups from across South Africa, a group from the UK and all their participants and facilitators. There were about two hundred people. On the first day I tried to take a photo of all the group in a circle and I couldn't fit everyone into the shot, even if I stood at the edge of the room. English was the language we spoke, with some translation, but there were at least six languages in the room and most of the participants spoke three languages.
>
> One morning I came into the hall and Sid (Andrew Siddall, facilitator, UK) had prepared two-hundred yellow triangles and two-hundred red triangles beautifully cut out in piles in the room. There was also a huge paper wheel, about

six foot in diameter, which he had stuck on the wall carefully. On the wheel spokes he had written, in beautiful calligraphy, different jobs or disciplines or activities: drama, visuals, movement, admin, pastoral.

Sid gave everybody – facilitators and participants – a yellow triangle and asked us to write our name on it and something that we could give to the project. He made it clear that this could be a skill, a quality, our profession, a competency, something we were good at. He encouraged us to write it in as much detail as we could: if the Give was playing the violin we had to detail any grades we had taken or what kind of music we played; if it were cooking, we detailed what kind of food was our specialty. Nothing was excluded. We could give a smile or carpentry skills or the ability to play a rhythm on an oil drum. We all wrote something on the piece of paper in silence.

Then Sid asked us to come back to the circle with our yellow triangles. He got out a stepladder, stood on it near the wheel so that he could reach the top. He asked everybody to decide where his or her triangle fitted in the wheel, for example, drama or movement. At Sid's request one of the South Africans started a call and response song. Gradually, one by one, two by two, people came and gave Sid a triangle, telling him where to place it on the wheel. He carefully placed each triangle on the wheel, all pointing out from the centre. A few songs and dancing later all the yellow triangles were on the wall. We looked at it and Sid asked, 'what can you see?'. We saw that the administration part of the wheel was empty, so that might be a problem, but that there were a lot of skills in drama.

Then we started again. Sid gave out the red triangles and we put our names on them and wrote something we hoped to Gain. Again we sang and ritually offered the red triangles to Sid who placed them carefully in amongst the yellow triangles on the wall.

Sid asked us, 'what more does this tell us about the project?' He was good at helping us identify where there were absences and also commenting on the positives – 'look at all these brilliant dance skills – it seems like we are going to make a really good movement piece'. He encouraged us to look at who wanted to Gain in the area we were going to Give and vice versa. We began to make connections.

The way Sid placed the triangles, with their points towards the centre and radiating out into the circle making beautiful patterns, made this collage of Gives and Gains looked like a massive sun on the wall. It pretty much filled the whole wall of the scout hall. It was a powerful image and stayed there throughout the whole project. Even if you didn't read what it was all about, its scale and colour made you smile when you came into the room. We then applied this approach of Give and Gain across all aspects of the three-week project in many different ways. When we met daily as a big group it was always beneath this 'sun' and we came back to talking about it all the time. It gave us a visual representation of ourselves as a company with self-allocated roles. We brought in an extra facilitator to work on admin – an area that we, collectively, were lacking. We made working groups that were responsible for each of the wheel areas. Sometimes we asked the participants to go to their Give groups and some time to their Gain group. So, whilst your tendency might have been to go to the area where you felt more confident, where you had something to give, you were forced to go to an area where you could gain. Sometimes we'd put people in a Give and Gain pair to make a piece of work. Sometimes we just checked whether everybody felt they were gaining what they said they hoped to gain. A couple of times we used it when somebody was excluded or not participating – deliberately locating them according to their Give or Gain. It acted as a ground plan or a map of how the finished performance might be made, what it might look like and what it might *be* like, because it has the sense of celebration of a group of individuals right there in front of you – all the time.

Making this Give and Gain wheel took half a day and talking about it extended through the whole project. Its main purpose was to affirm that in this project everyone – facilitators and participants – were equal in their capacity to learn from one another and it asked us all to take responsibility for this.

THE GIVE AND GAIN WHEEL

Depending on the size of the group it will take between one and four hours.

Prepare in advance:
- Some coloured card or paper cut into the shape of long triangles: these should be about eight inches long. You will need one red and one yellow triangle for each participant and facilitator.
- A 'wheel hub' on the wall of the workshop space: mark out a circle on a large piece of paper (about a metre in diameter) and divide it into sections like a wheel, with the spokes extending out beyond the circle. Each section should represent an aspect/activity/area of the work you are doing: for example, Producing, Acting, Digital Media, Documenting, Dancing, Pastoral, etc. These headings will vary according to the aims of the project. There will also need to be a section for 'miscellaneous.' These areas/aspects/activities should then be marked around the inner ring of the circle each by its own section. Stick the paper securely on the wall with masking tape.

The activity:

- Explain the premise – 'We believe that everyone, facilitators and participants, has something to Give and something to Gain from this project. We need to tell each other about the things we want to Give and the things we want to Gain so we can help each other Give and Gain.'
- Explain the areas/activities/aspects that will go towards making up the project by showing the 'wheel hub' and ask if anything is missing. In some projects you may want to define these areas as a group at this point, rather than filling in the headings in advance.
- Give each person a yellow triangle and invite him or her to write his or her name and a skill or capability they are able to/want to Give to the project – which would sit under one of the headings. Encourage them to be detailed: for example, Grade Eight piano, jembe drumming, singing Beyoncé songs, comedy acting, gumboot dancing.
- Give each person a red triangle and invite him or her to write his or her name and a skill or capability they would like to Gain from the project.
- Everyone needs to stick his or her red and yellow triangles on the wheel extending out from the appropriate heading. The long point of the triangle needs to point towards the circle. It helps if someone who understands what the finished wheel should look like goes first. A participant/facilitator may need to help to make it look beautiful.
- There are many ways of doing this, depending on the nature of the group and the number of participants: (a) Everyone sings a song while participants one by one go up and stick up their triangles. (b) Each participant goes up and reads out their triangle to the rest of the group before sticking it up. (c) Using recorded music or live percussion each participant dances to the Give and Gain wheel to stick up their triangle. (d) When participants are less confident about declaring their Give and Gain individually, you can support people by inviting them to work in groups, or to attach them whilst other work is going on.

Reflecting:

- Lead a reflection – what can we learn about the project and each other from looking at the wheel? Leave the wheel on the wall throughout the project and keep coming back to it.

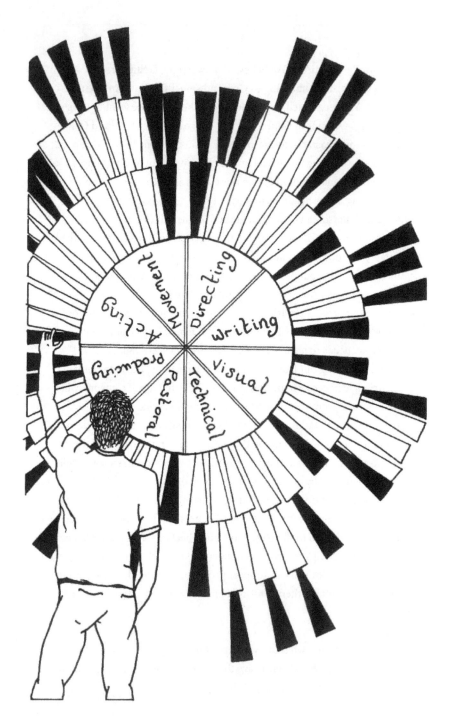

FIGURE 3 Give and Gain.

Creating the Give and Gain wheel is almost a performance in itself.

Principles of Give and Gain

Lucy Neal (director of LIFT 1979–2005) draws on complexity theory when explaining the importance of Give and Gain to Phakama's work.

> Phakama creative practice is a journey of discovery where any one individual is engaged collectively and is bound to discover a great deal more as a result of collaborating with others. They don't know what that will be. That is the practice. A resilient system is one that has the most ways of connecting with itself. By doing the Give and Gain wheel, you are not only showing what's in the system but saying 'this relates to that'. Phakama maximises the relationship between things. It is a resilient and strong system, one that communicates well with itself, that knows what's happening with itself. (2014)

Give and Gain establishes a principle, elaborated throughout the book: Phakama works with what there is in the room. Give and Gain begins to identify the particularity of this in terms of the skills, capacities and interests of each person. This shapes not only the content of a performance, but also its form. Give and Gain challenges traditional deference to job titles, age, culture or experience and it encourages alliances across age, class and gender divides. It invites everyone to sign up to a contract of equity. It is not a nod to collaborative practice but it puts it at the centre of the creative process: it is explicit and celebrated. It was notable, during interviews, how easily participants and facilitators articulated the importance of Give and Gain and its principles in four specific ways. First, making the Give and Gain wheel begins a process which extends beyond the exercise, informing all areas of practice and is surprisingly unfamiliar and difficult to evaluate. Corinne Micallef (2014) considers her experience of trying to be true to the ethos of Give and Gain:

> In the arts, it's supposedly collaborative, but is there time for that to really happen? Do people default into hierarchy, who's in charge, and split the division of labour? I think collaboration is the most natural thing in the world, but it's also incredibly ambitious to try and do that in a creative context. Sometimes there were things to unlearn, habits of efficiency, or 'we have to get it done'. Give and Gain goes back to something a bit deeper that's about trust and that can't necessarily be evaluated. In every individual moment people are Giving and Gaining. You can never say where it starts or stops.

Secondly, Give and Gain presents itself in a visual form, displayed throughout the creative process: a constant reminder of the contract of shared responsibility and a promise to be responsive to everyone's talents and needs. Andrew Siddall (2014) stresses this importance:

> It's immediate for everybody to see. It's not one person who sees it – everybody sees it. It grows. Not only do I see myself but I see where everybody else fits. I see where our strengths and weaknesses are. You can almost shape the show from that first few minutes when you see that visual. You can see where our interests are, not just as facilitators but as the entire group.

Thirdly, making the Give and Gain wheel takes time out of an already tight creative schedule but is essential in a process that draws everything from the people gathered in a room. Siddall articulates the value given to the emphasis and time allowed for this practice:

> Many people work collaboratively, particularly in the arts. The difference with Phakama is that we make a point of stating this and then spending time exploring what it means with everybody who's part of it. It's making it explicit. We'll spend three hours doing Give and Gain and giving people time to think about what they can offer and what they want to take away from it.

Lastly, Give and Gain must include everyone, coordinators, facilitators, participants and therefore everyone is cast as both teacher and learner. This promotes equity in both status and practice: everyone will be doing in this project – no one will simply be telling others what to do.

Phakama facilitators are articulate about how much each project teaches them about relational practices. Ali Zaidi was one of the four practitioners from the original UK facilitating team that took part in the first Phakama project in South Africa in 1996. For Zaidi (2015), 'connectivity, collaboration and compassion' continue to be pivotal in his art making. Reflecting on the influence of Phakama on the importance of 'co-authorship' in his work he said:

> It was all about getting people to understand that the philosophy of participant centred work means that each person brings a gift. I can now articulate this mantra better because I use it all along in my practice: in order to create a *feast*, each person brings their special dish/ 'gift' to the table. Collectively each person's unique 'gift' and specialism creates an authenticity, which otherwise is just not possible.
>
> At the time we didn't use the word 'gift', instead we called it, 'the special thing that you can bring'. We used the analogy of a wheel. In order to get the wheel rolling we needed to assess who brought what, and then view the gaps. My special gift that I had taken to South Africa was visual aesthetics. It was also about the use of materiality, because my practice had been very much about mixing different

mediums. One of the gifts common to all of the UK facilitators was the gift of working with people. We were good at communicating. We didn't have any pre-judgements and we strived to acknowledge people for who they were.

The practice of Give and Gain is the basis of how I create. It's not about a singular voice. It is about co-authorship. It's an important stance because it's a position of learning and teaching simultaneously. It is the principle of mutuality. It is the principle of a hug. You cannot hug or shake hands unless both parties share a similar intention. If the energies are not equal, then one can become the abuser and the other the abused.

Early in a project Give and Gain allows everyone to see how the work is going to be made, by the group together. It values the competence of each individual and gives them shared responsibility for the whole group. It also allows them to see themselves as part of a community from whom they can learn and 'care with'.

Cultural Contexts

South Africa and Ubuntu

Phakama's imperative to create structures for the voices of all participants to be heard developed from the specific historical and cultural context that led to and shaped the first international collaboration. In 1996, two years after the end of the Apartheid regime (1948–94), South Africa was still reeling from the violence that had been perpetrated upon it. The rhetoric around rebuilding South Africa as the harmonious multicultural 'rainbow' nation was prevalent. The Truth and Reconciliation Commission (TRC) was established by the Government of National Unity to allow both perpetrators and victims to voice their experiences and for some to be brought to justice. However, also emerging was the understanding that 'rainbowism' operated as a way to silence the complaints and concerns of black people, that the work of the TRC was more about appeasing the guilt of the white population, and that the developing democratic society would simply become a 'post-apartheid apartheid' (Fikeni 2016).

In the first Phakama project, described by Tony Fegan in the following pages, the deep-rooted inequalities experienced among the South Africans, coupled with the inequalities inherent in the colonial histories, were very raw. Allowing everyone a voice, creating time and space for everyone to tell his or her story, was paramount. But Give and Gain is about more than giving everyone a voice. It understands that everyone's experience is interconnected.

In 2009, Phakama South Africa did a project called *Mutu* at a high school in Maitland, a semi-industrial, racially mixed suburb which houses a large percentage of the African refugees living in Cape Town. *Mutu* is a Setswana Word meaning 'human' and thus referenced ubuntu. Ubuntu is a Bantu expression, which literally translates as 'personhood' or more loosely as humanity or humanness. Although it is thought to have originated in South Africa it appears in many African languages and has formed the philosophy behind a variety of postcolonial African freedom movements. Archbishop Desmond Tutu, reflecting on his time as chair of the TRC, popularized and globalized the term in his book, *No Future without Forgiveness*:

> [Ubuntu] speaks of the very essence of being human …. We belong in a bundle of life. We say, 'a person is a person through other people'. It is not 'I think therefore I am'. It says rather: 'I am human because I belong.' I participate, I share. A person with ubuntu is open and available to others, affirming of others, does not feel threatened that others are able and good; for he or she has a proper self-assurance that comes from knowing that he or she belongs in the greater whole and is diminished when others are humiliated or diminished, when others are tortured or oppressed, or treated as if they were less that who they are. (Tutu 1999: 34–5)

During the anti-apartheid campaign and within post-apartheid rhetoric ubuntu was reclaimed as a philosophy on which to build the new nation. Its importance became formalized when written into South Africa's Interim Constitution in 1993: 'There is a need for understanding but not for vengeance, a need for reparation but not for retaliation, a need for ubuntu but not for victimization' (Truth and Reconciliation Mechanism 1993). Ubuntu has, at its core, the notion of taking responsibility for and having empathy with 'the other'. It resonates with Tronto's ideas about the ethics of care, discussed in the previous section, and the sociologist Richard Sennett's ideas about cooperation which we will look at in the next section. 'Caring with' is the only possible response in ubuntu because the 'self' is created from and maintained by your relationship to 'the other'. As Michael Onyebuchi Eze (2010: 190–1) elaborates,

> This idealism suggests to us that humanity is not embedded in my person solely as an individual; my humanity is co-substantively bestowed upon the other and me. Humanity is a quality we owe to each other. We create each other and need to sustain this otherness creation. And if we belong to each other, we participate in our creations: we are because you are, and since you are, definitely I am.

It was in this climate that Phakama developed a process that explicitly acknowledges the interconnectedness of all its participants and the responsibility and care we owe each other. With ubuntu each individual both gives to and gains from the group, the community, the society, the world he or she is part of.

Progressive Education

The development of Give and Gain is also influenced by progressive education movement of the 1970s, which saw arts practitioners, led by the pioneering work of Dorothy Heathcote and Gavin Bolton, champion a child-centred approach to learning. This was the climate in which Tony Fegan, director of Learning for LIFT, had worked as a comprehensive school teacher in 1970's multicultural London and was fundamental in shaping the approach developed during the first Phakama residency.

Heathcote and Bolton are pedagogical philosophers and practitioners influenced by the American philosopher, psychologist and educational reformer John Dewey (1859–1952). Dewey developed a radical set of pedagogical theories at the turn of the twentieth century. Rooted in 'action' as opposed to absorption of knowledge, his emphasis was on the importance of democracy in the classroom. He believed in experiential learning that required students to work collaboratively and cooperatively, to problem solve and apply critical thinking (Palmer 2001). Drawing directly on Dewey's theories and influence, American humanistic psychologist Carl Rogers (1902–87) developed his person-centred therapy which focused on the self-understanding of the client and the therapist as, in Rogers' words, facilitator. He understood that in order for a person to 'grow' psychologically they need an environment in which the following characteristics can flourish: genuineness (openness and self-disclosure), acceptance (being seen with unconditional positive regard) and empathy (being listened to and understood) (Rogers 1959). He applied this understanding to education, believing that a person learns only those things that are perceived as being involved in the maintenance or enhancement of the structure of self, and therefore any threat to the self of the learner has to be reduced to the minimum. He understood that a person cannot teach another person directly, a person can only facilitate another's engagement with learning (Rogers and Freiberg 1994) with the implication being that

> teachers who either naturally have, or are trained to have empathy, genuineness (congruence), and who prize their students (positive regard) create an important level of trust in the classroom and exert significant positive effects on student outcomes including achievement scores, interpersonal functioning, self-concept, and attendance. (Rogers and Neilson 2013: ii)

Like many learning environments, Phakama draws upon these ideas by placing emphasis on facilitation of learning rather than instruction, generating the material from the participants' own interests and concerns, and creating a safe space in which the learning can take place. But, perhaps most importantly, the practice of Give and Gain as outlined in this chapter ensures that a 'differentiated perception of the field' is facilitated and therefore a possible change in self-perception, particularly in relation to competence, might take place. Participants and facilitators are asked to see themselves with new eyes, to celebrate their skills, experiences and competencies freshly. It also invites everyone to reflect on the areas of practice where they feel less competent, encouraging everyone to move out of their comfort zones, to widen their horizons, to stretch beyond what is already known: to learn. In Part Three of this book, interviews with people who have been involved with Phakama evidence this 'flourishing'.

Another significant influence was Paulo Freire's (1921–97) critical pedagogy, developed through working with adult learners in impoverished areas of North Eastern Brazil, which informed *Education as the Practice of Freedom* (1967) and *Pedagogy of the Oppressed* (1968). He believed that education, in any form, could not escape the relations of oppression inherent in any social interaction. He saw education as a political act which therefore has two primary functions. First, it must develop critical consciousness, enabling participants to construct themselves as subjects in the world and thus regain their humanity. Secondly, it must provide the capacity for participants to question and ultimately change their historical and social situation. Importantly for Phakama, Freire describes a dialogic exchange between teachers and students, believing they have much to learn from each other. His pedagogy is based in questioning, reflection and participation. Freire's ideas were the foundation for Augusto Boal's theatre-based critical social enquiry, Theatre of the Oppressed, and were central to the Black Consciousness Movement associated with Steve Biko in South Africa from which the township arts practice described as the 'theatre of struggle' emerged (Palmer 2001).

In the UK, practitioners also began using theatre and drama as processes to support educational engagement. Dorothy Heathcote and Gavin Bolton (among others) in the 1960 and 1970s began to explore a participant-centred approach they called 'process drama' in which drama was used as a learning medium. In particular, Tony Fegan sites Heathcote's idea of the Mantle of the Expert as an influence. This approach, again, put the learner at the centre of the learning. Dorothy Heathcote always began a class by engaging with what the children wanted to do. It also repositioned the power in the room. The children become responsible experts in the classroom who are engaged in an enquiry for which it is necessary to solve problems and make decisions – which they find themselves able to do. The teacher becomes the enabler rather than the transmitter and their role is to create conditions whereby a mantle of leadership, knowledge, competency and understanding grows around the child. The approach is based on doing, in the belief that this mantle grows through 'usage' (Heathcote 2009: 1–2).

The work Fegan describes in his case study does not put the young people in a fictional context. The making of a theatre piece is a very real problem, which needs to be solved: How can we share our stories with another group of people who will witness them in a week's time? The Give and Gain approach, however, applies the principles of the Mantle of the Expert. It has, at its heart, a clear repositioning of power – teachers and students are experts and learners. The first project was built around the idea that 'everybody has a story to tell' which ensured that the work came from the participants and that they were experts in their field – but also crucially so were the facilitators. As with Heathcote's fictional contexts the work allows, both in its process and in its creative practice, the participants to imagine society anew, one they want to live in. But in the same way that Heathcote's students are able to move in and out of the fictional context to learn things they are not expert in to take back to the fiction, so the facilitators in a Phakama project give full responsibility to the 'expert' participants, but are always available to catch them should they stumble.

This sharing of responsibility for young people to envision the work and their world sat well in the particular cultural moment that framed this first project. Young people, school children, were critically involved in the fight against apartheid. Some of those young people were now trainee facilitators for this project. Now in power, the African National Congress was clear about the positioning of young people as collaborators in the rebuilding of the new South Africa. This, coupled with the spirit of ubuntu, both necessitated the invention of Give and Gain and allowed it to resonate with the experience of facilitators and participants alike.

In the following case study Tony Fegan, LIFT's Director of Learning (1993–2007), describes *Bulang Dikgoro/Open the Gates*, the initial partnership project between LIFT and Sibikwa Community Theatre, based in Benoni. Benoni was a white suburb of Johannesburg near Davidton, a black township, and Actonville, an Asian suburb. In addition to Give and Gain, Tony describes two other aspects of this first project that remain embedded in Phakama's work. First, its aim was to introduce arts educators and artists from South Africa to new ways of working through the arts. Training has remained central to the work and later in Phakama UK's projects, *Tripwires* (2010–11) and *Spotlight* (2013–15), it became paramount. The impact of this commitment to training is explored in the final part of this book, Celebration. Secondly, the performance was to take place in the warehouse in which the training happened and thus it imposed the notion of site-specificity – something that had already infused much of LIFTs practice and is integral to Phakama's. Engagement with site is addressed in the second part of this book, Making the Performance.

References

Eze, M. (2010), *Intellectual History in Contemporary South Africa*, New York: Palgrave Macmillan.

Fikeni, L. (2016), 'Lwandile Fikeni's Ruth First Speech on Rage in the Rainbow Nation is Indispensable', *Mail and Guardian*, 18 August, http://mg.co.za/article/2016-08-18-protest-art-and-the-aesthetics-of-rage-social-solidarity-and-a-post-rainbow-sa (accessed 10 October 2016).

Heathcote, D. (2009), 'Mantle of the Expert: My Current Understanding'. Keynote address to the Weaving Our Stories: International Mantle of the Expert Conference, University of Waikato, Hamilton, USA. Unpublished keynote address.

Micalleff, C. (2014), Interview at Queen Mary University of London, 16 December.

Neal, L. (2014), Interview at Queen Mary University of London, 16 December.

Palmer, J. (2001), *Fifty Modern Thinkers on Education*, London: Routledge.

Rogers, C., H. Lyon and J. Tausch (2014), *Becoming an Effective Teacher: Person-Centered Teaching, Psychology, Philosophy and Dialogues with Carl R. Rogers and Harold Lyon*, London and New York: Routledge.

Rogers, C. (1959), 'A Theory of Therapy, Personality and Interpersonal Relationships as Developed in the Client-centred Framework', in S. Koch (ed.), *Psychology: A Study of a Science. Vol. 3: Formulations of the Person and the Social Context*, New York: McGraw Hill.

Rogers, C. and H. Freiberg (1994), *Freedom to Learn* (3rd Revised Edition), Upper Saddle River, NJ: Prentice Hall.

Siddall, A. (2014), Interview at Queen Mary University of London, 16 December.

South Africa's Interim Constitution (1993). Available online: https://peaceaccords.nd.edu/ provision/truth-or-reconciliation-mechanism-interim-constitution-accord (accessed June 2016).

Tronto, J. (1994), *Moral Boundaries: A Political Argument for an Ethic of Care*, London and New York: Routledge.

Tutu, D. (1999), *No Future Without Forgiveness*, London: Rider.

Truth and Reconciliation Commission (n.d.). Available online: http://www.justice.gov.za/ trc/ (accessed 12 June 2015).

Truth and Reconciliation Mechanism (1993). Available online: https://peaceaccords. nd.edu/provision/truth-or-reconciliation-mechanism-interim-constitution-accord (accessed 12 June 2016).

Wagner, B. (1999), *Dorothy Heathcote, Drama as a Learning Medium*, Portland, ME: Calendar Islands Publishers.

Zaidi, A. (2015), Interview at London Metropolitan University, 20 March.

CASE STUDY
BULANG DIKGORO/
OPEN THE GATES
(BENONI, JOHANNESBURG,
SOUTH AFRICA, 1996)

Tony Fegan

Description: This month-long 'experimental residency' for artists, arts educators and young people was the genesis of Phakama. The site-specific promenade performance, *Bulang Dikgoro/Open the Gates,* was inspired by the stories offered by the participants about surviving the day-to-day realities of life as a teenager in Benoni and their aspirations for life in post-apartheid South Africa.

Place: Benoni, South Africa.

Date/Duration: July 1996 (with follow up projects and evaluations until January 1997).

Partnerships: LIFT, Sibikwa Community Theatre Company.

Facilitators: Sibikwa Community Theatre Directors: Phyllis Klotz and Smal Ndaba; South African Facilitators: Caroline Calburn, Trevor Engel, Manya Gittel, Donald Legodi, Benedict Mashiyane, Pogiso Mogwera, Martin Mgwenyana, Raphael Mchunu, Pandora Ngubane, Jabu Masilela, Ephraim Hlophe and Shirley Mzizi; LIFT Facilitating Team from the UK: Ali Zaidi, Beverley Randall, Andrew Siddall, Tony Fegan.

Participants: Fifty young people from Johannesburg and its environs.

Funders: British Council and South African Arts Council.

Facilitators Coming Together

Since the fall of apartheid, Lucy Neal and myself from LIFT and Phyllis Klotz and Smal Ndaba from Sibikwa Community Theatre had begun to speak about a professional arts exchange between arts education practitioners in South Africa and London. From these discussions emerged *Bulang Dikgoro/Open the Gates* (1996), the project from which Phakama as a process, a network, an organization was born.

The month-long project was to focus on training arts education practitioners from across South Africa, particularly those outside the main metropolitan areas, who, previously, had few professional development opportunities. Phyllis recruited successfully via the networks she had across the NGOs and Arts for Development sector. This resulted in an eclectic group of adults who were prepared to dedicate a month of their lives working with a group of artist practitioners from London whom they had never met. The training would culminate in the team all working together to produce a performance with local young people.

Klotz and Ndaba insisted that a culturally diverse group of practitioners from the UK would be an essential part of any exchange. Like the South African artists they recruited, the cultural profile of the UK team should reflect the complex cultural aspirations of South Africa's 'Rainbow Nation' two years after the elections. The London team was drawn from artists and producers in LIFT's networks.

The project base was a large, ground floor space beneath Sibikwa's headquarters, in a series of industrial buildings within a car repair yard. It was heated by portable gas heaters during what turned out to be the coldest July and August in thirty years in Johannesburg.

The London team agreed from the outset that we would place an emphasis on listening and looking throughout the exchange. We agreed that

1 We would always review the day's work and take on board the responses of the group.

2 We would plan each evening for the following day.

3 We would not come into conflict with each other whatever the circumstances.

4 Although English would be the main language of communication, we would ensure that the other languages present would be part of the process.

5 Time would be spent ensuring that all comprehended conceptual issues.

Although I was coordinating, it soon became a group-facilitated process with each playing to our professional strengths and discovering some we didn't know along the way. Once we had passed the polite initial two days of welcomes and induction meetings, some challenging issues of a philosophical and political nature began to emerge in the workshop space. The first five days involved some practical sharing of what people knew about, bringing people together to work. Warm-up games were shared. Some of the South Africans who were working in classroom drama or youth arts were familiar with them and contributed their own. For others it was a revelation that you would get up and do what you might expect the young people to do.

Our key focus was a response to the idea that 'everybody has a story to tell'. First, everybody shared how each had come to be in Benoni. The work employed a number of practical processes such as partnered timelines, hot seating, personal testimonies, freeze frames, drama games and song. It was hugely confessional, with people telling their life stories and professional experiences, many of which had been informed by the apartheid era.

Some important factors emerged which had an impact on all our relations. It was clear that there was a huge disparity between individuals' experiences in the Northern and Southern Hemispheres and also between black and white in South Africa. This was informed by the colonial legacy and Britain's tacit and overt support for apartheid until recent times. The impact of growing up and living in the apartheid era was expressed explicitly. There was a definite split in the group between those of us over forty years old and those younger in terms of experiences or aspirations. It was painful, full of tears, remorse, hope and, sometimes, sheer hysteria. We debated potentially oppositional ideas about how to work with participants. Some defended director/choreographer/designer-led practice while others advocated devising processes or particular methodologies such as forum theatre or forms such as traditional African dance. We also debated what kind of performance might emerge from the familiar 'theatre of struggle' form that would reflect the reality of the young people we would be working with. The ongoing and most contentious conversation, however, was the one around the roles of teacher and learner. It focused on the challenge to the status of the teacher when an emphasis was put on a learner-centred process. The conventionally acknowledged social respect for the teacher, whatever the circumstances, came under immense scrutiny.

Emerging Methodology

We had to find a simple way of demonstrating how a disparate group of adults with no experience of working with each other, let alone collectively facilitating young people to make art, might work together with equity. In our wide-ranging discussions and practical arts workshops we were beginning to be aware of our individual talents and skills. There was a huge interest in the Londoners' experience of site-specific work. We listened to the successes that the South Africans had experienced in creating work in communities. If we were hoping to share our professional practice of work with young people, we needed a structure that would harness the painful political histories and personal experiences.

'Everybody has a story to tell' became a framing device to think about the important issue of historical resolution. The TRC was just beginning its work so the idea that in order to achieve equality we had to hear all the stories, however painful, was common currency. All agreed that, whatever our past, the focus of working with young people to enable/facilitate them to step into a new future rang true.

The framework led us to talk deeply and explore practically how you facilitate a genuinely child/participant-centred process. This raised all sorts of issues of status, culture and age-appropriateness around what young people were allowed to say and do. The most contentious moment emerged from a discussion about young people being defiant if they held an adult's gaze and the lack of respect that entailed in some societies. This heated debate was stopped when one of the oldest black South African practitioners recounted his experience at the hands of some white men in his home town. He recounted how he was forced to step off the pavement and to look down as the men harangued him while a group of young black boys witnessed his humiliation. He could look neither the white men nor the boys in the eye, and yet he knew that the white men were focusing their hatred at him through their eyes. It was a moment of revelation and it had a transformative effect on us all. It created a space to reflect on the larger history we had all been grappling with and how it had played out for one man in our midst.

We then approached the issue of 'holding the gaze' at first quietly concentrating on seeing our reflection in our partners' pupils. For many this was the first time they had experienced seeing their image in another's eyes in such a public setting. There was a sense of wonder and stillness. Then gradually after some time as we moved from person to person we began to play ridiculous games of holding each other's gaze until the other laughed. It went some way to acknowledging the new territory we were all stepping into together and was a practical sign for the focus we would need as potential co-facilitators. This was a breakthrough and dispersed some of the tension relating to the historical rhetoric that had been present. We began to look at how experiences impact on us emotionally, individually and collectively. We had stepped over a line and started to work in small creative teams of threes and fours to respond to stories we wanted to share.

Workshopping

We agreed to break down the tasks of running sessions together. Some of the participants with previous participatory drama experience paired up with those who were new to the work. A London team member joined each group. Each small team ran the warm-up session every morning and led creative discussions and practical improvisations with words, music, dance and visual arts/design, exploring how we might work with young people.

We set up a series of workshops exploring the organization of an arts project. We broke it down into the following areas: design with Ali Zaidi; text with Tony Fegan; technical and production design with Andrew Siddall; music with Pogiso Mogwera and Martin Ngwenyana; dance with Shirley Mzizi and Caroline Calburn; and production with Beverley Randall. We ran a carousel process of workshops to ensure that we all could be involved or lead in our strength and also try out something we were less familiar with or confident in. Some of the exercises (listed below) we did in these early workshops formed the basis of our work with the young people and have developed in to the practice described throughout this book.

MY BOX OF OBJECTS

This exercise was used to enable the adult facilitators to learn more about each other. Later in the project, we used it with the young people to aid the creation of a fictitious character.

- Each participant chooses objects, personal to themselves, and puts them in a box.
- Other participants interpret the box and speculate about what it says about the person who curated it – telling their imagined story.
- The person whose box is being discussed can only respond after others have made their interpretations.

In later projects we saw this kind of exercise developing into some aspects of Cultural Tours and it continues to be used as a way of introducing individuals and groups.

MY TIMELINE

This exercise helped the facilitators to see what history, experience or knowledge they shared. Later in the project, we used it with the young people to develop a fictitious character's history.

- Participants, starting in the present and going back in time to childhood, identify significant events in their lives and professional development.

- Participants present these, in relation to others, on a timeline across the floor – this can be done with post-it notes, shells, beads or any other small objects.
- These are then mapped alongside national and worldwide changes.

We continue to use timelines, made of random objects or post-it notes. In some ways this exercise is the forerunner of *Drawing the Body* and *Map of the World.*

THE MINUTE TEXT

- Individual participants are asked to write a title and the first line of a story on a piece of paper.
- Each participant reads their title and sentence to the group, who write and share back the next two lines of the story.
- Participants then choose one of the lines offered by the others.
- Starting with the new line participants continue to write their story for exactly one minute.
- Stories are shared with the group, who give feedback and explore common themes.
- Repeat writing for two minutes, then ten minutes, etc. until a rough story has emerged.
- Split participants into groups. Each group chooses one story, not their own, to interpret in movement, drama, song or visual art.

This exercise became a metaphor for what the process was all about – how everyone contributes, how material is generated, shared and added to the creative process. This exercise went on to form collective writing exercise *Poetry Cuts.*

HOW TEXT IS ALTERED BY SITE

This exercise took the Irish myth of the *selkie* or seal-woman in which a human male steals a *selkie's* sealskin – preventing her from returning to the sea, and leaving her with no option but to marry her 'captor'.

- Read/tell the story to the group.
- Participants make notes of images that strike them.
- Split participants into groups and ask them to share images and recreate them somewhere in the building or its environs.

On this project one group worked indoors, one in the intermediary space and one group outdoors. The latter group created footsteps on the 'beach' that were a powerful reminder of the mythical women's journey from seal to a human. This was a key exercise for most on this project, in understanding the performance territory that we found ourselves moving in, as well as discovering the wealth of what the site had to offer – something Phakama has built upon ever since.

Give and Gain Wheel

Through these processes we arrived at a point of understanding about how we might work and create a performance with young people. The collective desire of 'giving voice' to young people gave rise to the Give and Gain wheel. Sid developed it into a specific practice (described at the start of this section). It emerged as a simple way of practically illustrating what range of skills and experiences were needed to develop arts work with young people shared with a public audience. It helped to disperse the anxieties that some individuals had about their lack of formal arts skills, training or experience working with young people. It drew attention to the collective process involved in making performance and emphasized that all could give and play a part and all had something to gain or learn from each other.

The conscious process of working out what skills we had or what ideas we could forge together to prepare ourselves to work with the young people meant that we brought together the emotional privacy of an improvisation process and the public spectacle of song, dance and design that inform theatre. After twenty days' work we had a joint team that was confident in working with each other and familiar with each other's practice. We were prepared to work with young people in an open and non-judgemental manner and to respond to whatever the young people might offer.

Working with the Young People

When the young people, whom Sibikwa had recruited via a series of workshops in local schools, came for ten days of workshops each afternoon after school, we were ready. At the end of that ten-day period, we literally opened the gates to an audience. The title of the show, *Bulang Dikgoro/Open the Gates*, referenced the process: that all facilitators and participants were opening new gates. In retrospect the project opened gates on a whole set of processes which would stretch over the next twenty years and four continents. It is impossible to capture the experience of those who witnessed the communal event which was the performance. However, it is useful to have a workable description of what we shared, of the work we did in those ten days, in order to understand the devising processes that generated and curated material for the performance.

Performance Map

We had six performance areas: two outside and four inside the warehouse. The audience, led by young guides, was presented with two open-air moments in sequence and four pieces inside. These inside pieces were short, repeatable loops which enabled the audience to experience them in smaller groups.

Opening the Gates Dance: My memories of this are the slightly shocked faces of the invited guests as they entered the yard at dusk under a huge bamboo arch: British Council officials; a South African Arts Council representative; Asian, black and white parents; Phylllis Klotz; the Sibikwa Community Theatre company. They were confronted by six blazing barrels and had to make their way through a contemporary dance piece to a small stage at the end of the yard. The heat from the barrels was palpable.

Shall I Go or Shall I Stay?: This told the story of an informal settlement where residents have been asked to move on by the authorities. It was presented as a deconstructed conversation about whether to try and stay put or pack up and go. This conversation became more and more fragmented with indecision as it was repeated.

A Township Drama: This scene was presented in the style of 'the theatre of struggle' protest plays which were popular in the townships of apartheid South Africa and made accessible to others by the Market Theatre, Johannesburg. It was high energy, declamatory and infused with song and dark humour. It dealt with the flood of guns into the townships at the end of the struggle and the subsequent violence and domestic conflict they contributed to.

The Whispered Confessions: In this scene, individual participants, holding oil lamps behind picture frames, whispered stories as if they were confessions. Each audience listener had to lean into the picture frame to hear each story.

The Oracle for the Future: This scene was presented in a covered space with a participant dressed as a prophetess/*sangoma* (traditional South African healer) situated at the top of a ten-foot wooden ladder. She wore a cloak with pockets containing paper scrolls that had prophesies for the future written on them. Spectators were asked to pick a number. An assistant climbed the ladder to consult the prophetess who then indicated which pocket the assistant should take a scroll from to give to the spectator. Other *sangoma* performers sat whispering phrases linking past, present and future.

My Soweto – A Lament: This was a central site with a beautifully set table with white linen, wine glasses and silver cutlery and an elaborate wire chandelier, amid a rock and rubble strewn landscape. A small culturally diverse group led by an inspiring young woman lamented the changing social and physical landscape of Soweto, while a group continually set and reset the table. Throughout, a reporter commented on the scene.

Sunburst – Praise Songs: The spectators were eventually escorted by young performers outside again where it had become dark. Amid singing and dancing they were led to the gates at the end of the yard where a huge sunburst, made of old car exhausts wrapped in paraffin wadding, was set alight.

Applying the Methodology

The fifty young people came from the black Township of Daveyton, the Asian community of Actonville and the white Benoni High School. We worked together for ten days after school and each session lasted for three hours.

The pastoral care of the young people was the responsibility of the young arts practitioners from Sibikwa Community Theatre, assisted by Beverley Randall (UK). Because the participants were not in residence, the pastoral care largely consisted of ensuring the young people from Daveyton had enough bus fare to get home after each workshop. From the start, the young people worked in mixed groups, and care was taken that all the young people could understand what was being talked about. English, Afrikaans, Xhosa and Zulu coexisted. English was the main language of communication but time was given for translation to take place.

Each session began with a physical workshop followed by a short reflection on the previous afternoon. The young people were invited to join small teams of facilitators who had opted to work inside or outside on site. Together they devised material. The decision on how it might be sited was negotiated with the larger group after the material was shared with everybody.

The most critical pastoral issue to emerge was the revelation that some of the young people from Davidton were experiencing familiarity with guns and violence.

The young people talked candidly to adults, often for the first time, about these experiences. These issues were eventually addressed publically via the fiction of the drama. It was a new experience to some of the adults that the individual social and emotional health of the young people should be a pedagogic concern for us all. I believe it marked a shift in some people's thinking: from the 'group identity' more important in the anti-apartheid struggle era, to the 'individual's rights' of the new era.

The 'everybody has a story to tell' starting point resonated with the young people immediately. It enabled them to go beyond the didactic rhetoric of the 'theatre of struggle' that they had inherited from the generation that had been on the frontline. That form had dealt with themes which were now, in 1996, already history. Our approach encouraged them to draw on their own experiences and perceptions and to present them with ambiguity. While they also embraced the songs, dances and the familiar texts of the inherited performance language, the young Asian, white and black South Africans were enabled to create a series of fictive worlds that were more complex and authentic. A mixture of dynamic, 'grab you by the heart' dramas were counterpointed with quieter, reflective and hesitant improvisations.

For example, the process of creating the *Shall I Go or Shall I Stay?* section arose from a role play which responded to the Bantustans (areas designated by the white South African government as black 'homelands' in the mid-to-late twentieth century), which were a major strategic device to segregate and exclude black South Africans during apartheid. Pogiso Mogwera (facilitator, SA) and Martin Ngwenyana (facilitator, SA) using Heathcote's 'the mantle of the expert', gave some young people the role of officials deciding who could move on from an informal settlement to a township and others were given the role of residents. The response from the young people in role as residents was one of huge indecision when it transpired that moved families would be split up. The resulting performance piece portrayed the emotional responses from characters that were practically rendered speechless by having to make this decision. In conversation the young people revealed the provisional nature of their own family's economic and social lives. They also shared their aspirations to be part of a new nation and the educational and economic dreams they had for their futures. All wanted to do well and matriculate from school, in contrast to their parent's generation who had been denied this opportunity.

The more intimate *Oracle for the Future* piece was a comment on the hidden nature of traditional beliefs and animistic practices (a belief that all entities – human and non-human – possess a spiritual essence) that coincided with Christianity in South Africa. These were a secret source of fascination for participants, particularly the young women, as the *sangomas* were often powerful women. The young women worked assiduously with Beverley Randall to devise a process that would demonstrate the expertise of divining a future for those who might visit their oracle. It resonated with their own, newly discovered, aspirations for the future.

Give and Gain modelled to the young people that the process they were involved in would be as equitable as possible. It was a constant reminder to the adults of our process contract. Also, the process identified that many of the young people instinctively knew what was needed to create a public performance event. Genuinely balancing Give processes and Gain processes was a challenge, especially when the time constraint of producing a public event often tempted us to cut the corners. However, it enabled us to identify different modes of expression that in a more conventional devising process might have been overlooked. The example below illustrates the strengths of Give and Gain, but also its limitations in working to time constraints. It demonstrates the danger of deviating from it being a genuinely open and liberating process and of ignoring it once it has been embraced by participants and facilitators alike.

Two of our South African facilitators, Manya Gittel, with forum theatre skills, and Trevor Engel, a carpentry teacher at a reform school in the Western Cape, worked with a small group of inexperienced and 'quiet' black and Asian girls. They were creating an intimate confessional improvisation that became *The Whispered Confessions*. This was a Gain group who had never performed before and could have, in a conventional theatre devising mode, been overlooked. However, their desire to be in charge of their story coupled with Manya's and Trevor's adherence to the learner-centred approach produced a moving piece of performance.

The piece needed an aesthetic design frame and, having spoken to the group about this and with the pressure of the performance in one day's time, Ali Zaid (facilitator, UK) and I went away that evening and came up with a solution. When we returned the following day and declared that we had found the solution, the response was overwhelmingly negative. Trevor and Manya stated that we had not consulted them and we were imposing our aesthetic ideas on them and the group. A protracted discussion resolved the dispute but it reminded me of the challenge of establishing an open creative process and then closing it down without notice. Give and Gain is at its weakest when there is no time to bring ideas to be explored properly and when the 'outside eye' role is not agreed. Ali and I had undermined Manya and Trevor's sense of creative agency in facilitating the group and had not involved them in our decision-making. In fact, the time we spent undoing our presumptions could have been used in exploring, in an open manner, the performance solution that we had come up with.

Another example was *A Township Drama*, created by a group of young people. They produced a performance piece full of tales of violence, drug use and guns suffused with a dark ambiguity. It critiqued the received view of communal solidarity exemplified by the 'theatre of struggle' aesthetic they used. This generated an anxiety in some of the adult facilitators. The piece palpably demonstrated that a significant majority of the group had experienced and witnessed such events. This was supported by other young people's reactions when they saw the piece. The fact that the scene was a made up of participants from all three cultural groups added to the frisson. Questions of 'can we show this?' and 'are they exaggerating?' coupled with 'how do they know this?' and 'what will the audience think we have been doing with them?' revealed the tension between the 'everybody has a story to tell' theme and the reality of adults wishing to preserve a status quo. There were anxieties of how it might reflect on facilitators personally, as well as in the official education and cultural spheres they inhabited elsewhere. There were also worries that we might be breaking the boundaries of hospitality that Sibikwa Community Theatre had extended to us by inviting us to be in Benoni.

However, it was the very diversity of performance responses and aesthetic styles that the Give and Gain process had enabled that meant *A Township Drama* was seen as part of a bigger whole. The whole performance was a complex reflection of the young people's reading of the new South Africa and the stories that had contributed to a post-struggle reality they inhabited.

The work was theatrically ambitious, disturbing and celebratory. Caroline Calburn (facilitator, SA) described the images that lingered in her training journal, 'Snatches of song, words … fractured sentences. Glimpses of realities all piled upon another, whispered secrets from mouths haloed by oil lamps, an oracle up a long ladder and a rainbow canopy surrounded by raging fire' (Calburn 1997). The emerging Give and Gain methodology was allied with a participant-centred approach and a willingness for the adults to facilitate individual young people to step into positions of shared artistic leadership. It encouraged time for experimentation within time constraints and it allowed the adults to test the balance between philosophical ideas and practice.

Reference

Calburn, C. (1997), *Open the Gates*, Project Journal, Personal Archive.

INTERVIEW WITH MILDRETT STEVENS, TRACEY-LEE GATES AND SHARON WAVERLEY

The three South African participant/trainee facilitators from Cape Town interviewed below did not participate in this first project but joined shortly after, in the late 1990s. The women, in their thirties at the time of the interview, reflect on their experiences as teenagers working with Phakama. They are Afrikaans speakers and would have been classified as 'coloured' under apartheid.

The interview confirms the importance of preparing the ground effectively – that the process of good hosting and the practice of Give and Gain can have lasting impact on people's lives. Mildrett, Tracey and Sharon consider ideas of identity, ownership, acceptance and belonging. They talk of Give and Gain giving them confidence, expanding their horizons, encouraging them to see things differently, to be engaged. They confirm that it showed them how to recognize the needs of others and build friendships and community. They explore how these things shape the form of the performance and discuss the thorny issue of cultural sharing which will be expanded upon in the next section. What cannot be captured on the page was the laughter and joy that filled the room during this interview.

Mildrett Stevens, Sharon Waverley and Tracey-Lee Gates (now Jacobs) joined Phakama in 1998 for *Ka Mor Walo Ka Seatleng/With a Suitcase in My Hand*. Mildrett went on to take part in many local projects and big international projects including *Call Me Not a Woman* (2000), *The Robben Island Peace Project* (2001) and the Grundtvig exchange with Swedish students (2002–3). Tracey also took part in *Call Me Not a Woman*.

Lucy Richardson: What has stayed with you from Phakama?

Mildrett Stevens: I remember names. Names are important because that's what we did in Phakama. Every week you have to say everybody's names, whether we're twenty or we are forty-five, you have to go around the circle and get everybody's names. And if I asked Caroline Calburn, 'Who is that boy?', she asks me, 'Who's "that boy"? Go and find out what his name is'. And that still stays with me. If I walk into a restaurant, the first thing I ask the waiter is, 'What's your name, please'. It's the same with the taxi driver, the bus driver, whomever I encounter. It is important for me to engage with names because it gives somebody a sense of belonging and ownership: a name is the only thing that you really own. That is what we were taught in Phakama. A name it is about valuing people, acknowledging them.

Sharon Waverley: For me, it is about performance. You might know this person can do the performance better than that person, but you won't say 'no, that person mustn't do it'. It's not about who can perform better, it's about how you can express yourself. I remember sometimes, I said 'I can't, I can't'. And then Caroline Calburn said, 'Yes you can, just do this'. And for me that was very important, because sometimes in your own life, people reject you because you can't do something better than others. But Phakama gave you acceptance to carry through the performance in the best way you can. So for me it's don't give up on a person, always push, always encourage, always motivate and you'll get the best performance.

Tracey-Lee Gates: For me it would be about looking at things differently. Like looking at that window, perhaps, and then not just seeing a window but something else, maybe [looking through it to see] a boat that's arriving. It's just the Phakama way of looking at things more deeply or in a different way, that's what I've learnt.

Fabio Santos: What does Give and Gain mean to you?

SW: What I gained is confidence in myself: the idea that I can be whatever I want to be. I was a fifteen-year-old girl, not knowing who she was and who she will become, but Phakama gave me a sense of belonging. You can be gawky, you can be strange, but they accept you for your uniqueness. When I make friends I always give my all, I'm always present in that moment. That is what Phakama has taught me. When you're with someone, make sure you give. It's not just about drama, but having an impact, a footprint, on the person's life.

MS: I concur with Sharon in terms of the gaining of confidence. I can get up on stage to talk in front of a crowd of thousands of people. And because of the confidence aspect I've made friends. I have been able to carve my path to the life that I have now because of the fact that I try to volunteer myself, to say or to do something new. I can really, really, really ascribe that to the fact that I was part of Phakama. What did I Give? A lot of my time. It was time consuming because of where we lived, especially when we had our rehearsals. We didn't have parents who had cars to come and fetch us. Sometimes there were no taxis. You had to walk and sometimes we did a walking bus ride, dropping people on the way. I was the furthest away so I had to walk alone or sometimes I had to sleep over with somebody who was closer. I've also given me, as a person: my love and attention and my engagement – whether with the facilitators or the learners, or the material, or with the place. It was really about being present and giving your all and making the best of it.

TLG: I've gained friendships all over the world that I cherish.

FS: What made you stay with Phakama?

SW: Where we come from we didn't have things to do, something to look forward to. We didn't have friends outside our own space and Phakama was the way of owning something for yourself. I had my family, they're all crowded in the house, but on a Saturday morning I could be Sharon and have attention just for Sharon.

TLG: Learning something that you've never learnt at school or at home. Going there and doing all those different activities and engaging with people. Not knowing what you're going to do or what to expect or what the end result may be. Just creating something.

MS: I mean the facilitators usually say 'This is the idea that we have towards a performance. What do you think? Let's hear what you have to say'. You know, that was *lekker*, that was nice.

TLG: Not always just speaking, but creating something to put in the performance. Maybe you don't talk that much but you can create something with your hands and it will be part of the performance and you will say 'wow! my work is there'.

SW: What I also liked about Phakama was when we all were about to finish, then we sat down, our legs crossed, and talk about the performance. And Caroline Calburn and Yvonne Banning, all the adults, sit with us, equal, as if to say 'talk to me, I'm on the same high level with you'. That created a sense of belonging and unity, that this is a safe environment to express yourself.

TLG: What made me stay was travelling opportunities, visiting places that I would never have been otherwise. Now I've been to Cape Point, Robben Island and a lot of South African tourist attractions which many Capetonians have never been to. District Six is not even far, we probably walk past the place all the time, but now we've gone in there and know what it's about. And going to Robben Island – just staying there and being able to go home and say to your friends.

MS: I've stayed on Robben Island for a week!

TLG: … and you're the coolest child ever. That is the difference between you and your schoolmates because they didn't get to experience that.

SW: I think it's the difference between us and our parents. Our parents' generation still say 'I can't go to Sea Point, what am I going to do there? I'd rather go to a place where our people will go'.

MS: My mother is now in a position where she will say 'I've been to Robben Island and I've done this and I've done that. Mildrett took me'. I took my mum to Robben Island for her seventieth birthday. Her church went to Johannesburg a while ago for a conference and I paid for her plane ticket. I had my first flight experience through Phakama, going to the North West Province with Mpotseng. I said to my mum 'When you're on the plane you can go to the bathroom and it's very small'. Now we take a drive to Sea Point or Green Point and we buy our food and we sit on the beach. My mother used to think that only white people did that. So through me, through Phakama, my family is also now more exposed. I tell my siblings or my younger nieces and nephews, 'Listen, this is not the only place'. I take them out. I've been speaking to them about university since they were at primary school, because I didn't even know that there was going to be university for me after I finished school. Because life has been handed to me, I'm handing it down.

SW: I also think it's very important to start exposing kids to opportunities at early stages. If I can compare myself with my other elder sisters, they are fifty-one and thirty-five and staying with my parents. They don't have a driver's licence. They haven't been exposed to other things. They don't travel. I'm the one that has moved out of the house, travelling all over, and I have to say it's because of Phakama exposing me to a bigger world. You're taught to be fearful, you're taught to be cautious about things. You are encouraged to consider 'what if this and this doesn't work?'. But my attitude is 'if it doesn't work out, I've experienced things'. So Phakama helped me make up my mind – it made the world bigger.

LR: Were there particular challenges raised by the Phakama process?

TLG: Within our Cape Town group we had Xhosas, Zulus, Tswanas. Sometimes, for example, the Xhosas would want to use a whole song in Xhosa, and we said 'We don't understand'. Then Caroline Calburn would say 'We're going to translate it so you understand what it means, but we will sing it'. We'd say 'Why must it only be a Xhosa song?'. Then another time we'll sing something Afrikaans and they would rebel because, maybe, now we have three Afrikaans songs and not even one African song. Then we have to compromise. We have to get to the point where we say 'Okay, then if not three Afrikaans songs, then at least two and some Xhosa songs'. In Afrikaans we say '*yster*', meaning having to carve iron. Sometimes you'd go home and you'd be very upset, but the next day you come back and you say 'Okay, we can look at doing something in another language. It's fine'. You have to learn Give and the Gain – that it's not just about my needs and what I want, but there's a whole lot of people.

MS: In the beginning it was mostly coloured people in Phakama. Then all of a sudden there was a group of African guys. We felt they were going to take over. But the transition into us becoming a group was very important. They were showing us what they could bring to a group. They were beautiful dancers and singers. But also in a situation like that, you lose something, and we lost the Afrikaans in our group. We lost our own identity.

TLG: It wasn't long after 1994. We had our democratic elections and our president, Nelson Mandela, was black. A lot of privileges came to the black people, the African people. We always felt as coloured people, we were sandwiched in between. We're not white, we're not black, and so we always kind of get lost. Four years down the line wasn't a long time to engage. We were secluded. We still had the racial slang in our minds that our parents used. In Phakama it was that territorial thing. We were here first, now you come. You've already won the election. Now you come and you want to do the dance, and everybody's now looking at you. We had to work with that and we had to work *through* it.

MW: We had to realise that for us to grow we had to embrace their culture. So Phakama was actually doing what the country was trying to do on a tiny little microscopic level. And it was the manner in which it was done – it wasn't forcing it. We also wanted to start dancing like them and doing the body movement we admired. We started to appreciate it. We wanted to embrace that.

SW: Honza, a participant from the UK, and I were very close. He would tell me about his origins in Grenada, the islands in the West Indies. In South Africa we know the West Indies from the cricket. We know it is black people. So I realized that coming from the West Indies to a white place, you want something better for yourself. It was the realization that, although we are different in the way we speak, in the way we are brought up, we both wanted to be better than where we're coming from. This was what we struggled with in our young lives. Honza was older than me and he was talking about drama, about making it good. That made our friendship very, very close. I was so young and he was genuinely wanting to be friends with me. That was exciting. We had to take them to our place and give them food and the thought that he wanted to come and experience my life was amazing. I can remember we phoned to tell our parents, 'Just make everything okay'.

MS: Everything happened in our community, in our culture. Venturing out into even being remotely interested in somebody from another culture or race was: 'What? Talking to a white guy?' Thomas, from Sweden, who I met through Phakama is white. That was where my mind set opened up and I thought 'I can interact with coloured guys and now with black guys and there's not much difference between my interaction with white guys. I can make jokes and talk about whatever.'

TLG: When I was in Genadendal on the *Call Me Not a Woman* project, I met a friend, Keeno, and we formed a strong bond – we were the same age and naughty. Eventually I had a baby and I named my son after Keeno because of that friendship. She would come to visit me from Genadendal and I would visit her.

LR: Are there moments from the performance that have stuck with you?

MS: I think it was Craig who was lying dead on the stage. He had to lie down and when the audience passed, I had to sing a song over and over. That was the time when we had gangs. Someone died and it was because of the coloured gangsterism. And each and everyone, even my family, who came to watch it, referred to that. Every person had a loss and the performance spoke to the losses they experienced.

TLG: In 1998, when we went to the District Six Museum, we learnt about what actually really happened there. People were forcefully put outside of the walls because they had to make place for white people and their new houses. I came across a story where a lady of seventy-five, Mary, had no family, no one to go to, and she ended up in Hanover Park in the backyard of someone she knew. And that was my performance, I went on as Mary, seventy-five years old with nowhere to go. I don't know why, but whenever I did that performance, I would feel this woman's pain. How can a woman of that age just be taken out of her house and become a backyard squatter? That is something I will always remember. Our parents lived in District Six.

SW: The audience did a ritual where we talked or thought about the person that we'd lost. Caroline Calburn said 'What is it that you would like to say to the person if they could hear you?' We stood in this big circle afterwards and then they would place a rock or a candle in the middle: it was a way of saying 'Okay, you're gone. I'm letting you go. I've said my last goodbyes and it's fine. I'm going to carry on.'

Every now and then when I hear the word teacher, I think of a scene. We were on Robben Island with the ex-political prisoners and we were walking around the graveyard. We learnt about the people who suffered leprosy. Caroline said we must think of a character. I was sitting on a rock under a tree and just started talking. I remember saying 'I'm a teacher'. And Caroline passed me and she said 'Okay, go on'. I said 'I'm a teacher, I teach children to read and write'. She said, 'Go on'. I remember, I was just sitting very forlorn. 'I went to the doctor and he diagnosed me with leprosy, I had a family and then all of a sudden I'm here on Robben Island. I couldn't teach any more, I couldn't be with the students anymore because I would make people ill also. I've lost my nose, my ears are about to fall off, I can't write any more, my fingers are gone. It's sad because I miss my family. All I remember is I'm a teacher, I could teach children to read and write'. They put that performance on a video recorder and it is in Robben Island Visitor's Centre. When people go there, even now, they can press the button and my story comes up. When I went with my mum in 2014, one of the other people pressed a button and I thought 'that's my voice, that's my story'. So I will always remember, even when I go there just for fun, I'll remember.

CULTURAL SHARING

Introduction

In the previous section we established that the Phakama approach was derived from the premise that 'everyone has a story to tell'. This section, 'Cultural Sharing', unlocks the process of negotiation and cooperation enacted in order for those stories to be shared and further explores the challenges involved in this process.

Phakama is interested in bringing together groups from different demographics. For example, projects have been international, interracial, intergenerational or have aimed to integrate asylum seekers with young British people or young Indians from a variety of social castes. Furthermore, on each project individual Phakama facilitators and participants bring particular cultural experiences and expectations. These may include knowledge, beliefs, attitudes, values, goals, conventions, social practices, ideas, customs, social behaviours and identity. They might be derived from wider cultural situations or emerge from within the individual's particular experience. The term 'sharing' is used because it holds the understanding that individuals are empowered to 'share' as much or as little as they choose. There is no imperative to 'exchange' but structures are in place which facilitate sharing, as and when individuals choose to do so. It places both the definition of culture and the decision to share it in the hands of each participating individual.

The sociologist Richard Sennett's ideas about cooperation as a necessary but not easy form of social practice frame our reflections through this section. First, they are applied directly to 'Map of the World', a Phakama exercise that makes explicit this modelling of negotiated cooperation in the context of cultural differences.

Then, through the lens of the project *Be Yourself* (London, 1999), facilitator Caroline Calburn (South Africa) explores the complexities of her experience of many years of cultural sharing with Phakama. She describes some of the challenges of cultural sharing, particularly when attempted in situations where there is extreme social injustice, while acknowledging the deep engagement with others that makes it worthwhile. She describes it in terms of 'pain'– reflecting the very personal and intense way in which cultural sharing can be experienced.

In her interview, Maylene Catchpole (UK) – participant, trainee facilitator, Phakama UK National Coordinator and board member (1997–2007) – draws on examples from throughout her life to emphasize the impact this work can have on an individual and their practice of working in participatory contexts.

Finally, Ananda Breed's essay reflects on the collaboration between Phakama and Creative Arts Team (New York City) at the CTW Festival of international theatre by young people that took place in Liverpool as part of the European Capital of Culture celebrations in 2008. In this essay, Breed develops the playful idea of telescopic performance through her exploration of international partnership, art making and Nomadic Theory.

Working Together

Phakama develops situations that bring people from different backgrounds and experiences together. It acknowledges and values difference in order to move towards making, together, a performance which expresses both individual and communal identities. At the core of all the interactions which take place is an ethic of care. Joan Tronto states: 'the fact that care can be a well integrated process should not distract us from the fact that care involves conflict' (1994: 109). The Phakama process does not shy away from the conflict which cultural sharing can bring. Instead it tries to hold it and provide mechanisms for dealing with it, inviting participants and facilitators to rehearse mediation of challenge and difficulties beyond the rehearsal room. This supports the building of deep relationships between people because they have learnt how to negotiate and trust each other – to face difficulty, as well as joy and celebration, together. As Maylene Catchpole makes evident in her interview in this section, this contributes to the kind of self-determined self-actualization Carl Rogers identified as being the central outcome of education.

In his book *Together: The Rituals, Pleasures and Politics of Co-operation* (2012: x), which discusses cooperation and difference, Richard Sennett identifies the kind of 'difficult' cooperation that is required when working with 'people who have separate or conflicting interests, who do not feel good about each other, who are unequal or who simply do not understand one another' (6). The social skills Sennett believes need to be in place to allow this kind of cooperation to flourish are outlined later in this section. Phakama's roots in post-apartheid South Africa have built practices and strategies for enabling 'difficult' cooperation.

Sennett acknowledges that cooperation 'requires of people the skill of understanding and responding to one another in order to act together, but this is a thorny process, full of difficulty and ambiguity and often leading to destructive consequences' (2012: x). He sees cooperation as a craft, just as Tronto sees care as an action. Importantly Sennett identifies that the craft of cooperation 'emerges from practical activity' (6). This resonates with the Phakama process of learning by 'doing' alongside others – a process that relies on social interactions. This section reveals that while the Phakama process is often challenging, it can result in deep, productive and sometimes transformative cultural sharing.

Phakama Practice: Mapping the World

Mapping the World is a process that celebrates, in microcosm, the making of a world together and the discovery of commonalities, while giving space to cultural differences. Fabio Santos, who explains this practice below, begins by describing the way the practice unfolded in *Strange Familiars* (London, 2003), a two-year project with a group of unaccompanied asylum-seeking minors. *Strange Familiars* culminated in an intensive residency and a performance, part of LIFT 2003, at the National Children's Home in Highbury, London. Fabio then considers how Mapping the World might be applied in other projects.

Phakama's interest in cultural sharing led us to examine notions of place and mapping. When we began working with refugees for *Strange Familiars*, the participants originated from many areas of the world and we wanted to find a way to acknowledge and explore this. The Mapping the World exercise emerged from this and Tab Neal, a facilitator on the project who had done work with masking tape and design in schools, led on this exercise.

We had an actual map of the world on a wall divided into six squares going from 'A' to 'F'. We split the group into six smaller groups and we gave a roll of masking tape to each participant and facilitator. Together we were going to re-create the map of the world on the floor – on a much larger scale – using masking tape. Each group had to recreate their appointed section of the world on the floor in all its detail. People looked astonished. It seemed like an impossible task but soon everybody was busy creating the map. The process is collaborative – decisions need to be made about who *does* what and who *knows* what. Individuals have to work with their group and each other: the group working on square A have to negotiate with square B as to how their lines meet. It is all about borders and connections. It takes observation, negotiation and action to recreate the map on the floor.

The exercise always starts like this, collaboratively preparing the map, preparing the ground. How the exercise plays out varies from project to project. Each facilitator brings a different element to it. It can lead to storytelling, to movement or to design.

In *Strange Familiars* we agreed not to ask the young asylum-seekers to describe their experience because they are repeatedly asked to do so elsewhere: to solicitors, social services and lawyers – they have to explain themselves. This exercise, however, gave the young people permission to talk about the challenges of home and exile from a starting point that was creative, not interrogative. We asked the young people to place themselves first where they were born and then in the place they had travelled to. Interesting, challenging, complicated and sad stories started to emerge about how people fled their place of birth and travelled to different countries until they got to the UK. We asked the participants to repeat their whole journey and, on each stopping point, make a physical picture of what that time meant or to make a vocal story collage. If people wanted to tell these stories they were given space. Other people did not want to tell that side of their story, which was also respected.

Then we explored individuals' journeys across the map. Tab gave the participants different colours of masking tape to mark their journeys on the map. We considered journeys that crossed as people traversed the world: for example, someone moved from Liberia and someone moved from Guinea and their journeys crossed. Yellow masking tape crossed with green masking tape. Then we suggested these crossing – pairs talked with each other about their journeys. A network was created on the map and networking began in the room. Stories with commonalities and differences started to develop. Issues of language and politics started to emerge. We asked the young people to go to a place they would like to visit and a place they would not like to go. In both cases, for some of them, it was their place of birth.

Mapping the World engages with socio-political issues. The *Trashcatchers* events (2008, 2010 and 2013) were about the environment. For these projects we asked participants, 'check the label on you clothing, see where it was made and go there'. All the UK participants moved to the East because their clothes were made in China, Pakistan or Bangladesh. They didn't realise that we bought so many things from other countries. On the project *Message in a Bottle* (2012), an international project with young people from six European countries, we asked them to bring an object from their home country that meant something to them and related to the project's theme, which was 'water'. When we did this exercise, we asked them to place the object where it came from and tell the story behind it. In both cases we saw transglobal forces of trade and human transport illustrated through the physical iterations of objects and bodies moving across this scaled-up map of the world. We saw how we interact with the world.

You can do Mapping the World with any group of people because you can ask any question of that map, of people's relationship to place. We thought it might be more challenging to animate the map if the participants had lived in a particular place all of their lives – as was the case when we did the exercise with a group of young people in Dorset, UK. However, it is surprising, with every group, how much of the world they encompassed in their responses to our questions. Partly because nearly everybody has a heritage which is more than just their local one. Mapping the World may hold your story of escape, but it also holds your dreams of the future, your imaginings, your favourite curry house, your American idol/ singer and/or the jumper that you are wearing on that day.

Mapping the World is about scale. There is a small map, there is the big map and then there is the real world, which is even bigger. Theatre works with scale.

It is about upscaling or downscaling, zooming in or out. So this exercise models life and it models theatre. The map becomes a metaphor – the world is much smaller than we think, and we can coexist if we want to.

MAPPING THE WORLD

Prepare in advance:
- For the map you will need: a large print of the map of the world divided with masking tape into six sections/squares (a, b, c, d, e and f), a thick black marker to make the lines (every country, continent, islands, etc.) on the map very clear. When the map is finished, pin it to a wall so everyone can see it.
- On the floor you will need masking tape to draw the six squares on the floor and give each square letters (a, b, c, d, e and f). The squares on the floor should be a mirror image of squares on the map on the wall.

The activity:
- Split the group into six smaller groups.
- Ask the groups to take their position in each of the squares on the floor and give each group at least one roll of masking tape per person.
- Each group needs to recreate as closely as possible the lines of the map within their square. Allow around twenty minutes for this. Encourage all to be involved.
- As the groups progress with their work, you can give instructions such as: (a) Remember to negotiate your borders with your neighbour. (b) Make sure that you don't leave any country out. (c) Some islands are very small and we must make sure that they are represented. (d) If you are not sure about a country, ask your colleagues and go and have a close look at the map on the wall.
- Ask everyone to clean anything that is not part of their work and stand at the edges of the map they created on the floor.

Sharing:
- Use the map as a platform for performance made from movement, memories, story-telling and imagination. Or place objects participants have sourced or made on the map to tell their stories. Use the map in whatever way you want as a platform for performance.

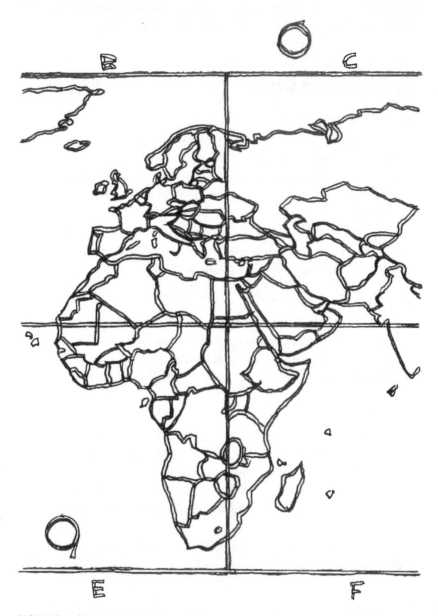

FIGURE 4 Mapping the World.

Active engagement in creating a world map encourages emotional connection and allows for acknowledgement of shared experiences.

Difficult Cooperation

In *Together: The Rituals, Pleasures and Politics of Co-operation* (2012), Richard Sennett defines three social skills, which we distil below, that are necessary for difficult cooperation:

1. Interactions should be dialogical (as opposed to dialectical): The interaction looks at the intent beneath the words. It does not need to seek resolution or reach a common ground. It values process.

2. Expression should be subjunctive (as opposed to declarative): The expression resists the desire for domination, for being right, leaving space for more interaction.

3. Social exchange should be empathetic (as opposed to sympathetic): The exchange addresses the other objectively with interest and wonder, and therefore promotes engagement.

Thus Sennett privileges opening up over finding closure, listening over telling, ambiguity over clarity and curiosity over identification. Mapping the World itself, like all Phakama practice, provides a structured space from within which this kind of interchange can take place. The exercise begins with a collaborative task which gives everyone shared ownership of the map. While the task is to recreate the map, the impossibility of doing that accurately and perfectly already demands creative solutions of the participants. They are not told how to do it, so it demands a solution reached at through dialogic interchange. The finished product may not be 'right' but it always captures the spirit and endeavour of those who made it together.

The map then provides a platform on which people can explore their own journeys and watch and listen to the journeys of others. Because it is like a stage it encourages listening, it gives the opportunity, as on a soapbox, to be heard. It does not prescribe the content of the contributions. Each contribution is an aspect of yourself rather than a demand to articulate your entire self. You can present it in any way you want. The places people are asked to go in the world are autobiographical, but also wished, or completely imaginary, or about the past and the future. It asks you to give a portrait of yourself, which is more than just what happened to you. To see and present who you are and who you want to be, to see yourself how others see you, and to see who you might become.

Sennett, when explaining 'subjunctive expression', draws on his background as a craftsman, his craft of musicianship and in particular the making of musical instruments. He too understands the concept of *yster*' (referred to by Tracey-Lee Gates, a Phakama South Africa participant in her interview in Give and Gain) that cooperative processes often feel like bending iron. He identifies that materials do not benefit from being hammered into new shapes but that always the application of 'minimum force' is needed. He applies this to social interchange: 'Only through behaving with minimum self-assertiveness do we open up to others' (211). The gentleness with which the Phakama facilitator moves around the space touching people to indicate their opportunity to speak allows also for them to opt out. Most opt in. Everybody is on the stage as the stories are being told and so everybody holds the stories. Everybody becomes a carer of that person telling that story, carers of each other. Each person's contribution is respected, so you respect the contribution of others. People listen with empathy, with curiosity with 'a sense of wonder'. When Mapping the World was practised in a training workshop at Theatre Arts Admin Collective in Cape Town, South Africa (2015) with a group of experienced arts practitioners, one woman began to cry as she spoke of the relationship she wished she had to her homeland, South Africa. No one moved towards her, no one said don't cry, everyone just let her do what she needed to do and listened. No one needed to identify with the story or control her grief. Empathy is extended, not sympathy.

Facilitators need to model this dialogical, subjunctive, empathic way of interacting because it underpins all the work. Sometimes objects are used in Mapping the World. Participants are asked to go to the map and place their object, and then leave the map before the next person goes. The facilitator might say something like: 'when you walk in the world be careful with other people's possessions, look after them'. So when you move you are careful and you are looking after other people, their objects and so their identities and their dreams. So when someone tells their story we know not only that we need to look after them and *how* to look after them because we have being practising it throughout. Participants care for each other's things whether physical, material things or experiences and dreams.

Mapping the World, and more generally the Phakama approach to cultural sharing, acknowledges that the world is full of glorious texture, colour and detail that is specific to each individual's experience of culture, but that we live in it and experience it always in relation to other people. This is exemplified in Beverley Randall's reflections on being part of the original facilitating team on the first UK/South Africa exchange programme *Bulang Dikgoro/Open the Gates* (1996). Cultural sharing is always embedded in the specifics of a particular cultural moment. Beverley Randall's reflections (2015) specifically highlight her experience as a black British woman visiting South Africa at this particular cultural moment in post-apartheid South Africa.

One day, one of the South African facilitators asked a question and he said, 'Okay Sir', to Tony. He must have felt something that made him see Tony, in this moment, as a white man, not as a fellow practitioner in the room. A few days later, I had an incident in a bank in town: I wasn't served. I wanted to change some money and there was a foreign exchange counter upstairs. I thought someone saw me so I waved and went upstairs. I was left sitting up there for a long time. Finally, I came downstairs and said, 'Will someone serve me?'. They were so surprised to hear this English voice and one woman ran across the banking hall saying, 'Oh, sorry, I didn't realise you were foreign'. I thought, 'woah, woah, woah!' I said, 'This is not a bank. How dare you call yourselves a bank if you think this is the kind of service that I'm used to having'. Finally, she put me in a queue and it was the wrong queue. And I thought, 'My God, the level of incompetence in this place'. At last they sorted me out, and I said, 'This would never happen in England', and I marched out of the door. By this time, I was enjoying speaking to white South Africans in that way because I knew there was nothing they could do. I came back and I shared the story and we all laughed except this one South African facilitator. He said to me, 'I want to tell you something'. He told me a situation where his boss, who was white, during the apartheid regime, asked him to go and pick up alcohol from a store. He said, 'Is it okay?' and the boss said, 'Yes, it is', so he went. This was a store where only whites could go to get alcohol, so he would have had to have permission or his boss needed to set it up beforehand. He walked in to the store and was not served and was humiliated by the experience. He said to me, 'I never thought that I would live to hear about a black person in a situation that you have just described'. I cried, because as much as I am a black person, I'm a black British person, my life experience is completely different. Of course there are racist situations all around, but nothing of that kind of calibre: I could shout back, but he knew there was nothing he could do.

In this story Beverley learns something about her own culture through the sharing of experience in one that is different to her everyday life. She sees her story through different eyes. In Sennett's terms the exchange is 'dialogical' – they recognize the intent beneath each other's words and do not attempt to reach a common ground, 'subjunctive' – no one is insisting that their experience is right, 'empathetic' – they are curious about and engaged with each other. There is no closure – sharing has instead opened both individuals up to new understandings and ways of experiencing the world.

Phakama projects are peppered with interactions of this sort – which run alongside moments of deep engagement, reflection and celebration. These ambitious projects often push people out of their comfort zones. The practices outlined in this book establish means of cooperation and therefore set up the opportunity for cultural sharing, but this process is not always easy. Interactions can be difficult and sometimes unresolved, but they are valued as part of the learning process. The experience of each project is very individual as people navigate their way through many exercises, many groups, many interactions. Sometimes dialogic interchange opens things up so much that there is chaos. Sometimes surprising things about culture and our multiple identities arise. Sometimes it is painful.

Caroline Calburn's following case study exposes the experience of living through the difficult cooperation Sennett imagines and the expression of this within the performance work produced. Caroline was one of the South African facilitators on the first project, *Bulang Dikgoro/Open the Gates* (1996), and a facilitator on all the large-scale international projects and evaluations sessions until 2006. She led Phakama through a series of extraordinary projects across South Africa which developed and shared the practice locally, sustaining the relationships between South African facilitators. Caroline, together with Trevor Engel and Andrew Siddall, led the process that led to Phakama South Africa becoming a legally constituted organization in 1999.

Here, in order to describe the complexities of cultural sharing in *Be Yourself* (1999), she also speaks about the years of practice which preceded and enabled it – evidencing Sennett's claim that 'the long-term work builds up the security of your practice' (2012: 201). A Phakama facilitator always works as part of a team and Caroline, therefore, draws attention to the importance of solidarity and trust. Throughout, Caroline focuses on her own learning through Phakama and the key relationships between facilitators. Her case study insists that culture includes cultural practices as well as cultural heritage in its definition.

References

Randall, B. (2015), Skype interview with Fabio Santos, 14 May.
Sennett, R. (2012), *Together: The Rituals, Pleasures and Politics of Co-operation*, London: Penguin.
Tronto, J. (1994), *Moral Boundaries: A Political Argument for an Ethic of Care*, London: Routledge.

CASE STUDY
BE YOURSELF (PHAKAMA SOUTH AFRICA AND PHAKAMA UK, TRICYCLE THEATRE, LONDON, 1999)

Caroline Calburn

Description: *Be Yourself* was programmed as part of LIFT '99 to be performed at the Tricycle Theatre in Kilburn, West London – a 200 seat professional theatre. It was a partnership/exchange between Phakama South Africa and Phakama UK. Eight facilitators from across South Africa travelled with twenty participants to London where they worked with seven UK facilitators and twenty participants. It was the first time Phakama had performed in a conventional theatre.

Place: Tricycle Theatre, London.

Date: July 1999.

Partnerships: LIFT, Phakama South Africa, Lewisham Youth Theatre (LYT).

Facilitators: Tony Fegan, Andrew Siddall, Lucy Richardson, Matthew Bugg, Graham Jeffrey, Ian Bald, Fabio Santos, Donald Legodi, Manya Gittel, Shirley Mzizi, Pogiso Mogwera, Anthea Hans, Liesl Hartman, Caroline Calburn, Ntokozo Madlala.

Participants: Twenty young people from the UK and twenty young people from across South Africa.

Cultural Sharing: The Background

Fragment of Memory 1
I have retreated from a tense structuring session into a small, crowded workroom where Sid has set up materials and a basic idea of how to construct miniature

model buildings. The room is peaceful and thick with the concentration and quiet chatter of a group of young people cutting, detailing with Stanley knives and covering with tin foil. Buckingham Palace is emerging, as is a tower and a few other London landmarks. Someone holds up his miniature to look and show. Another is trying hers out with its tiny internal light and the room breathes and sighs. This is a welcome break from the fraughtness beyond. Donald Legodi, a facilitator from Seshego in the Northern Province of South Africa, is next to me, constructing idly. 'The torture of cultural exchange' he says into the silence after a few moments. We lean into each other. I'm feeling it: a heavy weight inside.

Phakama: Be Yourself was Phakama's fifth international residency and had been commissioned by LIFT as part of the LIFT '99 festival. Controversially, and for the first time, a Phakama project was to take place in a theatre building and to perform in a conventional auditorium: the highly respected Tricycle Theatre in Kilburn.

As a South African organization, Phakama had been going strong for four years with a remarkable body of international and local work behind us, a thorough five-year plan with projects planned right up until 2001, and a stable group of about two hundred young people collectively working weekends and holidays in provinces of South Africa: Gauteng (coordinated by Shirley Mzizi and Manya Gittel), the Northern Province (renamed Limpopo in 2003, where Phakama was part of BAAGI Arts under the leadership of Donald Legodi), the Western Cape (coordinated by Caroline Calburn, Trevor Engel, Yvonne Banning, Liesl Hartman, Andrew Siddall, Sonwabo Masepe, Mpotseng Shuping, Anthea Adonis and Mandla Mbothwe) and the North West (coordinated by Pogiso Mogwera). Many of these facilitators had worked on more than one international project together since 1996. There was strong kinship, a deep understanding of the way Phakama worked, a shared vision and a growing maturity – all forged from the fires of creating processes and performances under extremely difficult working conditions and with very few resources. We began to see ourselves and behave like family – affectionate, fractious and loyal. And it is among family that is the safest place to truly 'Be Yourself'.

This choice of project title was perhaps, in its naivety, pointing to our growing maturity. The choice also had much to do with the general trajectory of previous projects: the facilitators would dream up often vague but suggestive project titles that would be used as a catalyst for the ideas and personal and imaginative stories of the young people. Titles often changed mid-project in response to the material and themes emerging. *Bulang Dikgoro/Open the Gates* (1996), a title found a week before performance, responded to the sudden liberation and joyful possibility of racial doors being flung open wide; *Wololo! Watch out!* (1999) was found mid-project by a group of youngsters responding to the then current fear that at the turn of the millennium there would be global catastrophe. *Be Yourself* had been decided early on. It had to as one of the many constraints of being part of a high-profile festival demanded: programmes to print, publicity to send out and tickets to sell. The title

Be Yourself had none of the creative energy of *Izimbadada/If I Were in Your Shoes,* (1997), the weight of the metaphor in *Ka Mor Walo Ka Seatleng/With a Suitcase in My Hand* (1997) or the lyricism of *Call Me Not a Woman* (2000) and I had personal doubts about how we were going to turn something so prosaic into an exciting piece of theatre. But what none of us had foreseen were the complexities of what it meant to be yourself, and how this was going to present itself, not in the artistic work, but among ourselves. Were we in fact ready to be ourselves, with all the acceptance, tolerance and understanding that that implies, and to deal with the fall out?

Phakama was busy percolating through layer upon layer of cultural sharing. In *Bulang Dikgoro/Open the Gates* in Benoni in 1996, the first cultural sharing that took place was quite literally opening the doors to two nations with a fraught political history. While the diversity within both the British and South African groups was acknowledged, the cultural exchange that occurred on this project was at a UK/South Africa level. The South Africans were bound closely together by the newly conceived national project of the Rainbow Nation. Mandela was our president, democracy was eighteen months old and we were still united in the dream. While we were proud of our national achievement, we still lacked self-confidence. Relations were polite, we all trod carefully. The UK team (who had a strong history of multicultural work) were sensitive, generous and open and the South Africans were hungry and willing, yet armed. Where tensions arose, colonialism was the issue. At times, the South Africans silently seethed that the British were telling them what to do. At other times it emerged openly: brought up for discussion by the UK team, or raised by South Africans, often with typical self-deprecating humour. However, where the British team were personally experiencing the racialized history of South Africa, as Bev Randall explains earlier, South Africans were united in political good will.

By late 1997 through to 1999, however, the cultural sharing had become racialized. 'Setting the stage for a shared future', Phakama's byline, which emerged during the evaluation session for the very first project and underscored all the work Phakama undertook in South Africa, now spoke directly to the South Africans at a race level. The South African facilitators were deeply committed to bringing young South Africans from different cultural backgrounds together and addressing cultural exchange at a local level – creating an opportunity for young black (the political use of the word to refer to all races not white) and white South African youth to meet, work, get to know and make friends with each other. We were building a new South Africa. It was our duty, but it wasn't easy. In 1998, in preparation for *With a Suitcase in My Hand/Met 'n Sak Onder die Blad*, Pogiso Mogwera (facilitator from the North West, South Africa) had travelled to all the schools in Mmabatho, to recruit Phakama participants. In one historically white school, he had been booed as he took the stage at assembly to introduce Phakama to the pupils. Despite the humiliation he had persevered and three young white girls joined the project. Trevor and I had managed a similar feat in Cape Town with Lindy, a young white girl whose mother drove her from Gordon's Bay to Grassy Park weekly (a seventy-minute drive with a detour through Kuilsrivier to lift another participant) to participate.

We spoke about race and racism. Among ourselves as facilitators we openly acknowledged our history. We trod on each other's toes and had to backtrack through four hundred years of history. We listened. We vented. We engaged. As one of the only white South African facilitators in the early years, I consciously tried to step back. I was confronted with my white privilege and all that it had given me. Phakama was my place of healing, the first time I was able to work alongside black colleagues, to give what I had and gain what decades of apartheid had denied me. We were challenged and we challenged each other. We worked with a deliberately cultural consciousness: at a strategic level through the choice of performance cities and sites; at a process level through food, creative exercises and cultural visits; and at an artistic level through language, songs, performance styles and aesthetic choices.

The process of deepening our understanding was made possible by our annual week-long residencies for facilitators (our first being held in 1997 in the Strand, six months after our first project in Benoni in 1996) that usually coupled as our AGM. These were extraordinary moments in the organizational history characterized by deep reflection on the previous project; debate around critical issues that were emerging both within the work, among ourselves and within the political framework that the work existed within; lengthy conversations around methodologies, aesthetics, life and art; moments of outrageous creativity; forward planning and strategizing; writing up of all discussed; exchange of experiences and approaches; endless problem-solving, negotiating and debate. They were a heady mix of intense work, wild friendship and love. And as the latter increased, as it did yearly, so the work and the depths to which it plumbed, intensified. We had raging fights each year, generally around issues of race and how we related to each other, colonization and who was trying to impose certain ideas, values, aesthetics or anything else that emerged – great offences taken, with walk-outs, but most importantly winding roads to finding each other again and to understanding better what had happened. By 1999 our experience and understanding of cultural sharing were beginning to shift to another level.

Cultural Sharing: *Be Yourself*

Fragment of Memory 2:
We are sitting in a circle on the stage of the Tricycle Theatre. I had been cutting strips of white paper and the group had all been scattered in their own worlds, juggling words and shifting strips of paper. Silently, one by one, they had come to a stillness that is particular to the completion of a task. And now we are sitting in a circle on the stage. Waiting. And into the circle is dropped the words of the first

poem. There is a visible shift in the room. The silence intensifies. Backs straighten. Whole bodies are listening. This is the London we visited – twisted and turned, cut, refashioned, juxtaposed into new meaning. Each poem is profound in its complexity. We see below the surface, deeply.

In preparation for *Be Yourself*, the South Africans went through a rigorous selection process to choose which of over two hundred participants were to travel to London. Each province was to send five young people to make up a group of twenty. The young people became amazingly adept at developing and managing selection processes, and were exceedingly generous in handing opportunity to each other. For many of them it posed the first and, probably in their eyes, the only opportunity to travel overseas.

In Cape Town, once selected, the whole group prepared their representatives for the visit. We made a large frieze of London based on the young people's impressions of a city they had not seen. Oxford Circus was in the middle: circus tent, clowns and acrobats. The frieze was animated through a soundscape, recorded and slipped into one of the suitcases. In London, the Phakama group from LYT had been planning the first week of the project. Through a process, carefully devised by four of the UK participants, Gemma Emmanuel-Waterton, Maylene Catchpole, Robert Hutchinson and Chinh Hoang, a series of day trips were organized to introduce the South Africans to the city – to the stories above and buried beneath its pavements – and an opportunity for the young Londoners to see their city through new eyes.

Through a variety of different tasks, the cultural visits became the raw material for the creation of performance. Experiences were explored, in typical Phakama fashion, through young people focusing on the various aspects of performance that they identified as an area that they wanted to learn in, or in which they were experienced. From Brixton emerged a series of characters; from Brick Lane, an intricate Indian design that Sherna Botto (participant, South Africa) and Chinh Hoang (participant, UK) laboured over that framed the stage like a typical proscenium. Andrew Siddall (facilitator, UK) and Liesl Hartman (facilitator, South Africa), with a group of young people, created a jigsaw floor that broke apart, like the earth being mined, from which South African gold nuggets were hung – the jewels in the crown.

During the process, personal stories drawing on cultural experiences were shared and bonds were made between everyone involved. On one of the cultural tours Beverley Randall (facilitator, UK) shared tales of her upbringing as the daughter of a West Indian immigrant in Brixton. During one workshop, when asked to share a story with a partner, a South African participant told how his mother had been detained during the struggle, and had given birth to him while in solitary confinement. It reinforced the necessity and value of cultural interaction – that we are part of a much bigger world. Early on, among the design group, it was decided a small mirror on the inside of each programme for the performance would confront the audience member on arrival – asking them to look at themselves.

Ideas began to flow after an initial setback when we realized that we had never worked in a theatre before. For three years our projects had existed on sites in South Africa – warehouses, museums, cultural centres – which somehow made anything seem possible. When a young person suggested, 'and then it rains', rain was possible in an empty warehouse where anything could be jimmied: so rain it did, on the heads of the Seshego audience during *Ka Morwalo Ka Seatleng/With a Suitcase in My Hand*. We had open fires without fire-proofing, offering possibly the most theatrical moments. But now, sitting in the auditorium of the Tricycle Theatre in Kilburn, London, every suggestion that was made was met with Health and Safety Regulations. Everyone felt constricted – Why can't we have miniature cars and buses on wires over the heads of the audience? Rehearsal rooms were only partially available to us and became bubbles of activity rather than homes. Tony Fegan reflects:

> This was not our own environment. There was no ownership of the space. We felt provisional there. The London experience was atomised into individual little cells. How can you compare packed lunches to the communal cooking of cows that fed us on *Call Me Not a Woman* up in Seshego.

While the Londoners were staying in their homes, the South Africans were accommodated in a London University hostel, Schaffer House, in Euston. The accommodation consisted of a series of self-contained flats with bedrooms, bathroom and kitchen areas shared between six people. This enabled artist tutors to be resident with the students.

As creative solutions were, ultimately, found, the segmented space of the Tricycle Theatre along with dislocated university living spaces, so different from South African sites we had worked in – mostly open warehouses and halls accompanied by dormitory-style living – were not aiding what was becoming an increasingly difficult project. The South Africans hated the food. 'We don't eat fruit in our food', they complained, referring to the plantain in the Jamaican cooking, a deliberate choice made by the London team. We knew from experience that if bellies were full, everyone was happy. Working days were too often punctuated by visits to see performances on in the rest of the LIFT festival, and visiting and running peer-to-peer audience development workshops. At a particularly critical moment in the rehearsal process we had to attend a reception hosted by Cheryl Carolus who was then the South African High Commissioner at South Africa House. Carolus had been instrumental in promoting and raising funds for the project and celebrating its success. Some of the young people returned from this reception inebriated and barely capable of working. Seasoned Phakama team members were lost in all the administration of trying to manage the venue and the festival and both sets of demands. There were a number of new facilitators and young people who had not worked on other projects and did not fully understand or buy into the Phakama process. LIFT asked all participating companies to perform at the LIFT Club – a late night free event which was curated each night of the festival by a different company. Extra pressure was placed on the group to prepare a performance for the LIFT Club Phakama Night, coupled with the pressure to produce an outcome for the festival. And trouble was brewing in the accommodation quarters of the South Africans.

As Maylene Catchpole describes in her interview that follows, some of the young Londoners had discovered the freedom of what it meant to be black in 1998 when they visited Africa for the first time to participate in *Met 'n Sak Onder die Blad/With a Suitcase in My Hand* in Cape Town. Now, in London, the South African team was dealing with the effect of living in London and its apparent freedoms, so different from South Africa. The noise, the pollution, the buzz, the people, the happenings, the history, the vastness of size and sprawl, the apparent wealth and opportunity, the complex transport system and the cultural diversity of the city all appeared to make the young people giddy and 'drunk'. With all this, coupled with the intense interest and praise from all those involved in the Festival, the young South Africans began to push boundaries. Residential rules were being flouted and when addressed by the South African facilitators, they were met with disrespect and arrogance.

Where the young South Africans were growing in a confidence, it felt that the South African facilitators, on foreign soil, were losing their agency, along with a capacity to be heard. Attempts had been made to raise the issue in facilitator meetings but had been moved over. And then, one of the young South African men accused one of the openly homosexual South African facilitators of sexual harassment. The story spread like wildfire among the young people and, with no proper procedures in place, coupled with a looming performance deadline, the facilitators moved into crisis mode. Attempts to resolve the situation led to dissent among the facilitators. Prejudice began to surface, blame apportioned and a rather heavy handed and closed approach was taken. In response, the young people rose up in anger, led by some outspoken young Londoners. They gathered like a force behind the complainant. Mutiny was in the air. Lucy Richardson (facilitator, UK) called for calm, attempting to refocus the group on the task at hand: we were here to create a performance and that was what we needed to do. With a collective in-breath, people stepped back from an emotional precipice and got down to the work.

The next morning, the session began with Matthew Bugg (facilitator, UK) leading a gentle physical warm-up and Tony Fegan (facilitator, UK) talking quietly about the need for respect, even in the face of lifestyles that might not sit comfortably with individuals: reminding everyone of why we are here and what Phakama is all about. The room felt fractured and bruised. I have no memory of how we returned to the work or even how the last of the performance was pieced together, except that some facilitators retreated into isolated bubbles and worked on what needed to be done. People kept busy, channelling the intensity of feeling into the work. The background track was silence. But we made a show.

Ultimately, the accusations were withdrawn. But the heady mix of a new city and its apparent freedoms, coupled with growing confidence and the cultural melting pot, had meant everyone was out of their depth: young people and facilitators. We had encountered a similar incident in Cape Town the year prior to *Be Yourself*, when the young people from Britain had come to South Africa on what was our first international youth exchange on South Africa soil – *Ka Mor Walo Ka Seatleng/With a Suitcase in My Hand* (1997). In the project report, Yvonne Banning (facilitator, South Africa) (1998) describes how it is ultimately the art and the young people's understanding of the images that they have created that brings people back to reality in a profound and renewed way.

> One of the most crucial learning situations I encountered was an allegation made by one of the young people of misconduct by an adult tutor. I was one of three tutors deputed to investigate and manage this potentially extremely damaging occurrence and to suggest steps towards resolving it satisfactorily. I took this difficult task on, in spite of my feelings of inadequacy, because I knew by this time that I could rely on the skills and resources of all the tutors to assist, and because the responsibility and decision-making would be shared by the whole group. I thus became involved in a fairly sustained process of talking to the tutor concerned, the young person, the tutor group and the ad hoc 'committee'.
>
> In fact, the two people themselves – the young person and the tutor – found their way to each other through the symbolic potency of the theatrical work we were making. In an extraordinary demonstration of how theatre can heal deep, private individual as well as collective hurts, the young participant used the fire ritual sequence in the performance to enact her own private reconciliation. During the ritual the participants collect a stone from the fire circle and each offers their stone to a member of the audience, who then carries it to the entrance of the chapel and places it on a growing cairn, reminiscent of the cairn of stones on Robben Island begun by Nelson Mandela. This young person, responding intuitively to the symbolic and feeling resonances of the ritual, spontaneously offered her stone to the tutor. This outcome would not have been achieved without the contexts that the project provides: the holistic morphing of theatrical and social; personal and collective; symbolic and real; trusting and daring.

Where the healing emerged from the fires in Cape Town, in London we were not so lucky. The performance was strung onto shards of pain, misunderstanding and strained relationships; beautiful and glistening. But for me there was no closure.

Cultural Sharing: An Audience

Fragment of Memory, 3

The stage is dark. A tiny star appears and floats in the blackness, like a firefly. And another, and another, until the darkness is filled with twinkling stars cascading down to earth. And then the stars become a twinkling city at night. And as the sun rises buses float down from the sky and park gently along the river between buildings. London at dawn. Large black arms creep between buildings, fingers trail water, heads rest on roofs. Bodies. A river of blood. Blood River. And then a voice next to me, whispering a story. To me. Only me. Heads crowd in to hear. And we're offered a bowl of water to wash our hands in, absolve ourselves. The bowls glow and the water is cool. And then it rains, water sprinkled upon the city, a libation, ululation.

Post-show conversations at the bar were not proving easy. While the performance was received well, elements seemed to have touched nerves. Tony Fegan (2015) recalls:

> I had a terrible fight with the brother of a friend who accused us of sanctifying Stephen Lawrence [through] the ritual of washing of hands and forgiveness. But Lyn Gardner equated it to Pontius Pilate, of washing one's hands of responsibility. The show was hard-edged. Other Phakama work had a softer, more redemptive texture.

Images were slippery, open ended, ambiguous, opaque, often unresolved. There were theatrical moments, during rehearsal, that had proved difficult, the telling of the Stephen Lawrence story in particular. Lucy Richardson had worked hard with a group of young people in resolving it. Fabio Santos had introduced wonderful moments of rhythmic dance connected to everyday London experiences of pickpocketing, like a contemporary Oliver Twist, and Matthew Bugg and a group of young people had created ingeniously spliced soundtracks from found sounds recorded during the cultural visits. Lyn Gardner (1999) had written a glowing four-star review in *The Guardian*:

> If I tell you that one of the most moving, exuberant and visually stunning shows to see in London is a youth production devised and performed by a group of South African and London teenagers, you will probably be skeptical. But *Be Yourself* is really terrific. The production uses the full height of the auditorium and repeatedly takes the show into the audience: you feel as though you have been thrust into the very heart of the city, into its smells, sounds and sights. It is an exhilarating and truly brilliant achievement.

There was a moment of complete satisfaction at a job well done. The performance had moments of real beauty, insight and joy. Sixteen years later, Tony and I recall *Be Yourself* in a conversation:

> It was a bitter show … a lament. The struggle to be yourself was a lament. You lose something in it. Being yourself comes at a price. How much can I be myself and how much must I balance this with my responsibility of co-existence? Our professional friendship allowed for things to go unsaid, and when push came to shove, we were pushed back into our own bubbles. (Fegan 2015)

Cultural Sharing: A Long-term Process

Be Yourself demonstrated that cultural difference is not just embedded in place or race but is also about different social practices. For me and others both gender and sexuality were experienced on this project as cultural difference. In all the four Phakama years leading to this that the facilitators had worked together on projects – the proximity of living and the close conversations – as a group, the sexual orientation of the facilitators had never been discussed. Where personal friendships had been forged there had been openness, but neither disclosure to the group nor covert behaviour. Rather, there had been an overt physical intimacy among all the facilitators regardless of gender. The affection displayed among the facilitators towards each other played a critical role in modelling behaviour for the young people. If the young people saw adults of different cultural backgrounds getting along, being able to communicate verbally and physically with each other, it was a message for them that they could too. In South Africa this was very important – and for me personally, an unequal liberation. But with this came a presumption by some of a homogeneous heterosexuality. The accusation made (and later withdrawn) on *Be Yourself* was perhaps an outcome of this presumption.

Phakama was committed to cultural sharing and all that that meant. It understood that a huge part of the negotiation of cultural difference is about negotiation of the self. Each one of us, at some point over the years, was forced to look in that mirror that the young people had stuck to the inside of the *Be Yourself* programme. As we had matured, we had moved beyond the broad categories of national difference and race, and were getting closer to the personal. And as we got closer to the personal, the more difficult the cultural sharing became. This was the privilege granted us by working closely as a large team over an extended period of time. Huge professional affection bridged the more difficult chasms. What has transpired is a web of relationships, that despite time, distance and difference, has remained intimate – a shared understanding. As facilitators we always knew that we were the generation that had the difficulties with each other – each of us a generation more closely scarred by colonialist relationships and the alienation of apartheid. Phakama's processes, however painful, moved us, the facilitators, towards self-actualization.

References

Banning, Y. (1997), *With a Suitcase in Your Hand* Project Report, Phakama SA archives.
Fegan, T. (2015), Skype interview with Caroline Calburn.
Gardner, L. (1999), 'Phakama: *Be Yourself*', *The Guardian*, 5 July.

INTERVIEW WITH MAYLENE CATCHPOLE

Maylene Catchpole was nineteen when she first joined Phakama. As a member of LYT she was invited to be involved in the first UK project *Izimbadada/If I Were in Your Shoes* in 1997. Since then she has been in *Be Yourself, Met'n Sak onner die Blad/With a Suitcase in My Hand* and *Call Me Not a Woman* and has been involved with Phakama ever since as Phakama UK's national coordinator and as a member of the board until 2007. Maylene trained as a drama teacher, working in comprehensive secondary schools in multicultural south-east London.

Maylene's interview is rich with examples of the way in which Phakama helped her to understand the nature and importance of difficult cooperation. She often refers to the challenges she faced but she also recognizes the space Phakama gave to the kind of interactions Richard Sennett defines as being essential to cooperation. She talks of listening and debating, of ambiguity and confusion, of curiosity and empathy. Her journey is one of discovery of the world, of other cultures and of herself. Most importantly it is ongoing, there is no closure: the impact of the work, of the challenges and the resolutions, still resonates in the work she does and the person she has become.

LR: When you heard, in 1997, that you could possibly go to South Africa or work with some South Africans in London, what did you hope you would gain from doing that?

Maylene Catchpole: Because I was in my late teens, I was quite open to new experiences and new challenges. I had an expectation that I'd meet new people, that I'd make friends and that I'd learn something from the experience beyond living in south-east London and being a teenager there.

LR: Do you feel that Phakama changed you in any way?

MC: It changed me in the sense that you discover your own identity when you meet people culturally different from yourself. You're very culturally aware, particularly as a young black Londoner, of where you're from. But when you meet someone who's very definite about the tribe they come from, the village they've come from, it makes you question 'where am I from?' 'How much do I know of my history?' I got a greater sense of understanding of who I was, how much I wanted to know about my history and my past. It also forged the vision that I can do anything and that I can aspire to dream bigger than south-east London, than going to university. The world is my oyster. Lots of the South African participants were doing things beyond what was expected of them. They would travel for hours and hours to get to projects. They pushed the boundaries of limited expectation. So I thought 'I can do what I want'.

LR: And were there challenges?

MC: Challenges come when you get people in a room and you want to have a democratic process and everyone's got a different opinion of what that might be. How do you resolve conflicts in a democratic way when you want to hear everyone's opinion when ultimately the decision has to be made about how the work moves forward or what work is chosen for a performance? The young people that were involved in Phakama from LYT were all close and we thought along similar lines. The participants that came from different areas in South Africa had different ideas of what they wanted. It was a challenge to set about merging and blending ideas together. Some of our biggest problems were informal conversations about the work and about social situations: how you queue up to get lunch; what food is acceptable to eat; whether you like this food or not; how you should interact and talk to adults.

LR: And did Phakama resolve any of those challenges?

MC: I think some were resolved and some of them were ongoing. Some of them were just us trying to find out where we fitted into the system and the structure. There were meetings where some of the older participants would mentor particularly the younger members of the group, give them advice and support. I think lots of what Phakama does in terms of Give and Gain helped us deal with that, not be domineering but guide people and see what happened.

LR: When you went into the project, did you have an idea that it was going to be about cultural sharing?

MC: I don't think I did at that time. I was aware it would be about encountering a different culture, that it would be a different experience from my own. But you go into it with a sense of fun and enjoyment. What can you learn about the arts, performing and theatre? Cultural sharing came second for me. You go there thinking about the kind of theatre you can make, the kind of art you can create, what you can contribute to that. You come away with a cultural experience that impacts your life and how you work in the future.

LR: You've talked about seeing the different ways that people are, their different abilities to do things, the different privileges that allow that. Was that the main thing – a notion of South Africa/UK cultural sharing?

MC: It was more than that. We were a multicultural group of teenage Londoners sharing the African theatre experience and the experience of the African young people. This was all framed by the context of post-apartheid South Africa. Most of the London group hadn't fully understood the reality of apartheid and its impact, and we weren't aware of how it would affect us. We were from a very multicultural background, we went to multicultural schools, we had multicultural friends – that was normal to us. But in post-apartheid South Africa, there were still very clear cultural and racial lines amongst the groups. From our point of view there were people that were, not deliberately racist, but had racist tendencies in how they interacted with others. It was noticeable. It was uncomfortable. We, the young people from London, were quite outspoken about it. Some of the young people from South Africa found that quite uncomfortable, some found it refreshing and some didn't know how to handle it. It was the elephant in the room that no one wanted to talk about. We were just so bold at the time, saying, 'Why are we not talking about it, because this is what it is.' It wasn't until we were in that experience and talking to the other young people that we realised what was going on. There was a privilege line. None of the young people from London were affluent but we saw how privileged we were compared to some of the other young people. When we visited the townships we saw the backgrounds that a lot of the South African participants had come from and the situations that a lot of them had been through. There was a divide in terms of how much money we had to spend outside of the workshops. We would have our money and some of the South Africans wouldn't have much and that led to sharing. The question of whose opinions were heard and whose were listened to more often came up. We didn't feel uncomfortable speaking our minds but some of the South Africans did. It didn't occur to us at the time that it could be because of their race. We just said, 'this is what I want to say, so I'm going to say it.' Whereas some of the South Africans would hold back what they wanted to say or think people were not listening to them, because of their race. We found that very hard to deal with because we were not used to that. I'm a young black Londoner who's used to being listened to. I will speak my mind if I want to, that's how it is. But it was different for a lot of the South African group.

LR: I remember when we arrived in Cape Town and the boys all had to sleep in a scout hut. They were completely out of their comfort zone.

MC: I think that's when you really find out who you are: when you realise what, to you, is acceptable; what you like and don't like. For example, you don't know you don't like sleeping in a scout hut. People are saying, 'yeah, that'll be alright, all bunking down together, that'll be fab. Hey, but it's cold. Hey, but the toilet's outside.' It's about your expectation of situations. Until you're faced with it you don't know what you will and will not like, what you will and will not do. Once you're outside your comfort zone you respond in very different ways. That brings out different things in different people at different times.

LR: How did that process of collaboration, of cultural sharing, of keeping things open, of trusting that everyone's got something to give and everyone's got something to gain, change the kind of work that was produced?

MC: It's almost like having a hundred directors and not having one central idea. There's never any one overall director of a project. It's like a hundred hands have made one scene, because everyone's had an input into the thought process, contributed an idea, suggested something, recommended something, brought their spin on it. That all goes into how that scene is then created. An example was in Mmabatho. We were working in two houses on opposite sides of a street and we created a picture out of grain and food on a table. It was a picture of a woman. Everyone had a notion of what the woman should be doing in this picture and the kind of things we could use to show this. We all had a hand in putting some grain down or putting some beans to make up this one image. And it was just part of a scene, a backdrop. No one person is in charge. It's a collaboration between everybody and if you want to have an input you can. There's no way you're ever excluded from anything. Even if it's not your specialism, your art form, your initial idea, you can have an input if you wish to. That's unique.

LR: Do you feel that *Be Yourself*, for example, represented you?

MC: No, but it represented the London I knew from someone else's eyes. The *Be Yourself* project was about showing South Africans our view of London. Showing them that it's a different London than the one they've seen through the media. They thought that we never had racism or any unjust incidents happen. We don't always see the significance of some of the landmarks, events, people, places we encounter on a day-to-day basis. When we took the young people to these places they saw something different that we hadn't seen, or had overlooked or hadn't thought about.

LR: Are there any conversations, events, images, pieces of theatre or relationships that are particularly important – something that happened that will always stay with you?

MC: When we were in Cape Town in 1998 for *With a Suitcase in My Hand*, we went to District Six – a multicultural area where people lived during apartheid.

It was very rare to live in a mixed community in Cape Town during apartheid. District Six was bulldozed by the government. When we went to visit it, all that was left was a church. We looked at this derelict land that had been levelled and looked at the church and we talked about the kind of people that may have lived there. We talked about how it might have felt to be removed from your home. We developed a scene for our performance that was a Truth and Reconciliation trial of a police officer who had been told to remove people from their homes, forcibly if necessary. I played the police officer. In creating this work, as a young black Londoner, I'd never fully understood the impact it would have on the audience. I was not prepared for the emotional response we got from the audience, some of whom had lived in District Six. You can look at something on paper and think you understand what happened. The sign says 'For white people only'. I can read that's what it says. But when you've lived through it and it affects your life, it's something very different. On a dark, cold night, when you deliver the lines, 'It was my job, I was ordered to do it', and you realise how many people are sobbing in the audience – you're not sure how to deal with that. It was something that I will remember for a very long time – that responsibility for delivering something in the performance that made the audience feel so deeply. Then there are conversations that happened afterwards in a very cold scout hut. How you deal with it when people come up to you and say things like: 'I used to live on that street', 'I used to live in this neighbourhood', 'My grandmother used to live here', 'So-and-so I know passed away during this time'. You have to realise that it happened and as a performer you've brought that back for them: that memory, that ordeal, that tangible emotion.

LR: What is the legacy of being involved in Phakama for you?

MC: It wasn't just the legacy of Phakama, it was the legacy of working with LIFT and Lewisham Youth Theatre. For most of my teenage years I was very, very shy. LYT gave me a voice. I had an interest in drama: Phakama made me have an interest in the world. It helped me feel my self-worth and my value in the arts-making process. LIFT then showed me other aspects of theatre that I'd never thought about and how to teach and deliver workshops. It was the experience of Phakama, supported by LIFT, that gave me that love of working with young people. It allowed me to see the journey that young people go through that isn't a tangible examination result, but a process of evolution of self-discovery, developing self-confidence, self-esteem. Lewisham Youth Theatre, LIFT and Phakama – all of them merged into this idea of the human experience: how we experience the world and then how we teach others. That's led me to be a drama teacher. It's led me to think more creatively about how I deliver things. It's helped me understand the world that I live in and find my path in it.

Partnerships

Phakama only functions in partnerships. Its ethos insists on bringing together individuals from different groups and organizations so that the cultural sharing can take place. These partnerships have been many and deliberately varied and through them, and the process of Give and Gain, the practice and network has grown. Mostly the projects take place in one physical location. However, a project is often preceded and followed by work in several locations. There are often individuals who are not present at the project location, but who are engaged remotely with the work. Thus the reach of the project is extended. At various times over the last two decades Phakama has expanded to develop new relationships with partners outside of the relatively safe 'bubble' of the international Phakama network – for example, *Message in a Bottle* (2014) with new partners is six countries or *Tripwires* (2011). These collaborations are not about starting new Phakama groups in different countries but to offer the practice developed to date and to learn from others outside the so-called Phakama family. Some of these collaborations are inevitably more successful than others.

In the final section of Part 1, Ananda Breed, a theatre academic with extensive experience of working with young people and indigenous performance practices, explores the complexities of international collaboration through the partnership of Phakama UK and the Creative Arts Team (New York City) during the CTW international festival of theatre with young people. During this process, collaboration between the companies, separated by geography, is facilitated through shared creative prompts, digital encounters, a representative of each company visiting its twinned group and, finally, time spent working together during the festival. Breed's essay considers how Phakama UK and CAT's distinctly different approaches to making performances grappling with race, globalization and migration, provoked moments where the negotiated effort of hosting and sharing cultural practices was brought into sharp focus. Breed's essay attends to the specificity of approach that may be masked by the general terms 'young people', 'participatory performance' and 'collaboration'.

WHEN TIME IS NOT (2008): ARTISTIC EXCHANGE BETWEEN PROJECT PHAKAMA UK AND THE CREATIVE ARTS TEAM (NEW YORK CITY)

Ananda Breed

Introduction

In this essay, I explore the artistic exchange between Project Phakama UK (here in referred to as Phakama) from London and the Creative Arts Team (CAT) from New York City, through an analysis of their partnership in the CTW project from 2007 to 2008. For the purposes of this book, I focus specifically on Phakama to highlight how their positionality and artistic processes opens up a kind of *telescopic performance* that gathers and concentrates information to project into the future to 'make shared spaces where the impossible can become possible' (http://www.projectphakama.org/about/ (accessed 16 July 2016)). CTW is a biannual festival and approach to making theatre, produced by Contact Theatre in Manchester (UK), that focuses explicitly on the creation of new works by young people: new works that would never have been possible without the contact between companies and artistic practices from around the world. Noël Greig, one of the founders of CTW, in his book, *Young People, New Theatre: A Practical Guide to an Intercultural Process* (2008), that grew out of this work notes, 'The project should be *youth led* to the greatest degree possible.... It is about the development of the *whole person*, and the decision-making process should be in the hands of the young participants as fully as your context allows' (16). Companies who participate in CTW have differing pedagogies and practices of performance making that range from youth-led to adult-facilitated productions, but all incorporate the ethos to encourage youth-led work. Practices often differ based on the performance-making culture and tradition of each company from different parts of the globe. Although the focus of CTW is on artistic exchange, the process also relies on companies negotiating their own artistic, geographic and political borders through performance: some may be rejected and some reaffirmed through the process. In this essay, I argue that the reaction between companies is often based on the micro and macro effects of political, economic and geographic factors. What kind of environment is created when companies from different regions of the world generate transnational productions for international festivals? How might multidimensional memories be triggered, uncovered and manipulated to negotiate power, race and conflict? What power dynamics are subsumed or further articulated within this mediation of transcultural performance practices? These questions will be explored through the performances themselves, interviews with Phakama participants and archival materials including correspondence between the companies and their artistic activities. While both companies' environs are situated in cosmopolitan and urban international centres – Phakama's location in London and CAT's location in New York – the concept of environment becomes further questioned through Phakama's politics of place. I problematize the concept of environment and place using Nomadic Theory to analyse the transnational subject to address both the fluid and restrictive issues concerning border crossing and border enforcement through international festivals like CTW. Rosi Braidotti's Nomadic Theory illustrates how subjectivity is constantly in flux in relation to geographic borders and the social imaginary.

Greig positions CTW as a 're-evaluation of the role of creativity and artistic processes in an evolving world' and asks the question: 'How do we release our human creativity in ways that may steer us, in a truly evolutionary way, from the seemingly self-destructive path we have set ourselves on?' (2). This essay explores how the creative process of exchange between Phakama and CAT might address these questions, alongside my own reflective engagement with the CTW project as an artist facilitator between 2007 and 2008. Greig expands on the specific role of the artist facilitator:

> With the *Contacting the World* project, a 'third party' exists in the equation. An 'Artist Facilitator' has a constant and impartial eye on the process, ensuring that the exchange is happening at a rate, and in a manner, that preserves the equality of input and outcome. This person is neutral and non-directorial in terms of the outcomes of the work. (20)

This framing of the facilitator is distinct and different from that of the Phakama facilitator. As an artist facilitator in CTW, I created monthly inspiration activities and coordinated the artistic exchange between companies alongside co-facilitator Aylwyn Walsh, developing a framework to facilitate the exchanges between companies. This role of artist facilitator is responsible not only for the generation of material in the devising process, but also of the collaboration, communication and relationship between companies and their distinctive practices.

During the year when I served as an artist facilitator, the festival was produced by Manchester's Contact Theatre and staged in Liverpool (UK) as part of the Capital of Culture events. Participating companies included The Other Side of the Mirror (Poland), Creative Arts Team (USA), Phakama (London), Al Harah (Palestine), Aarohan Theatre (Nepal), Evan Youth Forum (India), Tiyatro 0.2 (Turkey), Afro Reggae (Brazil), Space 3 (Manchester), Positive Impact (Liverpool), Die Zwiefachen (Germany) and Barefeet (Zambia). The random process of drawing names from a hat produced the twinning of Phakama from the United Kingdom, and CAT from the United States. Over the span of nine months, twinned companies exchanged exercises and shared their processes towards a culminating event when all of the companies performed their productions during a week-long double-billed festival. Greig notes that the twinning process is most fruitful when it is based on a *partnership of difference* stating: 'Its value is rooted in placing two diverse groups in a creative dialogue with each other. The differences may be ones of ethnicity, culture, language, community, gender, sexuality or class. It is through this diversity that you will discover the unique creative nature of your project' (15).

The twinning between Phakama and CAT inherently brings out particular social, cultural and political nuances concerning issues including immigration, migration, conflict and culture. Additionally, the politics of place and environment come into question when one considers the selection process of the participating companies, not only selection committee process, but also the ability for companies to be granted visas from their home and host countries to support travel to the UK and to, potentially, visit the home of their twin company. Thus, most participating CTW companies represent government-sanctioned and relatively commercially and economically viable organizations. Issues of permission to travel were very much in play in the case of Phakama, as the CTW company included participants of both refugee and non-refugee status: there were five asylum seekers and the remaining participants included British youth and one young woman who was incarcerated in a semi-open prison. Artistic Facilitator Aylwyn Walsh notes the issue of terminology: 'At the time, the company was apt to avoid "refugee" as a term, as some were still awaiting asylum and they didn't want to create a hierarchy between those that had refugee status and those that did not, so the term that was used was simply "new Londoners"' (Walsh 2016).

In order to consider what is shared and what is specific in both Phakama's and CAT's approach, it is helpful to detail how each company articulates its mission and process. Phakama's commitment is

> to the practice of cultural exchange and celebration of shared experience by promoting a participant-centred and non-hierarchical educational philosophy through the medium of the arts. We believe that cultural exchange, arts activities and arts education are central/key to the empowerment and development of young people and communities. We believe that cultural exchange takes place when different cultures exchange their beliefs, values, customs and arts willingly in a spirit of equality and trust through a process of negotiation. (Banning, Calburn and Richardson 2006: 152)

CAT Youth Theatre 'provides young people with hands-on opportunities to create original theatre experiences from their own ideas that will stimulate: creativity; self-esteem and resiliency; broader horizons; a strong sense of community; reflection on what it means to be a theatre-maker and an active, engaged citizen in society; social awareness and activism through theatre'.[1] The mission of CAT 'contains a complementary commitment to develop and disseminate, locally, nationally and internationally, the pedagogy and methodologies on which the work is predicated; and to work with, train and otherwise support the many adults who share the lives of the young people either in personal or professional capacities.[2] Both CAT and Phakama focus on cultural activity to address contemporary social and political issues. However, how each company engages on a political and social level within the frameworks of their cultural contexts differs. Helen Nicholson remarks on the difference between socially engaged performance in the United States and the United Kingdom stating 'patterns of history and geography mean that they are differently nuanced' (2015: 22). While socially engaged performance in the United States emerged from the civil rights movement and protest theatre related to the Vietnam War, socially engaged theatre in the United Kingdom responded to the Troubles in Northern Ireland and Second World War bombings (Nicholson 2015: 22). Yet, what both companies have in common is how they 'pose essential, challenging questions about our individual and social selves and encourage the formation of a critical relationship to our world.[3] The different sociopolitical and cultural make-up of Phakama participants themselves in terms of differences related to ethnicity, citizenship and political experiences inherently negotiates some of these variances within the company itself.

---

[1] See http://www.creativeartsteam.org/programs/cat-youth-theatre (accessed 28 June 2016).
[2] See http://www.creativeartsteam.org/approach/mission (accessed 28 June 2016).
[3] See http://www.creativeartsteam.org/approach/mission (accessed 28 June 2016).

Rosi Braidotti's conceptualization of transnational mobility and subjectivity that argues for a feminist theorization of nomadic subjects is a useful frame to hold these considerations. Braidotti extends bell hooks' approach towards postmodern blackness of a kind of yearning 'for the construction of empathy – ties that would promote recognition of shared commitments and serve as a base for solidarity and coalition' (Braidotti 2011: 22). In this way, I consider environment – beyond the immediate environ of place – as the in-betweenness of transnational forces alongside considerations of mobility and non-mobility as a yearning for the construction of empathy. CTW creates a yearning towards the other for the construction of empathy, addressing Greig's question concerning how artistic practices might release human creativity in an evolutionary way. The CTW model of collaboration brings together two companies with strong identities and bonds that have been forged by their specific and different approaches to making theatre. Each company offers a provocation to think about how this may extend beyond the parameters of each group.

Exchange – Hidden and Visible/Invisible Places

In *Young People, New Theatre,* Greig provides an in-depth account of the CTW process detailing inspiration activities and accounts of how companies responded to the artistic stimuli towards the development of their twinned productions (Greig 2008). Through the inspiration activities each company developed questions that acted as a provocation, a stimulus and a navigation tool through the collaboration. Phakama noted that the devising process for their production, *When Time Is Not,* was guided by the following questions: 'How do you stay connected in a city of strangers? How can you fit the whole world in one place? What do I bring from my past to help my future? Where can I get the bricks to build my life?' CAT noted that their artistic process was guided by the following questions: Do the ghosts of our past nourish or contaminate our future? What do we gain and what do we lose when we hold onto our secrets?' (personal archive, 2007).[4] These precise and particular questions were shaped over time. Each month an inspiration exercise was delivered from the artist facilitators to the CTW companies through Facebook, email and phone (depending on the companies' accessibility to particular technical modes of communication). Companies responded to the exercises by creating a 'mini' performance work shared between all companies on Facebook as a digital film clip, photo album, drawing – or whatever form best represented the companies' interpretation of the inspiration exercise.

One of the exercises, 'Figures in a Landscape', invites young artists to select a physical landscape to serve as another character in the development of the work, to

---

[4]These questions come from monthly global review documents circulated among participating companies that update all companies involved concerning responses to artistic exercises.

allow characters and dialogue to emerge in relation to the landscape. This exercise, alongside the exercise, 'Hidden Histories' had a significant impact on the artistic twinning between Phakama and CAT. The 'Hidden Histories exercise' 'starts with a process of "retrieval" – researching into the past or recent histories of "place": those things that do not always get into the 'official histories' (Greig 2008: 81). 'Touring Spaces: Making the "invisible visible"' has resonances with Phakama's Cultural Tours exercise detailed in the Hosting section of this book:

Activity One: Places and Voices not often seen or heard

- As a company, have each member nominate various sites in your city/town and village that are not often seen and heard.
- Choose five of the places (eg: fruit stall, temple, alleyway, doorframe, abandoned train station, public restroom, etc.)
- Send your list of five places and five character types to your twin. (eg: bus driver, old woman choosing fruit, homeless woman, young boy playing, etc.)

Activity Two: Making your cast
Integrate your list with your twin's so you now have ten possible places as sites and ten potential characters. Select characters and sites that are most interesting and stimulating to your company.

- Go to the different parts of your city/town/village and interview five different people that you find there. You are collecting information that you will use for developing characters. (They can be used for developing your performance later in the process.)

Activity Three: Making your setting
Now, impose the space and character onto your own location: collectively create a physical map (this could be 3D or a drawing) that illustrates the physical relationship between the places and the characters.[5]

The following examples developed by Phakama illustrate the generative influence of the inspirational activities in the shaping of particular characters and scenes in *When Time Is Not*. One particular exploration of characters took place at the IMAX London, the largest screen cinema in Britain. The character of Mosombo, a young man from Rwanda, has been in London for a month. During this time, he has been to the Refugee Council where someone recommends he visits the IMAX theatre. Although he doesn't have money to see a movie there, he ventures to see the environment himself. While there, he bumps into the character, Mohammed,

---

[5] Artistic inspiration activities were retrieved from the author's own personal archive.

from the Refugee Council who is with a group of young people. Mohammed invites Mosombo to watch a movie with them. At first, they cannot decide which movie to watch – a documentary or a fiction. Mosombo convinces the group to watch the fiction stating: 'If they are in a dream house, they should watch a fantasy film.' The character of the usher enjoys IMAX as 'a fantasy world where everything can be re-invented and re-imagined.' Another chance encounter is between Benito, a receptionist from an abortion clinic, and Alfred who works for the African Burial Ground in New York City. These constructions of place – both the cinema and the worlds of the movies – and characters present an 'as if' scenario. Braidotti extends the practice of 'as if' as a 'technique of strategic relocation to rescue what we need of the past so as to trace paths of transformation in our lives here and now … for opening up, through successive repetitions and mimetic strategies, spaces where alternative forms of agency can be engendered' (Braidotti 2011: 27). In this way, the social imaginary provides generative agency towards one's own reflective subjectivity in a world rife with issues concerning globalization, migration and sovereignty to evoke fluid boundaries that enable a state of 'becoming'. Cultural practices like CTW establish artistic frameworks for the performativity of a nomadic subject. Although the culminating festival itself allows for the crossing of borders, the process of creating work through the artistic twinning and monthly artistic exercises allows for an ongoing process of crossing borders, both real and imagined.

Other varied characters come into contact with one another at the IMAX cinema. These characters and their behaviours represent issues concerning religion, nationality, human rights and gender. However, differences and commonalities between the characters are superseded in the scene by the urge to connect. Character descriptions include the additional following examples:

(a) ALDI shopper – Dawn is 54 and is a widow. She is Jewish although she doesn't practice the religion. Her husband was Austrian and died of a heart attack when on holidays in Austria. She is quite lonely and going to shop at ALDI is one of her favourite distractions. She is friends with her neighbours but only visits them rarely. She doesn't have family, so she loves talking to people around…and to observe everything, especially the way young people act and behave.

(b) Seller from Chinatown – Yin is 28 and has been living in China Town for the past five years. She works in a take away shop that is owned by her uncle. She has a baby girl (who is) one year old and is married to a Chinese man named Xyon. Yin doesn't have many American friends … and has hardly left Chinatown since she arrived in the United States because everything she needs is there. When she leaves China Town she likes to go to the movies and to the malls. She understands and speaks a bit of English so she can work with customers. Yin's uncle allows her to take her baby girl to work. She likes living in New York because she feels at home.

(c) Boy from Rwanda – Mosombo Farmato has been in London for only one month. He left two younger sisters and one younger brother back in Rwanda. His sisters are called Kissi Farmato and Girsei Farmato and his brother is Toma Farmato. The Refugee Council helped him with papers and (London) is now almost like a second home. He is living in a house with four other boys. He doesn't work, but the Refugee Council pays his travel expenses and gives him all the meals for free. Here he met people that he identified with and that gradually became his friends, almost family. Mosombo tries to dress like most young people in London, because he doesn't want to stand out. He says if you live in London you have to wear your cap and look like a 'gangsta'.

(d) [Alfred] dresses as an African and has recently done a DNA test to trace back to his ancestors. He was very happy to discover that he had an African heritage. He has mixed feelings about working in the African Burial Ground: sometimes he feels it is quite a noble job and that he is paying homage to his 'ancestors' (as he calls them). Other times he gets really annoyed by the tourists and start being snappy at everyone for no reason. Alfred truly believes he is African, but actually this embodiment of the African identity is just a reflection of his hidden Western middle-class guilt. (personal archive, 2007)

In these examples, we traverse between London and New York, between examples of varied forms of migration and immigration. These real and imaginary characters, created by Phakama, share a desire not to stand out in this new location which is almost like a second home.

During the artistic exchanges, both companies focused on place and variations between the present and the past. Phakama focused on the construction of characters, of new cities and identities. Their idea was to build a new city, a mix of New York and London, or even a mix of the many different cities involved in CTW. They explored the consequences of chance encounters. CAT focused on the theme of hidden histories and the guilt of America's past, particularly its treatment of indigenous populations and slavery, and how we identify with the places where we live. Their production illustrated a kind of haunting that resides with capitalism – that capitalism was created from slavery and continues to operate through the exploitation of transnational trade deals and the overriding monopolization by corporations. CAT attempts to acknowledge America's painful past marked by the genocide of Native Americans and the extortion of African Americans. The artistic journey between companies provided a platform for these varied issues to be explored by company participants. The overt thematic material of CAT has resonances with the historic context of socially engaged performance in the United States, whereas Phakama's nuanced approach to working with issues concerning human rights and identity politics may be derived from the multiplicity of experiences and sociopolitical and cultural frameworks of Phakama participants.

Company Exchanges

As part of the CTW project, there were also in-person exchange visits between participants. Companies nominated one representative who was involved in the CTW project (with practical theatre skills) who would act as an ambassador for their group, and as a key player in the development of the work of both twin companies. Some suggestions to maximize what could be gained from the visit included: to review and respond to the work of the twin company; to take some representations of the work that your company has developed thus far as a result of the collaboration; to offer a practical workshop; and to explore the environments that the twin company inhabits, to consider 'What is the "feel" of the city, town, district or area? What are its textures, mood, and atmosphere?' These questions resonate strongly with Phakama's commitment to residency, cultural tours and hosting. Two young people from Phakama worked with CAT in their home city and one young person from CAT visited Phakama in the UK. Some of the sites visited in New York City included the African Burial Ground, the World Trade Centre and Ellis Island. The stimuli and resulting political and social commentary of these resonant sites informed the production. The materiality and architecture of each site allowed for an embodied experience of affect that could be translated back to one's company following the company visits. However, inherent differences in how both companies considered access, safety and citizenship were revealed through communications between companies in the lead up to and duration of the visit of Phakama participants to New York during this process. In terms of transnational encounters and collaborations between young people, there were some sobering examples of when the 'as if' scenario of global citizenship diminished when faced with practical considerations of mobility concerning visas, passports and entry across national borders. The possible limitations of mobility are presented in an email exchange between Santos, the then former artistic director of Phakama and the director of CAT in March 2008:

> It will be a problem for the Phakama team to travel by themselves to Penn [S]tation for the following reasons: [d]ue to the USA's very tight immigration procedures, it may happen that one of our young people (or indeed both of them) is held back. It is therefore imperative to have some one from CAT at

the airport in case … immigration wants to talk with someone to confirm the reason why they are travelling to the USA. Plus, they are arriving at 19.40 in the evening in a new city and it would be nice to have some one there to welcome them. Phakama will pay for our three members to travel from the airport to wherever CAT is taking them, but they will need some one to guide them in your city. Can you please let us have your mobile numbers (in case … immigration decides to contact you – or the Phakama team needs to get in touch), as immigration problems are very likely to occur and I want to try as much as possible to minimise the related traumas for our young people …. Please do confirm that there will be someone there to welcome them at the airport. (Santos 2008a)

Within the email exchange, hosting, immigration control and trauma are all raised. These issues are further nuanced in relation to communication and each companies' relation to guiding or hosting the other. In another email exchange, Santos notes the discomfort experienced by some Phakama participants when queried about their Refugee status:

Some of the questions that CAT asked of [the young people] related to being refugees a while back (when did you arrive in the UK? Did you ask for refugee status somewhere else? etc) have created a little bit of tension and discomfort amongst the team. Some of our young people feel that people who know them personally can only ask such questions. Others feel that they have no problem answering them. However, the general feeling is that the whole question about being refugees should not be a priority for this collaboration as they feel that they have 'been there done that' …. They are very interested in going beyond labels and to talk about who they are as people. And let's not forget that all … involved in Phakama who are refugees have some painful memories that they'd rather forget about. Of course, the fact that some of them are refugees plays a huge role in shaping who they are. But they, as some of them eloquently put 'are much more than that' …. One thing that the Phakama team would like to ask is that CAT answer exactly the same questions (both the ones about being refugees and what that means to them, and the ones related to home) in any way they want. We feel that in this way we can have a more creative conversation. (Santos 2008b)

This engagement between companies explicitly calls into question issues of mobility and negotiations concerning labels, stereotypes and representation. Phakama unequivocally noted their interest to go beyond their refugee status to claim their identification as individual subjects and to further explore what happens when individual subjects come into contact with one another. Santos suggests that CAT answer exactly the same questions, thus also bringing into dialogue the fact that

America is shaped by migration and immigration, thus questioning the very notion of refugee and asylum from both a historic and contemporary perspective. Braidotti states:

> rethinking the bodily roots of subjectivity is the starting point for the epistemological project of nomadism. The body or the embodiment of the subject is to be understood as neither a biological nor a sociological category, but rather as a point of overlapping between the physical, the symbolic, and the sociological .... The body refers to the materialist but also vitalist groundings of human subjectivity and to the specifically human capacity to be both grounded and to flow and thus to transcend the very variables – class, race, sex, gender, age, disability – that structure us. (2011: 24–5)

Key to this engagement with embodiment is the ability to create political fictions, to transcend categories and social codes towards 'consciousness-raising and the subversion of set conventions' (Braidotti 2011: 26). If we were to perceive the exchange between Phakama and the CAT as a 'political fiction', what would that fiction look like? How would that fiction be written? And towards what kind of subjectivity? I argue that the political fiction created by Phakama within the exchange was based on the re-articulation of space (i.e. the focus on creating a new city), relationships and positioning of power (as articulated through email exchanges and the focus on characterization).

In an interview with Ines Tercio, Phakama's general manager at the time of *When Time Is Not*, she noted the importance of Phakama's process to focus on individual lives versus the label or stereotype of participants as refugees: 'Phakama tried to get to know the participants in the American company and to interweave their stories in the play. The American company started with a fixed theme of slavery based on the refugee experience. Participants in Phakama reflected, why is their focus on slavery instead of turning it upside down?' (Tercio 2016). Phakama's approach to performance making is to go between the real and the fictional, which may come from the nuanced influence of performance making from various performance traditions from around the world. For instance, the aesthetics of political theatre in South Africa (where Phakama was initiated) does not necessarily focus on realism or verbatim-related performance usually associated with the United Kingdom and the United States as text-based traditions of performance making, but rather embraces the fictional and abstract as often being able to communicate more about political issues than its real-life counterpart. Yvette Hutchison (2009: 211) states:

> In the South African sociopolitical context there has been no clear division between the real and fictional for two reasons: the obvious is to ensure the safety of both the sources of stories and the performers. The second is more subtle and interesting, and relates to an African philosophical approach to truth

that is not predicated on the binary systems prevalent within the European Enlightenment tradition of thinking, and thus does not place such a high value on empirical proof to validate an inquiry or conceptual position. In the African context, the story is itself important as a mode through which we can know ourselves and explore our history, identity and collective value systems. It is no less true for being fictional or constructed. At some level it may even suggest greater truth, abstracted beyond the specific.

The aesthetic variances between CAT and Phakama might have been informed either directly or indirectly by their historic political and cultural contexts. When asked about whether there was anything distinctive about Phakama's approach to making work, Tercio stated: 'The social time working together is important with exchange…. Eating together is as important as talking about the African burial site. It is important to interweave the social into the workshop time together'. Phakama uses social interactions to encourage a nonlinear space to allow understandings between people to unfold.

The title of Phakama's production, *When Time Is Not,* was based on a story offered by a participant, a resident of a semi-open prison, about visible and invisible places. When asked where she felt safe, she stated that there was a park bench with the inscription 'When Time is Not' on the back. Whenever she wanted to feel safe, she would go and sit on that park bench. The phrase resonated with the group and it became the thread that guided the rest of the devising process through timelines and frameworks that structured stories around the concept of time. It is useful to quote Tercio (2016) at length concerning the evolution of the production:

We worked on timelines from our lives, interweaving timelines from participants' lives and those from CAT as well – not knowing which stories were true or not. Characters and stories and places were explored. These were familiar to participants like an African taxi, airport, and market. There wasn't a straightforward narrative. There is the idea of journeys and growing up and key moments from people's lives. Each person stepped on a stepping stone …: '1995 my baby brother was born. I stopped being centre of attention. 1987 Mugabe consolidated his power in Zimbabwe and we had to escape.' There were big moments in the world … interwoven with personal experiences. Then the production turned into a celebration in true Phakama style, for participants from New York to come onto the stage. Scenes that stuck out in my mind include a scene with (audio) recordings from participants in New York. Also there was a beautifully choreographed scene when one participant is passed from lap to lap, from baby to walking, a metaphor for growing up, their first kiss, when escaped. 'When Time is Not' was the thread weaving threads of personal stories and time. The idea of timelines and physical and metaphorical lines [were] woven into what we were creating.

It is worth noting in the context of this book, that there were many differences between *When Time Is Not* and other Phakama projects and productions. Santos, the artistic director of Phakama at the time of the production noted that he didn't think it was their strongest work for a variety of reasons. The traditional theatrical staging of the festival production didn't allow for the site-specific responses that often locate Phakama within the local community and sites of discourse. He stated:

> It was a massive challenge to make a play for a traditional staged performance. Phakama wanted to do something site specific, but Contact (for logistical reasons) said no. It would have been extremely difficult to manage twelve productions happening all over the place. So the process, for us became a conventional way of creating work, and Phakama is not used to that and not very good at that. Phakama is good at creating work with the materials, people and spaces we have. It's about people exploring who they are in unconventional spaces, thus you reinvent yourself and the space with the audience. (Santos 2016)

Phakama aspired to work with these challenges by using the auditorium in unconventional ways and to create a collage of different representations where characters 'talk about everything – about going to a party and then losing one's parents or baby. Then they will switch to a moment that is true about a fire and how their parents were killed, followed by drumming and dancing' (Santos 2016). Phakama addressed the issue of representation through a collage of many things to reinvent themselves alongside the audience.

The space of *When Time Is Not* emerged from what Tercio refers to as 'aspirational space versus inhabitable space versus memorable space versus transitional space' (2016). The IMAX cinema was identified as an aspirational space for most of the participants due to the cost of the tickets and the technological advancement of engaging with cinema in 3D. ALDI supermarket was an inhabitable space due to the cheap price of groceries for most young people. Taxis were used as both a memorable space and transitional space due to the usage of taxis in both West Africa and New York. It was something that both companies could relate to. In one scene a taxi was signified with a set of steps going up and down to exemplify time while participants joined the taxi. It was a celebratory taxi with movement and song. In terms of transitional spaces, one scene was located at an airport. There was a blackout and the school children with their teacher go to an airport for light. Planes were arriving and departing during the lesson. Phakama makes a subtle statement about the difference of access between countries, as the only place that had access to light during the blackout was the international airport. In terms of borders and border crossing, Quinn (2016) states:

> There are too many borders between countries including economic borders. Phakama works across borders and nationalities, so you get to meet people who

you wouldn't normally. It's intrinsic. It's a part of the Phakama performances that people cross borders and are accepted into new communities.

I would posit that the CTW project served as an aspirational space for the interweaving of stories and characters between Phakama and CAT participants. Following the CTW project, some Phakama participants visited CAT participants who hosted them while in transit from various parts of the globe, illustrating the sustainable connections and relationships between company participants beyond the CTW project.

Conclusion

In this, final, section, I link the CTW project with my broader experience of participatory performance practice in very different international contexts and offer a brief conclusion based on potential limitations and challenges of the CTW exchange. My focus on social interactions and the varied negotiations of cultural forms (song, dance, music, art, etc.) has been an intrinsic part of working with young people for projects where I've served as a lead consultant in post-conflict settings like Rwanda, Indonesia and Kyrgyzstan. Sharing stories and engaging with one another on an informal level is important to create a working dynamic towards the unique creative nature of a project. One particular exercise that I've used involves a mapping of place to understand how power and access works on a purely geographic as well as metaphorical level. How does one place or space overlap with another place or space? What can we learn through the crossing of borders, both physical and spiritual? Sandro Mezzadra and Brett Neilson use the image of the iconic taxi driver in New York to explore borders and border crossing in the introductory chapter of their book entitled *Border as Method, Or, the Multiplication of Labor* stating: 'Issues of territory, jurisdiction, division of labour, governance, sovereignty, and translation all collapse into the urban space that these drivers traverse' (Mezzadra and Neilson 2013: 2). They note that borders create a '… blueprint for the colonial partitioning of the world and the regulation of relations between Europe and its outsides' of an *already global* space' (Mezzadra and Neilson 2013: 4). In this project, Phakama focuses on the *already global* space by resisting the social and political fetishization of the refugee subject through a reconfiguration of relationships and spaces to, returning to Greig's ambition for CTW to 'release our human creativity in ways that may steer us, in a truly evolutionary way, from the seemingly self-destructive path we have set ourselves on' (Greig 2008: 2). Phakama encourages artists and the world at large to consider *When Time Is Not* – if there was no time and we had the ability to live our lives freely as explored through interwoven social interactions and fluid environments.

The CTW project provided a rich opportunity for young people from both CAT and Phakama to reach towards the other. Perhaps it's the reaching that enables creativity and growth on both artistic and sociopolitical levels. At one point during the exchange, participants tried to see each other through an art exhibit, *Telectroscope,* that virtually connected people from either end of a giant telescope located between Tower Bridge in London and Brooklyn Bridge in New York (Ryzik 2008). Due to time differences and potential human error, participants never managed to see one another through the telescope. But, perhaps it's the desire to see and to meet the other that created newly inspired works in the case of the twinning between CAT and Phakama.

How does this case study provide new insights to practitioners and scholars engaging with Phakama's work? I would suggest that the focus on telescopic projections might inform new artistic practices. I coin the term *telescopic performance* to illustrate a process that is not necessarily focused on the intercultural or interweaving processes commonly associated with transcultural performance practices, but rather on the projection into time and environment that makes this particular project and the work of Phakama unique. As a telescopic performance, the methodology collects artistic material from a range of varied sources and projects them with the intention for us to see in new ways. The focus is on the projected future, demonstrative of prospective memory that involves remembering to carry out intended actions towards the future (Baddeley, Eysenck and Anderson 2015: 361). This aligns with Braidotti's 'as if' configuration of subjectivity alongside the notion of political fictions to consider art forms through an engaged subjectivity with a prospective other. 'They (Phakama] speak to you (from other times, places, continents) of the varied experiences, values, beliefs, dreams, hopes and memories of a diverse collection of people separated by all kinds of geographic, cultural, social, linguistic and ideological differences … a vision that is both theatrically [and] socially collective' (Banning, Calburn and Richardson 2006: 151). Telescopic performance literally transfers subjectivity and place in a way that layers alternative and place based relations to intentionally *blur* boundaries and borders. This essay engages with the notion of a projected layering of place and space to encourage an 'as if' construction of political subjectivity towards transnational nomadic subjects.

References

Baddeley, A., M. W. Eysenck and M. C. Anderson (2014), *Memory* (2nd edn), Hoboken: Taylor and Francis.
Banning, Y., C. Calburn and L. Richardson (2006), 'South Africa, London & Lesotho: Landscapes of the Heart', in Michael Etherton, James Gibbs and Femi Osofisan (eds), *African Theatre Youth*, Oxford: James Currey.

Braidotti, R. (2011), *Nomadic Subjects: And Sexual Difference in Contemporary Feminist Theory*, New York: Columbia University Press.

Greig, N. (2008), *Young People, New Theatre: A Practical Guide to an Intercultural Process*, New York: Routledge.

Hutchison, Y. (2009), 'Verbatim Theatre in South Africa: "Living History in a Person's Performance"', in Alison Forsyth and Chris Megson (eds), *Get Real: Documentary Theatre Past and Present*, New York: Palgrave MacMillan.

Mezzadra, S. and B. Neilson (2013), *Border as Method, or, the Multiplication of Labor*, Durham: Duke University Press.

Nicholson, H. (2015), 'The Silence within the Noise: Reflections from the UK on "A Vibrant Hybridity"', in Jan Cohen-Cruz (ed.), *Remapping Performance: Common Ground, Uncommon Partners*, New York: Palgrave Macmillan.

Quinn, S. (2016), Interview with the author, London, United Kingdom, 18 May.

Ryzik, M. (2008), 'Telescope Takes a Long View, to London', *The New York Times*, 21 May. http://www.nytimes.com/2008/05/21/arts/design/21tele.html (accessed 23 May 2016).

Santos, F. (2008a), Personal Communication, 5 March.

Santos, F. (2008b), Personal Communication, 3 May.

Tercio, I. (2016), Interview with the author, London, United Kingdom, 18 May.

Walsh, A. (2016), Personal Communication, 16 July.

PART TWO

MAKING THE
PERFORMANCE

INTRODUCTION

When you go into a Phakama process there is no expectation that we are going to produce something that has a predetermined shape or staging. We will produce something, but nobody knows what it's going to be. It might have a theme around it, but there's no script, there's no narrative, there's no specific story. There will be a date and start time for the performance. But that's about all you know. If you've any experience of Phakama you'll bring a hat and a coat and some gloves.

SIDDALL 2015

Devised performance is closely connected to the context and moment of production, and new practices have been invented to extend contemporary notions of what performance might be. Devising has, therefore, the flexibility to enable theatre makers to address matters of personal concern, to interrogate topical issues, and to extend the aesthetics and reception of performance.

GOVAN, NICHOLSON AND NORMINGTON 2007: 4

I'm inspired by David Roman's notion of 'critical generosity', through which he argues that performance should be taken on its own terms, and read through the exigencies of a social moment, offering cultural criteria equally as important as more straightforward aesthetic ones.

DOLAN 2005: 33

Each Phakama project culminates in a performance that is distinctly different from any other, informed by the people who make it and the particular context they are working within. Some projects have involved scores of young people coming from different countries working together in residence for a short period of time and staged in outside spaces (*Message in a Bottle*, 2011–13). Other projects have engaged a smaller group of people, living in the same city but with very different cultural experiences, gathering weekly to create work staged in the space that they meet (*The Robben Island Peace Process*, 2001, *Ten in a Bed*, 2015–16 and *Three*

Percent, 2014). However, despite the variance in scale, location and rhythm of the devising process there are certain characteristics that can be identified across all of Phakama's work. Part Two of the book is divided into five subsections to consider the collaborative creative strategies and approaches that generate and shape the material of Phakama performances.

The first section examines the characteristics of Phakama's aesthetic of togetherness focusing specifically on a layered co-authorship; the use of site and found materials; and the role of the audience as both witnesses and participants in the aesthetic experience of Phakama.[1] We have identified specific exercises adapted in projects in very different contexts. We detail their structure and illustrate examples of performance materials or understandings that have been generated or made explicit through them. In this section we draw upon projects including *Tripwires* (UK, 2011), *The Child I Curry* (Lesotho, 2003), *Landmarks of the Unknown* (Japan, 2015), *The Robben Island Peace Project* (South Africa, 2001). We build upon the theoretical frameworks of care (Joan Tronto) and collaboration (Richard Sennett) developed in Part One and engage particularly with Jill Dolan's work on *Utopia in Performance* (2005) to consider new understandings about the practical politics at play in the staging of Phakama performances.

This is followed by an interview with James Hadley, Arts Council England (ACE)'s Relationship Manager who supported Phakama UK's development from 2008 to 2014. James's interview considers the transformation of site and place through extensive partnership making and collaboration, focusing on two projects, *The Trashcatchers Carnival* (UK, 2010), a collaboration with Emergency Exit Arts, Transition Town Tooting and a network of local organizations in Tooting, south-east London as part of the Transition Town Network supporting the development of resilient communities and environmental justice; and *From Somewhere to Nowhere* (UK, 2010), a collaboration with the Orpheus Centre, an inclusive performing arts and residential college for young adults with physical or learning disabilities.

Sara Matchett is a theatre maker and academic based in Cape Town, South Africa. She first worked with Phakama in 2000 and collaborated on many Phakama projects in South Africa and India as well as having an ongoing relationship with the Phakama group in Western Cape. In this section, Matchett's essay 'Catalytic Conversations: The Aesthetic Weave and Social Weft of Phakama's Creative Practice', considers Phakama as a welcome disruption of the dichotomy between 'community' and 'mainstream' theatre practice and considers its influence on theatre makers and academics whose teaching, making or producing work is informed by a commitment to social justice and cultural equity. By focusing specifically on *Call Me Not a Woman* (Mmabatho 2000), Sara examines how this project provoked new understandings about geographical and psycho-emotional landscapes that dared to counter 'master narratives' of the ways of the world.

---

[1] Within the broader field of participatory performance there is a rich field of enquiry around aesthetics. See, for example, White (2015), Winston (2011).

The penultimate section of this part is a case study of *The Phakama Way* (Pune, India, 2002) by Vidyanidhee (Prasad) Vanarase, a theatre maker and academic from Pune, who has taken the lead on sharing Phakama practice locally and nationally. *The Phakama Way* was a month-long residency set up to support arts workers address barriers between different Indian castes and involved over thirty community leaders, theatre makers, university lecturers and school teachers to share ideas, exchange processes and develop a locally based Phakama methodology with the guidance of experienced facilitators from South Africa and the UK. The project culminated in a site-specific performance with young people from Mumbai. In this case study Vanarase details how Phakama upended assumptions and expectations about traditional roles of theatre making, particularly the authority and vision of the director and the repositioning of the audience from passive spectators to an integral part of the performance event.

Phakama performances usually take place beyond commercial theatre frameworks, in found rather than designated 'cultural' venues with established structures for press and marketing. This has meant that the work is often off the radar of the media. However, there has been some local and national press coverage of specific Phakama projects in different countries that reveal much about the public reception of this work. In the final section of Part Two, we have included Charlotte Higgins' article about *The Street Is My Backyard* (Argentina, 2006) featured in the British newspaper, *The Guardian*. Higgins attends to Phakama's engagement with site and particularly the cultural context that surrounds the production – the performance traditions and skills that people bring and share – as well as an almost tangible quality of the pressure of making a show with such a compressed, intensive devising process.

Layered Co-authorship

In *Making a Performance: Devising Histories and Contemporary Performance*, Govan et al refer to devising as '*processes* of experimentation and sets of creative *strategies* – rather than a single methodology' (7). In the following section we outline how specific creative strategies have been used within Phakama's practices to generate performance materials in response to the specificity of each context. Within this process, all of the work we describe in Preparing the Ground – Hosting, Give and Gain and Cultural Tours – inform, enable and, at times, directly contribute to the material of a performance. They establish an approach, an ethos to working collaboratively and equitably. In this section we have identified three specific examples of structures that have facilitated experimentation to generate performance material: Four Corners, Poetry Cuts and Drawing the Body.

Issues of authorship, authority and representation are always at play in any devising process. The difficulty in modelling the idea of collective authorship, where responsibility for all aspects of a company's work is shared equally regardless of skill or experience, is detailed in accounts of British performance collectives of the 1970s and 1980s that were part of the alternative theatre movement.[2] In contemporary professional theatre, there are a number of companies who devise their work based on ensemble but acknowledge the director as having a distinctive role within it (such as, in the UK, Frantic Assembly, Kneehigh, Complicite and Forced Entertainment).[3] For Phakama, the commitment to collaborative authorship and shared responsibility is realized through a layering of authorship: where each person has the opportunity to create and shape ideas through a continued sharing and shaping of material. The following three examples – Four Corners, Poetry Cuts and Drawing the Body – detail this principle in practice and we have given both the structure of specific exercises and in-depth descriptions of how these have unfolded or been adapted in specific contexts. While our focus has been on detailed structures for co-authorship the exercises inevitably reveal other areas of consideration – site, found materials and audience – though we attend to this in greater detail in the sections after this.

Phakama Practice: Four Corners

Four Corners is a structured approach to devising that explicitly models sharing, cycling and the layering of ideas to collaboratively author material. The following example is drawn from the devising process for *Tripwires* (London, 2011), a collaboration between Phakama and Index on Censorship, an international organization that has, since 1972, promoted and defended the right to freedom of expression.[4] *Tripwires* was a peer-training project with young people using the Phakama methodology to address issues of censorship and freedom of expression in a globalized world. The project ran for eight months with eighteen young people from East London, recruited from organizations working with young people such as Theatre Royal Stratford East as well as networks of young people engaged in politics including Tower Hamlets Youth Parliament and Young Mayor.[5] In addition to working with the team of facilitators, unusually in this project, Phakama and

---

[2] For further reading on the politics of devising practices, see Heddon and Milling (2005); for collectives and collaborative practice in the context of the alternative theatre movement, see diCenzo (2006), Hanna (1991).

[3] See Radosavljevic (2013).

[4] For more information on the range of campaigns and approaches initiated by Index on Censorship, see https://www.indexoncensorship.org/ (accessed 10 May 2016).

[5] *Tripwires: Freedom of Expression* (https://issuu.com/thinkgrowth/docs/tripwires) is a digital publication written by the project participants, reflecting on the process and issues engaged with during *Tripwires* and subsequent project working with young people in Palestine, Free2B, set up by six group members. The *Tripwires Documentary* by Mile End Films (2011) is available at https://www.youtube.com/watch?v=RNlxBJzDstE (accessed 2 May 2016). For a review of the performance, see Natasha Schmidt, 'What Does Free Speech Mean to Young People?', Index on Censorship Free Speech

Index on Censorship curated a series of workshops with visiting artists whose work has been subject to censorship and resistance: they spoke to the group explicitly about the political contexts they steered through and against in their arts practice. These included Martin Rownson, a British editorial cartoonist and writer whose satirical cartoons regularly feature in *The Guardian* and the democratic socialist newspaper *Tribune*; Htein Lin, a Burmese painter and performance artist who maintained his practice covertly through six-and-a-half years of imprisonment as a political prisoner; Gurpreet Kaur Bhatti, a writer whose play *Behzti* (Dishonour) (Birmingham Rep., UK, 2004) provoked outrage in the Sikh community for its portrayal of sexual abuse and murder in the *gurdwara* – the production was subsequently cancelled as the theatre said it could 'no longer guarantee the safety of the audience' (Hingorani 2010: 177) and Bhatti was forced into hiding;[6] and Belarus Free Theatre, a dissident theatre company that continues to use theatre as a form of direct action to denounce the dictatorship in Belarus, where censorship and human rights violations are strategies of government, despite the real and ongoing threat to their lives.[7]

Tripwires culminated in a site-specific public performance at Mile End Park Arts Pavilion in East London. Each scene unfolded to reveal a situation that compelled the audience to consider the provocations that permeated throughout *Tripwires*, 'one man's freedom is another man's offence. Where do you draw the line?' What is and isn't acceptable in human behaviour? What acts compel an intervention? How do you intervene? Natasha Schmidt (2011), deputy editor of the Index on Censorship magazine, details moments from the production:

> the stoning of a young woman presented as a circus attraction; a catwalk that drew out the themes of the objectification of women and beauty as alienation; the 'free space' that leaves participants dumbstruck and lost for words; the waiting room where preferential treatment can be bought and sold. Audience participation was crucial to the unravelling of each absorbing and often uncomfortable scenario. The tacit question asked by each scenario was: where do you draw the line?
>
> Voices came from unexpected places, disorientating, challenging and bringing the audience into the debate. Music, movement, singing, storytelling all contributed to a thoroughly atmospheric account of what it's like to be young, vulnerable, charismatic and ready to confront life, whatever it offers up.
>
> Later, the audience was invited outside the theatre equipped with individual headsets, the voices of the TRIPWIRES performers' in their ears. Film,

---

Blog, 23 April 2011, http://blog.indexoncensorship.org/2011/04/23/what-does-free-speech-mean-for-young-people/ (accessed 2 May 2016).
[6]See Hingorani (2010); Kaur Bhatti (2014).
[7]For more on Belarus Free Theatre see Livergant (2016: 241–57); Wade (2001).

movement, singing, visual art – and a sculpture of a burning man – all played their part in creating a dynamic, inspiring and memorable experience.

Fabio Santos details how Four Corners was used in one of the sessions where a musician, a movement artist (in this case a capoeira specialist), a theatre maker and a visual artist worked with the group to generate material that informed the production.

The young people were asked to bring in an object that said something about themselves. The group was split into four smaller ones and each chose one of these objects to work with. Then, each of the four objects was placed in a different corner of the room. This object was the stimulus for creating a short piece.

Each group also had a specific area to work with – sound, movement, drama and visual – and this informed each piece they made. So, for example, one corner had an Afro-Comb as the object and the movement group made a piece in response to it. In each of the other corners, small groups responded to the selected object through drama, sound or visual articulation.

Each group shared their work, going around the space in a clockwise direction, observed closely by the other three groups. Then each group left the catalyst object in its original corner and moved clockwise around the room, continuing to carry their skill with them.

When they arrived in a new corner, they repeated the piece they had just seen performed but adapted it to accommodate their particular skill/element. So, for example, the sound group arrived in the corner with the Afro-comb object and replayed the movement piece that had been made there and added a sound dimension to this.

Again, each group shared their work, one by one, and then rotated around the room: each piece had strata of the textures of different and additional elements of skill. When the groups arrived back in their original corner they had contributed to four short performance pieces, made by the entire group, layered with consideration of each of the four skills. The groups then refined and shaped this collage of devised material.

With Four Corners the principles in this iteration were: the object stays in a particular corner, the skill travels from corner to corner with the group, and the group attends to this aspect of performance making at every stage of the devising process.

In *Tripwires*, the devised material inevitably engaged with the themes of censorship and freedom of expression. For example, the Afro-comb, which belonged to Kishorn, one of the participant's, opened up a dialogue about what it means to be a black man in London and how aspects of identity can be expressed fully – or not. This exercise was highly generative and was the catalyst for one key scene about the stoning of a woman in the final performance.

FOUR CORNERS

Prepare in advance:

- The group offers a collection of objects for consideration – the invitation for this object can be open (bring something that means something to you) or specific (bring something that resonates specifically with the theme being explored).
- Identify four corners/locations within the working space.

The activity:

- Create four groups, each one responsible for a specific area of practice such as visual, music, movement, drama.
- Each corner/location is home to one object that stays there throughout the entire devising process.
- The four groups choose a corner to begin and respond to the object in this corner through their specific area of practice.
- These short pieces are shared with the other groups, one at a time and in a clockwise direction, while being carefully observed by the group to their right.
- After all the groups have shown their work, they move around the room in a clockwise direction to the next corner.
- The groups examine the object, recreate the piece they have just witnessed staged in that particular corner and add an additional layer of *their* group's art-form-specific response.
- Once again, the groups share this work, now with two interwoven layers of response.
- The process is continued until each group had travelled to all corners and four short performance pieces are presented, including all four art skills elements (visual, music, movement, drama) and contributed to by all.

Sharing:

- The four complete pieces can then be performed.

Note:

For the visual element of this exercise, the groups can make use of whatever is available in the room: tables, chairs, paper, magazines, participants' own clothing, etc. Extra material can also be brought in in advance if needed.

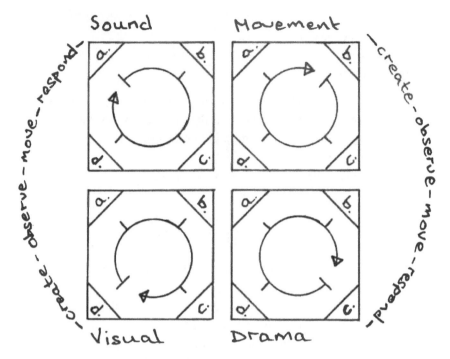

FIGURE 5 Four Corners.

Circles within squares: Four Corners relies on incremental layers of devising and results in four unique end products from shared source material.

Phakama Practice: Poetry Cuts

Poetry Cuts models another structure for shared and equitable collaboration. Lucy Richardson reflects on how this exercise was developed and adapted during a training week in Lesotho with fourteen artist facilitators with different disciplinary skills from six Southern African Development Countries and the UK as part of *The Child I Curry* (2003).[8] This British Council-funded project was developed in response to the United Nations Convention on the Rights of the Child (UNCRC) Article 31, 'Children have the right to relax and play, and to join in a wide range of cultural, artistic and other recreational activities'.[9] The aim was to bring together practitioners, some with experience of education work but few with any participatory arts experience, to consider how these ideas might be explored and articulated by young people themselves. The UK and South African Phakama team was tasked with training for a week and then, together with the recently trained facilitators, delivering a project with young people over two weeks in Lesotho. These

---

[8] The Southern African Development Community is a regional organization with fourteen member countries – Angola, Botswana, Congo (DR), Lesotho, Malawi, Mauritius, Mozambique, Namibia, Seychelles, South Africa, Swaziland, Tanzania, Zambia and Zimbabwe.
[9] See http://www.unicef.org/crc/files/Rights_overview.pdf, 3.

facilitators then returned to their own countries to develop work with the young people they worked with, informed by the Phakama approach. The original training and production of *The Child I Curry* in Lesotho led to two regional projects of the same name in Botswana (2004) led by Jessica Lejowe and Boipelo Moagaesi and, in Mauritius, Christophe St Lambert and Sylvain Polydor.

The training week took place in a space that had a big garden and a hall. We asked the group to write, in their notepads, a response to the idea of childhood for ten minutes. They had to keep their pen on the paper – to keep writing: they didn't need to read it out, it didn't have to make sense but it did have to respond to the idea of childhood. Then we asked them to read their own work and to underline five lines or phrases each – preferably not a whole sentence but a group of words. We prepared strips of paper and got them to write out their phrase on five separate strips of papers. Then we asked the group to get into smaller groups of four and to put their strips of paper in a pile. There were now twenty strips of paper with four people. They muddled them up. We asked them to take one strip randomly and put it in somebody's shoe and then arrange the other nineteen strips of paper to make them into a poem on a large sheet of paper. They had to use everything that was there. Some phrases could be used more than once so there were some blank strips of paper on hand to write repeated lines. Each group had five minutes to work together before they passed it to the next group. Then we introduced a new set of rules. This group was allowed to change four words. They passed the poem on again and then the last group had to stick the strips of paper down and perform the poem. At this point, they took the strip of paper out from the shoe – that was the title for the poem.

The groups were invited to find a site in the centre or in the garden and decorate it, using the poem as a stimulus. The groups performed their poems in these locations. It was a key moment in the training because, very quickly, the groups made a piece of performance that grew from one word 'childhood'. No one person directed it. The performance depended on each person's contribution. This helped the group understand what you might do when you hadn't much time to think or rehearse; ways of engaging with site; and, ultimately, it modelled the Phakama ethos that the performance depends on shared responsibility.

POETRY CUTS

Prepare in advance:

- Choose a particular theme for consideration.
- Gather paper, pens and glue and prepare five strips of paper for each person in the group.

The activity:

- Invite the group to individually free write about the chosen theme for ten minutes, trying not to stop or self-edit.
- Each person reads their work to themselves and identifies five lines or phrases that stand out to them.
- Everyone is given five strips of paper and writes these lines or phrases on them.
- In groups of four, people pool their strips of paper and muddle them up.
- One of the strips of paper is removed from the pile and put in a safe place, ideally a shoe, without being looked at.
- The group is given five minutes to read the remaining strips of text and shape them into a poem. All the materials must be used. Everyone contributes to the curation process.
- Each poem is then passed to the next group and some new rules are introduced for example, they can change four words.
- The poem is then passed to another group that sticks the strips of paper down on a large sheet. The 'hidden' strip of paper is revealed – this is the title of the poem.

Sharing:

- Each group is invited to find a site and decorate it, keeping the poem in mind as a focus and catalyst.
- The poems are performed in these selected and staged sites – sometimes read, sung, or in a chorus.

Phakama Practice: Drawing the Body

Drawing the Body has been used in many Phakama projects. It is, in many ways, the visual articulation of Phakama's commitment to participant-centred practice and layered co-authorship. By drawing around each person, cutting out these outlines and placing them with reference to the group, the individual and the relationship of the individual within the group are visually articulated. Drawing the Body is an exercise that has a very specific starting point but can be adapted and developed to respond to the particularities of the context. In this section, we map the practicalities of the exercise and detail how it was adapted in different contexts.

DRAWING THE BODY

Prepare in advance:

- You will need a large roll of paper, something to draw with and scissors. Potentially you may also need glue, other found materials to decorate the outline with.

The activity:

- Somebody lies on a large piece of paper, choosing the shape they want to make with their body. The shape may be a response to something as simple as, 'make a shape, any shape' or something more considered, 'find a gesture that says something of you, repeat it, expand it and now lie on the paper in this shape'. You can experiment with the invitation.
- Another person draws around the outline of the body as carefully as possible. Every detail is included – every finger, every bit of clothing, every wrinkle and fold of cloth.
- You can write on the outline, draw on it, decorate it. For example, you could ask people to think about feelings and write them where the heart is; you could invite people illustrate their thoughts in the head; in your feet, you could think about where you have travelled to, where you'd like to go.
- You can decorate the person – maybe with items collected from the local environment like grass, earth, stones, twigs or bottle tops, sweet papers etc.
- You can paint or colour your person.

Sharing:

- Each group finds a place or a way to present their 'paper person', possibly beside their flesh and blood counterpart.

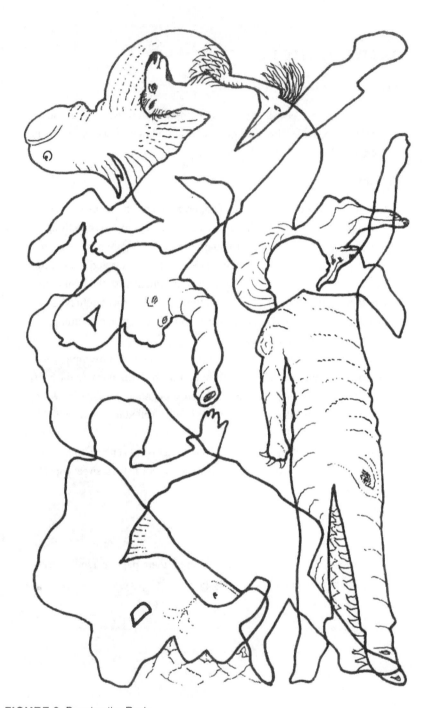

FIGURE 6 Drawing the Body.

Interlocking outlines in Drawing the Body create endless visual possibilities in the spaces between the lines.

Lucy Richardson describes how the initial structure of the exercise acted as a catalyst for collaborative practice that informed the narrative of the performance as well as the scenographic landscape for *The Child I Curry* (Lesotho, 2003).

We split the larger group into smaller ones. Each of the smaller groups choose an individual to be the person who was drawn around. These bodies were drawn on brown paper and the outline was decorated with found, natural materials from the garden of the place that we were staying. The groups found things in the garden that we hadn't even noticed and worked in such detail and with such care. They made hair out of grass, clothes out of stones, flowers for eyes, shoes made out of earth. Each small group worked together, sticking these materials within the outline. The outlines had texture and weight. They were absolutely beautiful: three dimensional, textured portraits of the individuals and their character.

We asked the group to take the outlines into the garden and find a home for them. Each group found their special place. When they came back, they picked up the bodies as if there were babies, cradling the head, or upright like puppets, holding the arms. There were glass windows looking out into the garden and as the groups walked out they began to sing, spontaneously: it was a funereal, sad song. Each group found their chosen place for the body and installed them with great care. Some figures sat on a chair, others leaned against a wall or were tucked in trees, some were hidden, some were prominent. And all the time the group was singing. Then the person whose body was originally drawn around went and sat next to the figure, in the same position that the body was placed. The bodies were very carefully created and attended to but they were also funny. One of them, maybe because the body became very heavy when decorated, had a walking stick and became on old man. So when the boy went to stand next to his decorated outline, he had a walking stick too and acted like an old man. This became part of the performance.

Drawing the Body is a collaborative task of care that brings the relationship of the individual to the group into the foreground. In the context of *The Child I Curry* the group had modelled the theme of the project – taking care about the ingredients (social, cultural, political values) you bring together in supporting a child to grow. It was only possible to do this work, with care, nuance and detail, because of all the preparatory work that had gone on before, establishing the framework of Give and Gain, of hosting.

Another adaptation of the exercise emerged in *The Robben Island Peace Project* (South Africa, 2001). Here the drawings of the body were inspired by the images of torture and servitude of the prison cells of Robben Island. However, the images that emerged were, in contrast, creative and liberating. In this version, all of the outlines of the bodies were cut out and then laid over each other on a large piece of paper. Shapes were identified in the gaps between the layered collage of bodies and then coloured in. The space between people became charged with imaginative potential, with metaphor: it was alive rather than inert. Andrew Siddall (2015), one of the lead artists, reflects on this exercise and how it enabled one of the participants, a boy who had been on the outskirts of the group and of the project, to become an integral part of it:

I worked with Liesl Hartman on Robben Island. It was a six months' long project building up to a show for Freedom Day. We took different groups of participants to Robben Island every second weekend and stayed there for four days. Every time we went over we took a few of the Cape Town team, some of the Cape Town teenagers came over and a group from Johannesburg or Botswana or Maputo, the kind of islands of Phakamas across South Africa. One particular weekend there was a boy from one of the more rural towns. He was on the edge all the time – literally standing on the edge of everything and not engaging very much. We did Drawing the Body as a mass group exercise, cutting out the body outlines and laying them over each other on a humungous sheet of paper. It was probably ten metres square and we had all the kids' and all the facilitators' outlines on it and they were all in different coloured markers. I asked everybody to stand around the edge of this huge sheet of paper with all of the outlines on it and to start looking for the shapes that they found in it. There was some head scratching, some looking and I kept gently encouraging people to look for the shapes in between the outlines – what they could see? All of a sudden somebody said, 'that looks like a crocodile!' And everybody went, 'what?' When it was pointed out there was a big 'oh yeah!' Then, 'Oh, there's a chicken!' Suddenly people started to see these shapes in the joins of the bodies, in the gaps between them. As we spotted them, we coloured them in. The boy who'd been on the edge throughout the project didn't know what was going on, he didn't get it: he was just standing off to one side. He thought we were completely bonkers. I said, 'why don't you go up on stage where you can see down and just watch. It's fine if you don't want to actually draw, but don't disappear, go and watch us do stuff and see what you think.' So he went and stood with his arms folded, staring at us as we were scrabbling about on the floor, colouring in the head of a bear or a chicken or a tortoise that somebody had found. We were at it for ages and ages and ages. Then he whispered, 'There's a bird. I can see a bird'. He stopped stock still on stage and was pointing at it. Everybody slowly backed away. Liesl identified the patch on the floor that was like a bird. It was extraordinary. From that moment the boy was completely in the project. He came down and coloured in his bird. It became his – his bird. And then this whole thing – a humungous thing of collaged bodies and found creatures – went up on the wall. It was there every week when we went back and became our wallpaper and this bird stood out for me.

Each of these exercises, Four Corners, Poetry Cuts and Drawing the Body, are structures of invitation rather than prescriptions for certainty: they create frameworks where individuals collaborate with the possibility of equity. Barbara

Heinzen, Chair of Phakama UK's board from 2005–12, reflects on this space of intentional openness as one of rare necessity that facilitates the possibility of genuine co-authorship, of cultural equity.

> What Phakama does is say, here's vaguely an area we want to think about: you define the problem, you define the language, you define the images. You don't know what's going to come out of it. There's a quality of invention that's not decided by anybody else in advance, there's no script, but there *is* a facilitated process that creates something on the fly, which also creates that emotional reaction of bonding. It's not that we did something together; it's that we *created* something together, we *understood* something together. (2012)

Sid's account of the boy in *The Robben Island Peace Project* who went from being on the outskirts of the group with little understanding or investment in what was happening to suddenly seeing the bird, understanding both the concept and willingly participating and committing to it, is a metaphor for the entire Phakama process. It illustrates the time, care and space required for people to take their place in the process, to become part of a collaborative endeavour: the offer is continually made throughout the process but unless someone is ready to 'see it', they will be on the outskirts looking in. However, only when people realize that they are not only invited but also necessary in the making and shaping of a production, does cultural equity become a possibility. The following exchange between facilitators involved in the first two decades of Phakama, discussing the particularities of this creative practice, highlights how an ambition for cultural equity is both embedded within and a consequence of this approach:

Andrew Siddall: Sometimes people use the word magic to describe the moment when all these different things come together to make a performance. I really want to question this and say actually it's nothing to do with magic, it's to do with an awful lot of people working really hard. It's very rare that you get so many people all completely focused on one thing. [*Sid points to each person*]: it's a bit of *your* brain, and *your* brain, and *your* brain and *your* actions *combined* that pop up with those things. And you never know whether it's 2% from here, and 20% from there or 50% from here and 10% from there that come together to create something. There is no directorial principle going on: there is not somebody telling us what to do.

Kelvin O'Mard: Working with Phakama, it was the first time as an actor, as a director, that I was able to work with a completely blank canvas and feel safe in it. In the beginning, I wanted someone to give me a script, I wanted someone to give me all the parameters. But I realised in this process that it was safe for me to have a blank canvas. I remember the young people saying to me, 'what are we going to do?' as we were taking them around Cape Town, or Robben Island. And I said, 'well, I don't know'. We really didn't know. That opportunity to work in a way that wasn't totally structured in advance or on my behalf hasn't left me.

Andrew Siddall: There is a lack of structure but there *is* a framework and that is really important. There is a timescale that's definite – you have seven days or eight days. And you have time periods through the day with break times – food is hugely important. One of the key words for me is sharing. Every single day, everybody sees what everybody else does. It's very rare for that to happen, to come together and spend so much time seeing each other's work. But its key. It allows everything to feed across the performance: what you have in one piece over there unconsciously feeds what we are doing over here. And the next day we give it back to you – in a different way. So the whole thing – despite the fact that there is no narrative, no pre-story that we are following – everything links and weaves together because we watch and respond to each other all the time.

Lucy Neal: The first property of a system – whether you are talking about the ecosystem, the body as a system, the education system – is that it has emergent properties. Phakama is a *system* for making theatre. If the dynamics of the system are in place, which Phakama does very well in its early stages, then you get these emergent properties – they appear to be improvised, they didn't necessarily come from one person, they appear to come from the places in between people, they came from this extraordinary quality of what happens when you interact and engage. Phakama is the practice of the in-between.

Lucy Richardson: I'm really struck by the fact that the first day of a fourteen-day project, where there *has* to be a performance at the end and we have few ideas, is spent doing 'Give and Gain' which is, effectively, nothing to do with the performance at the end. I remember the first one I did I was so frustrated – when are we going to get on with it?! But that's what you are saying – it's a brave thing to do, to give time and space to building that system.

In addition to generating material that informs the content of the performance, these exercises, like all of those referred to in Part One build a system of communication which accelerates facilitators' and participants' capacities in understanding *what to do* with this material: how to shape it, how to edit this supported by the facilitators. While the responsibility for the dramaturgical structure, scenographic curation and consideration of audience experience through the site of performance is shared by everyone, it is important to acknowledge that the artist facilitators' specialist skills fine-tune the aspects of the performance. This is only possible because of a commitment for all work to be witnessed and open to response from all participants and facilitators. This could, potentially, sound like some impossible dream of collective endeavour that can only result in a collage of compromise. However, the negotiated reality offers something different: a space of what David Roman refers to as 'critical generosity', staging the sharing of material with the whole group so that they can respond, inform and develop aspects of it. That is only possible through careful attendance to detail, reflecting Joan Tronto's proposals for care and democracy, evidenced throughout Phakama's approach to Hosting, Give and Gain and Cultural Sharing.

The process of shaping the performance from the material resonates with the structures and imperative of, particularly, Four Corners and Poetry Cuts. Time is critical – it is not so much about having an abundance of time but about how time spent early in the process allows for systems of communication to be established so that the group, of twenty young people or one hundred and twenty, has both the capacity and authority to act. Andrew Siddall (2015) describes this process:

> We are absolutely definite that we start the day as an entire group – always. Every single morning, we meet as a group, then we go off and we do our individual stuff and we do our group stuff. At some point before lunch, we come back together to share material and to discuss what we see. After lunch, we spin off again, to a different group or back to the same group. My job, a lot of the time, is often looking at material and going, 'what *is* going on? how can we join it together or make something?' I'll take a team of makers with me and we'll think together, 'what does this group need? How can we help them to show what they are doing?' So we are going, literally, around the group, around the outside of all the activity and bringing that into the performance. So even if everyone hasn't seen everything, there are other people in the group who have. In the late afternoon, we'll see a group doing stuff and say, 'it needs something else and we're not quite sure what it is but it needs a bit of direction here.' Someone else will say, 'I think I can add something to that!' because they see something that they can put in. And someone else will go elsewhere, because they have done what they can for that group. It's about shared ownership.

This commitment to shared ownership is inscribed across all aspects of a project as it builds towards a performance. Lucy Richardson (2014) reflects on this sense of membership of more than one designated group within a project:

> In Cape Town I felt like I was in at least four different groups: the facilitator group, the London group, the theatre group, the pastoral care group. The young people were the same – they were in different groups with different people. You are not just one thing, not just The Theatre Person.

Each person's ebb and flow from one group's area of responsibility to another is both fluid and informed by a sense of purpose and direction. If you were to imagine an animated diagram detailing an aerial view of a day in the life of a Phakama project, you would see moments of large group gathering, moments of dispersal with pockets of smaller groups and a constant weaving of people between all areas over the course of the day. It is this circling of bodies across the devising process, bringing layers of knowledge and insight about what is being made in another part of the building at another moment in time, that creates this layering of authorial and curatorial perspective.

Working with Site and Found Materials

The performance, held at Sibikwa's home in the dusty industrial area of Liverpool Park, transformed a courtyard and three linking rooms into a site-specific performance space. Every object was punched or textured, picking up on South African urban wire-art. Each of the seven performance spaces had their own design identity created out of found objects such as corrugated iron and cold drink tins and basic material like sand, stone, paper, hessian and tin foil. Perforated paraffin tins and oil drums spewed fire, windows adorned with intricately cut paper … . *Bulang Dikgoro's* creative process began when each teenager was told to bring three objects in a small cardboard box which would establish their character's lifeline. The stories of lives affected by physical and emotional violence, abuse, racial brutalities, insecurities and aspirations grew out of this collection. On the night, the performers vendored these lives in word and action. The audience, divided into staggered groups, traced the biographies, revealed in the seven phases … the final stop in the journey contained the source – the embryonic boxes mounted on walls with brassy bottle tops. (Sichel 1996)

Sichel's newspaper feature about *Bulang Dikgoro/Open the Gates*, the very first performative iteration of the emergent Phakama process, is necessary to quote at length as, in it, she identifies a number of characteristics of Phakama's aesthetic that continue to inform this practice over the next two decades: promenade performance in non-traditional theatre spaces; scenographic elements and props developed from found materials and natural resources; and the integration of audience into elements of the performance. She also reveals aspects of the process: the relatively short timescale for devising the performance; cultural sharing among people who may live near each other but who have different life experiences; and the small box of personal objects, 'the embryonic boxes', as catalysts for the interplay between personal experience and wider social structures.

Phakama's work rarely takes place in a theatre venue; it is characterized by an engagement with sites that are, usually, not traditional theatre spaces. Over the past two decades, work has been staged in sites including museums (*Breaking the Glass Box*, the Horniman Museum and Gardens, London, UK, 2004) and youth community centres (*The Street Is My Backyard*, in *Defensores del Chaco*, Argentina, 2006). On the very rare occasion that work has been staged in a theatre building (Tricycle Theatre, London, *Be Yourself*, 1999, *When Time Is Not*, Liverpool, 2008 and *The World At My Feet*, Jakarta, 2010), the devising and structuring process continued to engage with this space as a site for consideration rather than a venue for performance though, as pointed out by Calburn and Breed earlier in the book, this offered more challenges than opportunities.

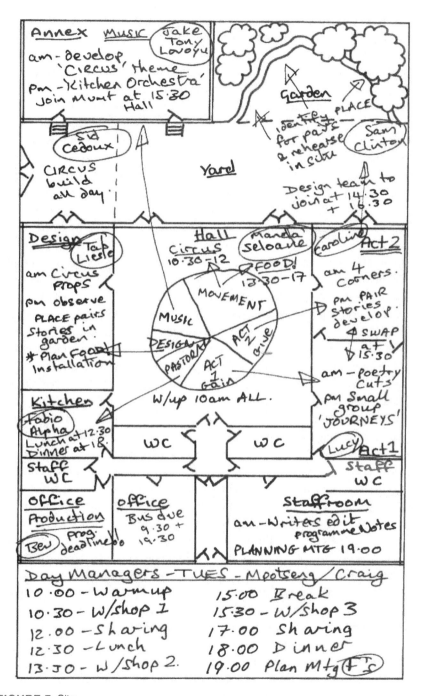

FIGURE 7 Site.

Shows are created on the sites they are performed in, so the Workshop Plan evolves into the Site Plan for the final event.

Phakama's practices and aesthetic are informed by a philosophy of attending to and responding to what is already present – the people who are there (their skills, experiences, dreams, concerns), the site that the work is made and performed in (the building, external space and the social and political contexts that shape them) and found materials that are recycled and reimagined from one defunct function to another of constructed possibility. This commitment to 'see with fresh eyes', to be alongside people, to re-consider the environment in which the project develops is built upon the foundation of an ethic of care that prepares the ground for a Phakama process.

It is helpful to contextualize Phakama's engagement with site in light of debates, in theatre practice and academia, about the emergence of performance practice in, to use LIFT's term throughout the 1980s, 'unusual sites'. In contemporary British, American and Australian theatre there has been a significant body of performance staged not in theatres but in a range of environments including factories, churches, tunnels, decommissioned prisons, hospitals, beaches as well as streets and public spaces such as parks. Some of this work explicitly engages with the history and function of the site (Tinderbox Theatre Company's *Convictions*, Belfast Crumlin Courthouse and Jail, 1998; biggerhouse's *Hair Raising* in JG's Hair Salon, Shepton Mallet, 2001) and some does not (Punchdrunk's *The Masque of the Red Death*, 2007), using the space as architectural opportunity to explore new forms of audience participation in and with the performance. There has been considerable debate about the terminology used to describe this work. In *Performing Site-Specific Theatre: Politics, Place and Practice* (2012), Birch and Tompkins consider differing academic consideration of this work: 'Nick Kaye and Miwon Kwon both chart the history of the form emerging from visual art and then being co-opted by theatre' while Michael McKinne argues that it emerged from the 1960s 'happenings' and environmental performance. They propose that 'whatever it's origins, site-specific performance was a significant form of theatre internationally in the 1990s' (Birch and Tompkins 2012: 6). This resonates with the findings from Fiona Wilke's 2002 survey of 'site-specific' British performance. It provides an insightful historical snapshot of the development of this contested term – and the practices that were accommodated by it – at the turn of the millennium. Wilke identifies the small number of companies that developed work in non-theatre venues between the 1960s and 1980s (including Welfare State International and Emergency Exit Arts) through to the wealth of twenty-four companies that emerged in the 1990s (including Lone Twin, Grid Iron and Knee High Theatre Company). Shifting sociopolitical and economic motivations have impacted on the development of this work in the UK and beyond. Baz Kershaw identifies how 'performances in theatre buildings are deeply embedded in theatre as a *disciplinary system*' (1999: 3) – by actively rejecting these architectural manifestations of cultural hegemonies, artists were creating alternative spaces for cultural practices. Funding also played a significant part in the development of a site-specific work. This played out in two ways: companies with very limited financial resources or access to cultural spaces called upon the potential of sites that were not economically prohibitive; and state funding streams, such as the Year of the Artist (2000) in the UK were also significant in investing in 'innovative new work for spaces and places throughout the UK, focusing on everyday areas where artistic activities don't usually happen or appear' (Wilkie 2002: 147).

When Phakama was initiated by LIFT in 1996, it evolved at a moment where the practice of site-specific work was gathering momentum. LIFT was committed to questioning not only who makes theatre but *where* theatre can happen and had produced performances in 'unusual sites' across the city, including *Urban* Man (London Zoo, 1995), *Visions of Earthly Paradise* (St Peter's Church, Vauxhall, 1996) and *Urban Dream Capsule* (Arding and Hobbs shop window, Clapham, 1999). Importantly, Phakama was launched in the same year as the *Out of LIFT* festival, a season of work that focused on 'theatre made for and by young people … commissioned, produced and presented … with the same production values as any other LIFT festival' in which 'Companies from Brazil, Denmark, France, Sweden and the UK worked in collaboration with young Londoners'.[10] Core to this was a commitment to creating public spaces for young people's voices to be articulated through artistic form and this was manifested through the range of non-theatre venues in which work was presented. Both the festival and the genesis of Phakama as a cultural practice making space for young people, resonates with Ngugi wa Thiong'o's argument that 'the struggle for performance space is integral to the struggle for democratic space and social justice' (1997: 29).

Phakama's practice of presenting work in non-theatre spaces was informed by its politics of democratic space making that reiterated the practicalities of the imperative for this work: the first projects in South Africa engaged large groups in a residential context where people lived and worked in the same space. Not only would it have been economically prohibitive to live and work in spaces that were away from the communities that were participating in the work, it would have run counter to the politics of work that committed to the process of making work that was responsive and attentive to the context of its production.

Additionally, by working outside of traditional theatre venues, the rules of *who* makes theatre, what its subjects may be, the forms of expression that may be articulated and the relationship with the audience will all be in play. It is, as Birch and Tompkins argue, 'more likely that those performances that take place outside theatre venues will be able to explore a more flexible rage of performance codes and strategies' (2012: 7). From the outset Phakama was a practical acknowledgement of its commitment to the cultural politics of working outside of the economies of professional theatre and established arts education practices.

So how does Phakama attend to issues of site in its devising and staging process? Archival materials related to *Kamorwalo Ka Seatleng/With a Suitcase in*

---

[10] LIFT Living Archive: http://liftlivingarchive.com/lla/year/1996.

My Hand in Seshego (18 September 1997) detail the particularities of some of the challenges of devising performance in a non-traditional venue. When the following fax was sent, two weeks before the residency and three weeks before the performance, there were some known entities:

> *Ka Morwalo Ka Seatleng/With a Suitcase in My Hand* will involve 100 young people and 15 arts practitioners from across South Africa and London working to bring to life their stories of migration past and present. These will be woven together through 6 days of workshops using music, dance, words and design into a large scale public performance incorporating 200 suitcases. The performance will be staged at Factory No 61 in the Seshego Industrial Area. (Lift Archive LIFT/1997/CE/023/004)

However, what the performance would be, in form and content, was still to be determined. How people would encounter and engage with each other could only be known when everyone finally met. Despite all the unknowns, practical production issues including power, water, access had to be attended to particularly when working in a warehouse building. This extract from a fax from Tony Fegan (LIFT) to Donald Legodi, the Phakama lead facilitator in Seshego, details the miscellany of materials that may be called upon (18 September 1997):

URGENT QUESTIONS

The power supply? Sid needs to know how many phases?

How many outlets?/power points are there in the warehouse. Are they on all the walls?

Is the floor concrete?

Do you have or can you borrow any electrical power tools eg fret saw, drill, etc. If not Sid will bring his tools but he'd rather not have to carry them if possible.

Can you get scrap metal and borrow welding equipment?

What sort of space do you have outside the building? Is there open space to build things and make a mess? Is there a water supply?

…

Not so urgent questions but things which would be great to have

1 We need basic tools – hammers, saws, axes, lots of nails and screws
2 Wood, Glue, Paint
3 Rolls of newspapers to write in

4 Cloth or big drapes like tarpaulin or canvas to hang
5 Lots of marker pens, Black board and chalk

(LIFT archive, LIFT/1997/CE/023/004)

Three weeks later, this list of materials had contributed to the transformation of the anonymous warehouse of Factory 61 into a performance venue. However, Phakama's responsiveness to site is not just about engaging with the architectural possibilities of a space or responding to threads of narrative related to the original function of a building. For Phakama, site encapsulates the experiential landscape of what has happened in that site during the devising process. Andrew Siddall (2015) reflects on moment from *Kamorwalo Ka Seatleng/With a Suitcase in My Hand,* which illustrates how the group responded to all aspects of site – from the architectural to the experiential – to inform how it curated the performance within it.

Seshego has very flat land. The warehouse was enormous with lots of windows but no glass so the wind would howl across it. One afternoon this purple cloud appeared on the horizon and the women who were cooking started putting everything away and the local kids were going, 'oh no!' – they knew what was coming. The purple cloud came like a sheet over the top of us and rain came in horizontally through the windows. It was such fierce rain that we hid everyone in a little room that had no windows in it. The wind, the lightning and thunder was ferocious. It went on for twenty minutes and people were terrified. And then it disappeared. We got huge brooms and, in a line, swept the water from the back of the warehouse out the front doors. We sang as we did it: a working song with everybody sweeping, pushing this water out. It became a great event in the life of the project. And because of this we had to put it in the show: we had to re-create this rain.

Ka Morwalo Ka Seatleng/With a Suitcase in My Hand was about a suitcase of stories. There was an oversized suitcase at the entrance to the site that the audience walked through to find stories. When the suitcase opened this story of the storm was told from within it. Part of my job was to make it rain in the warehouse for this story in the suitcase. So I duly rigged up. The water pipe was half a mile away outside and as it was the only one, there were only a few moments where I could have it when the women in the kitchen didn't need it. Because the water would take so long to come through the tubes and up in the roof and then rain, I had to time it before they got to that point in the story. There was a bit of a song in the story and that was my cue, but I had to be ready for it. I couldn't be at the tap because I couldn't see, so I had a line of three people and I gave the cue to somebody else, who passed it on and passed it on, and the tap got turned on then the water started coming back along this immensely long tube: there was a sprinkling of rain. There was a gathering of older women around this little story: it was a magic story so they were already entranced with it, staring into this suitcase as a participant told a story. Then the little song started, their feet started and they joined in with the clapping and the chanting. All of a sudden it started raining on them from the roof. And they went wild with joy: whooping and dancing and whirling each other round. And we had to hold the show for ages while they did it, they took over the show with pure joy at having called up the rain. These tiny little technical bits were like moments of sheer magic.

Performance staged in a traditional theatre space demands that all the stage action – across varying locations and times – is played on one stage, layered with sets and settings (Chaudhuri 2002). In Phakama's site-based promenade work, each scene is played out in a different setting within the performance space. There is a fictional frame layered on a site which does real work in advancing the narrative elements of the piece. Unlike the work of companies such as Punchdrunk (UK) that dress unusual performance spaces to disguise them, Phakama stages sites to reveals metaxis – the layers of fictive and real in operation at the same time. This sense of playful interrogation of space, through the staging of scenes in different areas within it, invites the audience to disrupt any predetermined idea of 'watching'. This is highlighted in Andrew Siddall's account of aspects of the staging of *Be Yourself* (1999) at the Tricycle Theatre in London, a 235-seat auditorium with seating on three sides.

When we did *Be Yourself* our audience was expected to sit down and watch us. But we were all going, 'but we've got to take them on a journey, to the park across the road, and maybe we should put the audience on the stage'. So we did what we could to subvert this – being *in* the audience. Anything but be on stage. We took them on a physical 'neck' journey in their seats and we managed to keep them in their seats until the end when they went on the stage. (Siddall 2014)

A little later in this section we expand on the imperative to bring the performance to the audience and to bring the audience into the performance.

Working with Found Materials

The commitment to attending and responding to what is present is further evidenced in how the Phakama process engages with found materials. In addition to working with materials 'found' within each participant – their skills and capacities as theatre makers who generate narrative rather than draw on the assumed authority of external sources or scripts – this process supports the construction of performances with readily available materials that are found, recycled and or have little cost. The imperative for this is about both economic access and developing capacity as an approach to collaborative creative practice.

Andrew Siddall brings considerable experience of creating large-scale, site-specific work in community contexts to his work with Phakama. He reflected on the influence of the Phakama approach on his practice (2015),

> I do a lot of work in schools, so that's all about what can you leave behind, what can you give to the teacher that they go, 'I could do that!' Not some scary thing that costs loads of money and is a special technique that only you can do. It's about enabling people to do what you've done when you're not there. That's really important. What can you leave behind, what's the legacy of this? Because theatre is ephemera, it disappears, it's just a memory: if you can skill people in some way then that's a much more solid thing to leave behind.

This articulation of both the use of found materials and the shift in perspective as to why and how this may be realized was most explicitly in *The Trashcatchers' Carnival* (2010). This year-long collaborative project with the residents of Tooting in south-west London, Emergency Exit Arts and Transition Town was financially supported through a Tipping Point Commission, an organization explicitly engaged in supporting arts practice addressing the challenges of climate change.[11] Since its inception, Phakama projects have been realized through a network of partnerships and collaborations. *The Trashcatchers' Carnival* was its most high-profile collaboration working with over one thousand local people through schools, community groups, businesses and the wider community. Some workshops explored environmental challenges, including peak oil, climate change and sustainability while others engaged in the design of the carnival itself – singing, dancing, storytelling and the construction of floats and costumes with recycled materials. The central motif was the Sankofa bird, a Ghanian mythical creature that flies forward towards the future with an egg in its mouth while looking back at the past. It is associated with the proverb, 'It is not wrong to go back for that which you have forgotten'. The metaphor of attending to the past as you face the future was animated through a carnival of enormous figures parading through Tooting High Street: baby elephants made from milk containers from the Sivayogam Hindu Temple; the Lady of Tooting, a figure that glided along the A24 road, buoyed up with hundreds of children's memories tucked up in her skirts; a six metre high giant gardener; and an elegant racing car made out of a side-board. *The Trashcatchers' Carnival* illustrates how Phakama's attending to site the immediate and local magnifies concerns that are ideological and global. This large-scale disruption of site is attended to in James Hadley's interview a little later in this section and in Lucy Neal's essay, 'Alive to the Music of What Happens', in the final section.

---

[11] For more information about *The Trashcatchers' Carnival*, the Transition Town movement and Tipping Point, see Neal (2015: 316–21); Transition Network, https://www.transitionnetwork.org (accessed 27 May 2016) and The Tipping Point, //www.tippingpoint.org.uk (accessed 27 May 2016).

Audience

> We can't measure the effectiveness of art as we can a piece of legislation, or a demonstration, or a political campaign for candidates or for issues. But I do believe that the experiences of performance, and the intellectual, spiritual and affective traces it leaves behind, can provide new frames of reference for how we see a better future extending out from our more ordinary lives. (Dolan 2005: 20)

Phakama performances are not staged for an audience, they are staged *with* them. Every detail in the planning of a show imagines the audience and the pathway that they might map through it. Often, the rhythm and shape of the audience's journey in a performance reflects the group's making of the process: the audience is welcomed as an ensemble of individuals, it comes together as one large gathering before breaking into smaller units that move around a site, encountering all aspects of the work, before returning to a collective body inflected by people's shared experience of being in and through something together. In *Utopia in Performance: Finding Hope at the Theatre*, Jill Dolan argues that live performance

> provides a place where people come together, embodied and passionate, to share experiences of meaning making and imagination that can describe or capture fleeting intimations of a better world … a way to reinvest our energies in a different future, one full of hope and reanimated by a new, more radical humanism. [*Utopia in Performance*] investigates the potential of different kinds of performance to inspire moments in which audiences feel themselves allied with each other, and with a broader, more capacious sense of a public, in which social discourse articulates the possible rather than the insurmountable obstacles to human potential. (2005: 2)

We argue that Phakama's process of devising and staging performance facilitates moments of alliance and a 'capacious sense of the public' that resonates beyond the moments of encounter. The following account of Phakama UK's collaboration with young people and artists in Japan illustrates the social work that performance can do in facilitating audience engagement with the young people through the structured spaces of performance.

Phakama was invited to Japan in 2015 by Sumiko Tamuro (Sintitulo) and Kaori Matsui (Asahi University) to share its working practices with theatre professionals in Tokyo, business and nursing students in Asahi University, Gifu and with young people at the Satsuki class of the Kani City International Exchange Association whose families had emigrated to Japan. The project culminated in a performance, *Landmarks of the Unknown* (2015), made by the young people at the school and the university students. In the following reflection Caoimhe McAvinchey details the audiences' shifting relationship to the performers and each other.

A foyer in a modern building on a Sunday afternoon. An audience of fifty people gather by the lifts waiting for the show to begin. In the distance, at the far end of the long corridor we can see a young man on a bicycle talking with a boy as they slowly make their way towards us. The audience tentatively looks around: is this part of the show? The cyclist and the boy arrive with us, grinning, welcoming us. The cyclist tells us about his bike and how it has opened up a world of possibility for where he might go, what he might do, who he might be. He then invites us to think about where we might adventure, individually and together. The audience is listening but still looking about: where are the other performers? We are guided into a room, bright with sunlight, and a rectangle with a map of the world is marked out with masking tape on the floor framing fifteen young people who look at us directly as we enter. We file around the perimeter of the room. And wait.

Later in the performance the audience is invited into two large classrooms situated across the hall from one another. Outlines of bodies have been cut out and placed on the floors of the rooms. Each body is outlined with blue electrical tape, holding it steady on the floor surrounded by a sea of blue crepe paper. These are Islands of Me, populated with the young people, holding an object that is special to them. When the audience arrives in the room, we are welcomed by a song and encouraged to weave our way around and through the islands. Then the young people invite us onto their island, one by one, talking with us about their objects and the story of why it matters to them. There is a hub of intimate conversations between people, sometimes in different languages. Even if people don't understand the words there is clearly a sense of 'this is me, I'm telling you something of me'. The audience listen to the young people's stories – the object and the conversation sparks off a memory or connection for the audience members and they engage in deep conversation with the young people. I find myself in a conversation with a participant from China who had three red, sponge, juggling balls. He tells me that he enjoys the feeling of the sponginess and that if people are sad he juggles to distract them. He asks if I know any magic and this sparks a long forgotten memory of my five-year-old self, meeting my great uncle Jack, a magician who lived in United States, who taught me a disappearing handkerchief trick when he visited Ireland in the 1970s. This section of the performance ended with the audience and performers stepping off the islands, making a great hand-holding circle around them, singing a song together. The audience is no longer separated from the performers but joined with them.

Almost an hour later the audience is in a corridor, huddling together, pressed up against the walls, laughing and waiting for the ensemble 'bus' of people hurtling its way towards us. There is erratic driving, flamboyant singing and intense scrutiny of a map that continues to unfold and spill with a limitless sense of possibilities over the heads of participants and the audience who have now scambled on this imaginary bus. We sway in the direction of travel, talking and jostling our way down the corridor before disembarking from our shared adventure of possibility. The cast disappear into the lifts and stairwells around us. The audience is back in the foyer where we started. We look at each other: we now recognise each other from the journeys to different worlds we have shared. We know that this is the show, that we are part of it.

In this example, the outlines from *Drawing the Body* became the set, the catalyst and the frame for an intimate conversation. The audience became co-authors within the scene, leading to genuine conversation and exchange. It is an example of performance as a practice of social life where conventional boundaries between the performers and the audience are ruptured resonating with Dolan's proposal that

> The aesthetics of these performances lead to both affective and effective feelings and expressions of hope and love not just for a partner, as the domestic scripts of realism so often emphasise, but for other people, for a more abstracted notion of 'community', or for an even more intangible idea of 'humankind'. (2005: 2)

References

Birch, A. and J. Tompkins (eds) (2012), *Performing Site-Specific Theatre: Politics, Place, Practice*, Basingstoke: Palgrave Macmillan.

diCenzo, M. (2006), *The Politics of Alternative Theatre in Britain, 1968–1990*, Cambridge: Cambridge University Press.

Chaudhuri, U. (2002), *Land/Scape/Theatre*, Ann Arbor: University of Michigan Press.

Dolan, J. (2005), *Utopia in Performance: Finding Hope at the Theatre*, Ann Arbor: University of Michigan Press.

Govan, E., H. Nicholson and K. Normington (2007), *Making A Performance: Devising Histories and Contemporary Practices*, Routledge: London and New York.

Hanna, G. (ed.) (1991), *Monstrous Regiment: A Collective Celebration*, London: Nick Hern Books.

Heddon, D. and J. Milling (2005), *Devising Performance: A Critical History*, Basingstoke: Palgrave Macmillan.

Heinzen, B. (2012), Interview, London, 16 March.

Hingorani, D. (2010), *British Asian Theatre: Dramaturgy, Process and Performance*, Basingstoke: Palgrave Macmillan.

Kaur Bhatti, G. (2014), 'Ten Years After My Play Behtzi Sparked Sikh Riots, I'm Back', *The Guardian*, 24 May. http://www.theguardian.com/commentisfree/2014/may/24/10-years-behzti-gurpreet-bhatti-birmingham-sikh-protest (accessed 2 May 2016).

Livergant, E. (2016), 'Belarus Free Theatre, Labour Mobility, and the Cultural Politics of the Border', *Contemporary Theatre Review* 26 (2): 241–57.

Neal, L. (2014), Interview, QMUL, London, 17 December.

Neal, L. (2015), *Playing for Time: Making Arts as if the World Mattered*. London: Oberon.

O'Mard, K. (2014), Interview, QMUL, London, 17 December.

Radosavljevic, D. (2013), *The Contemporary Ensemble: Interviews with Theatre-Makers*, London: Routledge.

Richardson, L. (2014), Interview, QMUL, London, 17 December.

Schmidt, N. (2011), 'What Does Free Speech Mean for Young People?' Index on Censorship Blog, 23 April. http://blog.indexoncensorship.org/2011/04/23/what-does-free-speech-mean-for-young-people/ (accessed 2 May 2016).

Sichel, A. (1996), 'This Landmark Event', *The Star*, 5 September (LIFT Archive, LIFT/1997/CE/023/004).

Siddall, A. (2014), Interview, QMUL, London, 17 December.

Siddall, A. (2015), Interview with Lucy Richardson, London, 20 March.

Wa Thiong'o, N. (1997), 'Enactments of Power: The Politics of Performance Space', *TDR: The Drama Review* 41: 3, 11–30.

Wade, L. (2010), 'Why Belarus Free Theatre Demands a Standing Ovation', *The Guardian* 10 December. http://www.theguardian.com/stage/theatreblog/2010/dec/13/belarus-free-theatre (accessed 2 May 2016).

White, G. (2015), *Applied Theatre: Aesthetics*, London: Bloomsbury.

Wilke, F. (2002a), 'Kinds of Place at Bore Place: Site-Specific Performance and the Rules of Spatial Behaviour', *New Theatre Quarterly* 18 (71): 243–60.

Wilke, F. (2002b), 'Mapping the Terrain: A Survey of Site-Specific Performance in Britain', *New Theatre Quarterly* 18 (2): 140–60.

Wilke, F. (2008), 'The Production of "Site": Site-Specific theatre', in Nadine Holdsworth and Mary Luckhurst (eds), *Concise Companion to Contemporary British and Irish Drama*, Oxford: Blackwell, 87–106.

Winston, J. (2011), *Beauty and Education*, London: Routledge.

INTERVIEW WITH JAMES HADLEY, PHAKAMA RELATIONSHIP MANAGER, ARTS COUNCIL ENGLAND (2008–2014)

In the UK, Phakama has been awarded support through various streams of ACE funding and has been a regularly funded National Portfolio Organisation (NPO) since 2008. ACE allocates each NPO a relationship manager who is actively engaged in supporting its development, thinking beyond a project to longevity and sustainability. James Hadley was Phakama UK's relationship manager in the London Theatre team from 2008 to 2014. In the following interview, the editorial team invited James to consider particular projects in relation to site and place and he reflects on how Phakama's practice has responded to local sites in the context of wider political issues around cultural equity, environmental justice and community identity. Hadley focuses on two projects, *The Trashcatchers' Carnival* introduced earlier in this section and *From Somewhere to Nowhere*, a collaboration between Phakama and young people who live and study at the Orpheus Centre, an inclusive performing arts and residential college for young adults with physical or learning disabilities.

What, for you, is the articulation of Phakama's practice? What performances are most memorable?

James Hadley: I think transformative is the key word, the experience of seeing the transformation of a place or a community. Often it would be a space that would be transformed – this is the bit of the process that, as an audience member, you get to engage with. But this would just be the cosmetic bit to show whole relationships, social dynamics and self-understanding had all been transformed. I was always aware that I was just seeing the cusp of the process when you come to the end and was trying to look back and think, 'what's happened in this process that's led to the end bit that I'm going to enjoy?'

The Trashcatcher's Carnival is always the big story I tell if I am talking about what represents the best of Phakama to me. It had been a very long process of Phakama developing partnerships, particularly with Emergency Exit Arts, Transition Town and all the partners locally, to try and reach an area where there wasn't much arts provision at all, where there were no theatres on the high street, and low arts engagement among most of the community. You had to convince people: it wasn't just saying, 'come and see our show', but actually saying, 'this is what this kind of arts engagement might be, this is why you might want to engage with it'. So really starting at the beginning. It was a very long process of engagement with school groups, engagement with community groups, community stakeholders; with a whole community from the ground up for over a year. I'd been sitting in the office hearing reports and wondering what was going to happen eventually? It's a real leap of faith as a funder because you don't see the process. You can sit in a workshop but even then you're only going to see a few hours of a much longer, gradual development process. You ask yourself if the end point is ever going to be any indication of what has gone on over such a long period of building partnerships and participatory work with artists, schoolchildren and local people wanting to engage with developing costumes and floats. It is a big ambition to build a carnival procession and sharing of food in a park with hundreds of people.

In the last week leading up to the event, I heard about various challenges in getting Tooting High Street – the carnival route – closed, which meant that it just wasn't possible to legally go ahead with the project. The police were not willing to close the road for a carnival. However, at the last minute, Lucy Neal found out that if you were going to stage a *protest* then the police had to turn up and safeguard the community. *The Trashcatchers Carnival* became a protest about peak oil prices, asking why should cars and the motorists own the high street rather than pedestrians? It was creative innovation, a wonderful reclaiming of the carnival as protest, making all the motorists stop.

When I turned up I hadn't realized how busy Tooting High Street is on a Saturday – with buses and people trying to ferry their children to various activities. As the procession gathered on a side street, with all these amazing partnerships having been developed, I was thinking 'this is going to majorly inconvenience a lot of people who aren't participants'. Gradually, just a small group lined along the sides of the street. There were lots of people who weren't involved, completely oblivious to what was going to happen, going about their business. Then the police turned up and they stopped the traffic: you could see the people stuck on buses and motorists go 'hold on, how long am I going to have to stay here?' And I thought, oh, this isn't very good! The procession was at least twenty minutes late starting, It was following its own organic scale of time. And I was still thinking 'how is this going to go?' When it started, there was a ripple of, 'oh, this is a bit of an inconvenience', and you could see people on the buses going, 'what's going on?!'. Then volunteers were handing out packets of seeds and people thought, 'ooh, there's something interesting going on here'. Gradually the floats started appearing on Tooting High Street, from the side street, and you could see the amazing energy of the schoolchildren and the participants; just how innovative the work had been, its scale. It was absolutely transformative in terms of the energy of the street: initially people were a bit grumpy and then, as the procession came down the street, shop owners were coming out of their shops, people on the buses were waving and the crowds grew and grew. Everything stopped and everyone focused on the procession. So, in those moments, quite apart from the wider procession and process, you saw a transformation happen with people in that space whose idea of what a high street was – an avenue through the middle of a community – was disrupted. People power changed how the space was used. It was astounding because Tooting has a very diverse population, yet suddenly everyone had the same shared focus on the carnival. Seeing the people that weren't directly involved actually getting on board with the idea and going 'this is something exciting', and engaging in that moment. It was really powerful; incredible knowing that there was a long, long tale leading into that transformative series of moments.

I would always come along and engage at the end of the process and see some kind of transformation that was only possible because of all of the work looking into the logistics, building the partnerships and gathering that level of investment from the participants. It was a deep metaphor for the impact Phakama's projects have in terms of gathering momentum and empowering people to make changes to their immediate location. Sometimes it's within their identity and sometimes their community, but sometimes it's the whole environment around them. It was a change of perception.

Another example was *From Somewhere to Nowhere* at the Orpheus Centre. It was really very different to anything else I'd experienced. For a start, I found myself in a car with three board members of Phakama – as an Arts Council employee, usually you only ever meet board members for an organization when you go to observe a board meeting – because there was no other way of getting to the Centre; it wasn't on the tube system but way out in the countryside. Kindly, and it's typical Phakama style, they said 'oh you can get a lift with someone'. It was a stormy night, and it felt like we were passing through the depths of nowhere, with no streetlights, travelling down country lanes. When we got there, there were loads of people gathered in a barn-like place. This wasn't an advertised performance and there was a sense of various participants and lots of people waiting. People had been working right up to the eleventh hour – bits of the show were still being redesigned because of the rain – it had been intended to be performed outdoors. The amount of work that had to be done to respond to the changing circumstances must have been huge, so there was a real frenetic energy about the space. And then when it started there was as incredible a sense of seeing how the Phakama process had been adapted to that space and adapted to the weather and the circumstances.

Many of the Orpheus participants were artists who had, in some cases, quite severe disabilities in terms of their sensory abilities and the creative process had been adapted so that each individual could participate fully. *From Somewhere to Nowhere* was a promenade through a series of locations developed around what would fit the artists' abilities and their creative vision – it was very much *led* by these individuals. I looked after Graeae Theatre Company[12] as well, and would see a lot of creatively integrated access, so this wasn't new to me. However, what was new was to see the individuals' creativity *leading* the process so that it wasn't a sense of fitting a disabled artist or participant into a process, but rather those disabled artists led the whole concept, the artistic vision, and there was a real sense of those individuals being the driving force within those environments that had been created. There were amazing challenges around the staging of the piece that had been turned into this wonderful thing where, yes, you have to have an umbrella to dash through the rain to get between A and B, but gradually, as it unfolded, you realized just how far you were travelling. Because you were being taken into a series of environments that were almost exotic to a traditional theatregoer, they were a very different paradigm because of the way they had been created and you were being let into a domestic space. It was studios and rehearsal spaces, dining rooms and a living room. It was a transformation of that space. Fireworks were meant to go off at the end, and I remember us all standing outside, waiting in the rain. It felt a world away from everything else because you were in the dark, literally, and you were being exposed to a foreign territory because it was a space that was very much owned by that community. So it was very much visiting somewhere else and being given access to a very different dynamic. The torchlight was a great metaphor, shining a torch into these little installations that people had made inside suitcases, giving incredible insights into people's dreams and hopes. Looking at their ideals of a holiday that maybe physically they couldn't have access to, but it was a really great metaphor for the creative leaps of imagination, going to these places. The rain was a great metaphor for the barriers negotiated. People were saying, well, there's rain, but this was reframed, the problem isn't the rain, the problem is with us integrating that, making that part of the process. So the team could have been all grumbly, saying oh, the show's ruined, we'll cancel it, but instead it's typical of the Phakama spirit that everything was just adapted to go with the circumstances that were given. So it was another great metaphor, I think, for that Give and Gain approach; the adaptability and flexibility, and the fact that there was a dialogue with the elements as well as with the people involved.

---

[12] Graeae are a British theatre company, founded in 1980 by Nabil Shaban and Richard Tomlinson, that 'boldly places disabled artists centre-stage in a diversity of new and existing plays' and 'pioneers a radical dramatic language by exploring the "aesthetics of access", creatively embedding a range of tools such as audio description and sign language from the very beginning of the artistic process'. See www. graeae.org (accessed 12 July 2016).

CATALYTIC CONVERSATIONS: THE AESTHETIC WEAVE AND SOCIAL WEFT OF PHAKAMA'S CREATIVE PRACTICE

Sara Matchett

To capture how Phakama has influenced my creative practice as a performance maker, evolving her signature in the landscape of South African theatre and performance, is a challenging task. The impact that Phakama has made on my professional and personal life has been considerable. Conversations with other artists who have collaborated on Phakama projects and contributed to this essay reveal the reach and duration of this influence. In the period covered in this essay (2000–5), South African theatre and performance was clearly divided into 'mainstream' and 'community'.[13] I maintain that Phakama, located on a continuum between 'mainstream' and 'community' theatre, through its creative practice, endeavoured to find synergy between the two.

I joined Phakama in 2000 and collaborated on numerous projects in South Africa and India over a five-year period: *Call Me Not a Woman* (South Africa, Genadendal and Mmabatho 2000), *Crossing the Red Ribbon Divide* (South Africa, Seshego 2001–2), *The Phakama Way* (Pune, India 2002), *Crossing Borders* (Cape Town, South Africa 2006). Over this period, I was also involved in regular Saturday creative sessions with young people who were part of Phakama Western Cape. All of the projects and creative sessions I was involved in have, in some way, influenced the kind of theatre that I make today, my performance-making practices with The

---

[13] Since 2005 there has been a definite shift in this regard, with theatre festivals, such as the Zabalaza Festival, performing annually at the Baxter Theatre, one of Cape Town's main theatre complexes. The Zabalaza Festival aims to develop and support new South African works and artists who are predominately from community-based theatre groups. Additionally, there have been free public performance festivals, such as Infecting the City in Cape Town which aims to explore how art engages audiences and functions in public space. These examples point to a more fluid relationship between fixed notions of 'community' and 'mainstream'.

Mothertongue Project, as well as how I facilitate learning environments within a university setting at the University of Cape Town (UCT).

The most notable aspect of Phakama that I carry with me into this work is the notion of conversations. Conversations are at the heart of what happened in Phakama projects. For the purposes of this essay, through a close reading of *Call Me Not a Woman* (2000), I will focus on the conversations between geographical and psycho-emotional landscapes; memory–story–performance; 'mainstream' and 'community' theatre; performers and audience. I conclude this essay with a reflection on Phakama's influence on my own and other artist facilitators' practice involved in various projects.

Call Me Not a Woman[14] occurred in two locations in South Africa: Genadendal, a small town in the Western Cape Province of South Africa, built on the site of the oldest Moravian mission station in the country, and Mmbatho, currently known as Mahikeng, the capital city of the North-West Province of South Africa. The performance took place in homes belonging to members of the respective communities. The decision to work in homes as sites of performances was taken by the artist facilitators prior to the start of the project. The particular homes we performed in were negotiated with the participants and resident artist facilitators once we arrived in the various towns. In Genadendal, a group of young people and artist facilitators from the Western Cape travelled to work with a group that had recently been set up by the art teacher at a local high school in the area. In Mmabatho a group of young people and artist facilitators from various Phakama projects in the country travelled to work with an established group in the area. All the participants and artist facilitators had prior experience of Phakama.

Call Me Not a Woman happened at a time when South Africans were negotiating the relative newness of our democracy. The South African Constitution took effect on 4 February 1997, the outcome of a comprehensive process of inclusive consultations and negotiations accomplished with an awareness of the injustices of the previous apartheid regime. Issues of inclusion were at the forefront of our theatre-making practices during the period I refer to.

Geographical and Psycho-emotional Landscapes

As with most Phakama projects, *Call Me Not a Woman* was a site-specific project. In Genadendal, performances took place in three geographical locations that make

---

[14]The title was inspired by Ellen Kuzwayo, a prominent South African woman's rights activist and politician, whose autobiography *Call Me Not a Woman* was published in 1985.

up the town: a Reconstruction and Development Programme[15] (RDP) house, a house in the more 'established' and older area of Genadendal, and the road that linked the two houses. RDP houses are a form of low-cost housing designed for people who previously lived in informal homes commonly known as 'shacks'. The size of an RDP house is typically 36 square meters. According to Raeesa Moola et al, 'there has been profound criticism with regard to the inferior building standards and quality of these housing units, as well as the lack of services and amenities in these development projects' (2011: 138). Additionally, it is not uncommon for between five and ten people to occupy these homes, resulting in overcrowding.

In the Mmabatho project the two houses that served as performance spaces were situated on either side of a main highway. One house was located in what was previously known as Mmabatho, and the other in the previously adjoining town of Mafikeng. Prior to 1994, Mafikeng and Mmabatho formed part of Bophuthatswana, a *bantustan*[16] area, commonly known as a 'homeland', that was set aside for people belonging to a specific ethnicity (in this case Tswana), by the apartheid government. Mafikeng became part of Bophutatswana in 1980, and was treated as a suburb of Mmabatho, the capital of Bophutatswana. After the collapse of apartheid in 1994, Mafikeng and Mmabatho merged and were re-incorporated into South Africa and in 2012 were renamed. Part of the Phakama performance involved a clothes-washing ritual that moved the audience across the road in both directions between the two houses. The South African Traffic Police Service was involved in the performance to stop the traffic and accommodate the washing ritual each time it occurred in the performance.

I contend that a key aspect of the site-specificity of the project was the notion of landscape. Here I associate two distinctive and oppositional sets of concepts associated with the idea of landscape: geographical landscapes and psycho-emotional landscapes. Geographical landscapes house concepts such as collective past/official memory, master narratives, geographical features such as mountains, rivers, as well as constructed features such as highways, houses and work/economic spaces, to name a few. Psycho-emotional landscapes are home to concepts such as conversations, personal stories/embodied memories, communities, homes, domestic spaces, dreams, hopes, disappointments and disillusionments.

By master narrative I am suggesting that a single narrative informed the structure of the towns that *Call Me Not a Woman* took place in. The master narrative of apartheid, in this instance, permeated the geographic memory of the place. Conversations, on

---

[15] South Africa's socio-economic policy framework implemented by the African National Congress (ANC) government in 1994.
[16] Territories set aside for black inhabitants of South Africa and South West Africa (now Namibia), as part of apartheid legislation. Ten Bantustans were set up in South Africa, and ten in neighbouring South West Africa (which was then under South African control). The purpose was to centralize people belonging to particular ethnic groups. In so doing 'independent' homogenous nation states were created for the various black ethnic populations in South Africa.

the other hand, suggest the exchange of multiple experiences, memories and stories between and within different people and communities. I argue that the potential for fracturing fixed geographic boundaries perpetuated by the master narrative, is realized through conversations. Apartheid as the master narrative had left traces of its existence not only in the structural makeup of the towns we worked in, but also in the psyches of the people of the town, where there was evidence of persistence of collective or official memory. In most small South African towns, segregation and zoning of the town was a direct result of apartheid planning. Traces of apartheid narrative remained embedded in geographical landscapes. This has impacted on the language and narratives of places. Ingrid de Kok attests to this, 'the segregation of space determined not only the unequal distribution of land and resources, but the unequal development of a hermetic set of narratives, and a rigidly closed civic language in South Africa' (1998: 68). It is precisely the notion of 'hermetic narratives' that disallows conversations to occur between different communities. Each community remains tightly sealed within their geographically segregated landscapes. Traces of apartheid narrative remained embedded in geographical landscapes and provided little room for personal memories to emerge and find expressions outside of their designated zones. The civic language associated with the master narrative de Kok speaks of, had yet to find a way out of its tightly structured geographic landscape, for, as she notes, 'Removing the physical "marks" has proved fairly easy. But the consequences of such physical marking are much more difficult to erase, for segregation has become the spatial imprint of our cities and the deep structure of our imaginations and memories' (1998: 70).

The choice to use homes as sites of performance in the *Call Me Not a Woman* project, engaged questions of how lived experience informs a site and how this in turn impacts on the performed story as well as on the memories of performers and audience. The energy of the people who inhabit a house invests the physical space with emotional and psychological meaning, transforming it into a home that is filled with stories and memories that give the space social and personal meaning. Architect Juhani Pallasmaa confirms this: 'buildings are devoid of emotion; a work of architecture obliges us ... to lend our emotions and place them in it' (2000: 1). The bricks and mortar of the house become encrusted with past experiences and memories, which ultimately impact on the experiences of people entering that space through what Marvin Carlson terms 'bleeding through' (2003: 133). Ongoing memories contained in stories and conversations of the external community, contribute to this process of bleeding through. Carlson also notes that 'fundamental to modern semiotics is the insight that any part of our perceived world ... is inevitably layered with meanings' (ibid). If one considers the house as part of our perceived world and the memories layering it with meanings, one begins to engage with what Carlson means when he says that 'how the 'something else' that the space was before ... has the potential ... of "bleeding through"' (ibid). Juhani Pallasmaa talks about 'experiencing a space ... [as] a dialogue, a kind of exchange – I place myself in the space and the space settles in me' (2000: 1). The notion of dialogue implies that the home as a site of performance contains memories that the performance and the audience encounter and kinetically dialogue with. I use the term kinetic because they do not necessarily verbally engage in dialogue or conversation with the house. The experiences of the layered memories bleed through the walls, floors and ceilings and seep into the experiences of the audience, whether consciously or not.

Call Me Not a Woman involved rehearsing and creating the performances in the various homes. The people who lived in the homes were invariably present throughout the rehearsal process and performances. We worked in kitchens, bedrooms, bathrooms and sitting rooms. My experience of this was that the layered meanings as well as aesthetic choices of the inhabitants (artwork, arrangement of furniture, colour and kinds of furniture, kitchen gadgets, utensils and linen) bled through and informed the creation and content of the performance pieces. The conversation between the context, aesthetic and the content became apparent. The arrival of the audience provided an additional layer of meaning, where audience and performers co-made meaning. This alludes to the notion of affect, which I reflect on later in the essay.

Call Me Not a Woman conceivably set out to explore what Cathy Turner in her reference to site-specific performance describes as 'performance … [as] an archaeological investigation of place' (2004: 376). Homes are filled with memories, traces of past, lived experiences. The home encapsulates these memories in its structure. It is precisely the notion of memory traces that warrants an archaeological investigation of the site through performance. Turner further asserts that 'since site is always a material trace of the past events, all site work is potentially archaeological' (ibid). By deciding to use homes as performance spaces, our starting point was conceivably the notion of psycho-emotional landscapes characterized by conversations, personal stories/embodied memories, communities, home and domestic spaces.

Memory–Story–Performance

In *Call Me Not a Woman* two communities were engaged in the creation of a performance that sought to dissolve the divide between them, created by fixed geographic landscapes. The project served to translate lived experiences into theatrical and performative experiences that serviced the needs of the performers and performance makers (made up of people from the communities we worked in as well as people from outside of the province and the country) and the audience (made up of members of different communities from the town and those who had come from outside to experience the performance). I maintain that central to this translation was the notion of story. In Andre Brink's view, 'Story [is] the outcome of a process of internalisation and personalisation; story as the construction of a version of the world; and story as the embodiment of an imagining or a complex of imaginings. ... Story explores a situation from the inside' (1996: 38).

This captures how I perceive story to work in the process of dissolving the divides mentioned above. A process of internalization and personalization is what happens in the psycho-emotional landscape when one explores personal, individual alternatives and responses to the collective or official memory of the geographical landscape. The reality it constitutes is real to the person constituting it and does not necessarily reflect the grand narrative of the geographical landscape. The embodiment of a complex of imaginings alludes to the multiplicity of experiences and personal interpretations of events, histories and encounters that are expressed through engaging with personal stories. This contrasts with the one-dimensional linear construct of a master narrative that leaves out the expression of personal responses and lived experiences, where, as apartheid South Africa attests to, experience becomes collective and is spoken for by the dominant economic and political discourse. The abolition of apartheid followed by the establishment of the Truth and Reconciliation Commission (TRC) evoked the emergence of personal stories within the frame of the TRC hearings. This emergence filtered into the theatrical domain. The TRC was set up in 1996 to provide space for hearings related to apartheid's atrocities and brought forth personal narratives related to human rights violations. The commission placed value on the expression of personal stories. However, as mentioned above, the persistence of apartheid geographical landscapes, in reality, did not easily allow for these stories to be shared across communities in the social domain. The 'spatial imprint' de Kok (1998: 70) refers to, appeared to remain in both the geographical and emotional landscapes of those who inhabited the communities we worked in.

Phakama's creative practice, because of its emphasis on multiple conversations across differences and shared experiences, provided a framework for these stories to be shared and experienced without having to structurally alter the geographical landscapes the homes were located within. In this way story acted as a catalyst for starting the process of fracturing the fixed geographical landscapes; it initiated and enabled conversations to occur between the different communities in which the homes were located. The homes in Genadendal and Mmbatho were within a 500–1,000-metre radius of each other, which made it possible for home occupants to converse with each other. The making processes and the performances served as conversation starters between the various home occupants, who had not necessarily communicated with each other prior to the arrival of Phakama. The performances served as catalysts for conversations beyond the performances themselves. These conversations occurred between the different home occupants, home occupants and performers, home occupants and audiences, as well as between audiences and performers. Theatre and performance provided a juncture for stories, which were articulated in action. This conceivably created a ripple effect among those involved in creating the performance and among audience members. The ripple effect seemed to inspire action in the form of further conversations and sharing of experiences between the different communities during the process of making the performances, during the performances, as well as after the performances. In this way the act of experiencing possibilities within the frame of performance potentially created opportunities in social situations for similar explorations beyond the performance. Michel de Certeau offers insights into the role of story in fracturing fixed geographical boundaries and altering people's psycho-emotional landscapes when he talks of stories as bridges:

> The story privileges a 'logic of ambiguity' through its accounts of interaction. It 'turns' the frontier into a crossing, and the river into a bridge. It recounts inversions and displacements: the door that closes is precisely what may be opened; the river is what makes it possible; the tree is what marks the stages of advance. ... The *bridge* is ambiguous everywhere: it alternately welds together and opposes insularities. It distinguishes them and threatens them. It liberates from enclosure and destroys autonomy (1984: 128).

This notion of story privileging a logic of ambiguity resonates with Phakama's creative practices that sought to fracture fixed geographical boundaries. Phakama processes, in my experience, provided participants with possibilities of restorying/ remythologizing or remodelling their lived experiences, where the construction of memories from past experiences and anticipated futures was not necessarily an account of fact. Carlson's notion of 'bleeding through' (2003: 133), where the narratives and memories embedded in the homes the participants worked in, influenced their making process as well as the possibility that performance provided for re-imagining and dreaming a different reality or past, invariably allowed for the seemingly impossible to become possible in and through performance. Story was at the heart of this process. Additionally, the idea of story welding together and opposing insularities is precisely what I think we achieved in the various Phakama projects I was involved in.

The key to the idea of story, within the framework of a theatrical event, which catalyses the transformation of fixed geographical boundaries, is the notion of memory. It is performance that transforms memory into story. The processes involved in performance-making organize memory in such a way as to become a story and is a way of making meaning out of memory. I would argue that performance-making processes and practices we employed not only organized and made meaning out of memory, but also triggered memories and allowed space for restorying these memories.

I am interested in Joseph Dunne's notion of life 'as a story waiting to be told' (1996: 150). This implies that stories are held suspended in the body, as memory, waiting to be told. The expressions of these memories, in the form of stories, are triggered by events and experiences. These events and experiences may not necessarily be directly connected to the person who owns the story, as Dunne notes, 'a person is implicated not only in one but in several stories – which, moreover, are not self-enclosed, since each may interlock with other stories belonging to one's own life or to the lives of others' (ibid.).

The idea of interlocking stories and 'stories belonging to ... the lives of others' is crucial to the role performance played in dissolving boundaries between communities that Phakama engaged with. It seemingly blurred the binary perception of 'us and them'. Through the sharing of personal stories, participants often noticed an aspect that mirrored their own experiences. This occurred across socio-economic and geographic divides. The performed stories, on being shared with the home occupants and audiences, often found further resonance. Paul Ricoeur endorses this by stating that 'the story of my life is a segment of the story of your life; of the story of my parents, of my friends, of my enemies, and of countless strangers. We are literally entangled in stories' (1996: 6). I maintain that the act of experiencing oneself reflected and represented in a story that is supposedly 'other' to you, is what begins to engage one in the possibility of exchange and sharing.

Associated with this is Cameroonian scholar Achille Mbembe's theories of otherness, difference and sameness. Mbembe recognizes the 'concept of the other [as] ... a quest for the recognition of difference' (2013). He locates his argument as emerging out of postcolonial theory, where the underlying principle is that of difference and otherness. He argues that the postcolonial emphasis on difference has evaded the question of sameness 'as a mode of worldliness [that takes] ... seriously what it means to inhabit the world' (ibid.). He emphasizes that by sameness he is not referring to the opposite of difference, but rather that 'there is one world ... we all share' (ibid.). He considers this as 'the world as home and the world as method' (ibid). His call to view the world as home and as method is a challenge to African philosophy and literature that he contends, has fetishized the notion in efforts of writing the self. He qualifies this by stating that 'the other says you are different and I myself say "oh yes", I am different, and on the basis of my being different I claim [a] ... set of rights. So everybody is in agreement' (ibid.). By re-envisioning sameness as a method of worldliness, he reasons that there is need to acknowledge 'that there is one world and that is what we all share ... the world as home and the world as method. And if we take that approach seriously ... we then become able to get out of the cul-de-sac of difference' (ibid.). This, I maintain, is at the heart of the idea of conversations between memory, story and performance, where the metaphorical act of translating lived experiences into performed stories/ theatrical events is evident. The experience of assimilating and making sense of someone else's life in relation to your own, in my view, is also a conceivable act of translation. This is particularly pertinent in Phakama's creative practice given that participants from different parts of the country, continent and sometimes world, lived in residence with artist facilitators from various geographical locations for the duration of project. Sharing living and working spaces, in my mind, required a level of assimilation and sense making of others. Mandla Mbothwe, South African artist facilitator, reflects on this (2015):

> Activities that in other projects I have experienced, were not considered important aspects of the creative process, like the washing of dishes, and cooking together, were considered valuable in Phakama projects because they made people come together.

Mbembe, in his reading of the act of translation, notes that translation

> forces us to inevitably confront an other and that confrontation with an other… is not necessarily a confrontation with an other who is an outsider. It is risky because it a confrontation with the other in ourselves; the terrifying other who is not external to us but who is in us.

Mbembe makes an explicit connection between the 'terrifying other' and racism. He notes that 'we face the other in ourselves and that in our inability to interpret that other [and] assimilate the other, we run the risk of [destroying the ego]. Racism [is] an instance of the destruction of the ego [that] sees an excess of otherness' (ibid.).

In Phakama projects, the impact of this realization through practice is what catalysed the possibility for conversations and sharing to occur across fixed boundaries. This, I would argue, initiated the dissolution of the impermeable quality of these fixed boundaries on the psycho-emotional landscapes of the people from the towns and communities we worked in. I believe that theatre and performance promoted a convergence of stories. Out of this convergence, transformation of memories and place and possibilities for cross-cultural communication were enacted, providing a means of experiencing and viewing a place through different lenses.

Community < > Mainstream

The key to Phakama's creative practice is the synergy between 'mainstream' and 'community' theatre that seeks to blur the divide between the two. I am reminded of Jan Cohen-Cruz's questions around notions of 'professional' and its binary opposite, 'amateur'. She notes, 'One of the biggest problems in negotiating the worlds of professional art and community may be mainstream critics ... the problem lies with an idea of professionalism that devalues community, indeed devalues any performance with a larger frame than a proscenium stage' (2004: 220). In popular South African perceptions during the five-year period covered in this essay, theatre and performance had little economic value. 'Community' theatre was further marginalized, in that it tended to be sidelined by 'mainstream' theatre practitioners. It was viewed as lesser and inferior. Mbothwe notes that 'it was reduced to community theatre in a very derogative way that implied that it was amateurish' (Mbothwe 2015). This was largely because it did not necessarily conform to 'mainstream' theatre norms and traditions that were typically defined by the spaces and geographic locations in which theatre was performed. 'Community' theatre, on the other hand, did not necessarily rely on theatre buildings and geographic locations that were more easily accessed by those who had transport and were able to afford the price of a theatre ticket.[17] 'Community' theatre was typically performed in townships[18] in non-formal spaces such as church halls, market places, bus stands, train stations and taxi ranks.[19] The architecture of these spaces meant that the fourth wall of the proscenium arch theatre space was absent, and thus often allowed for and encouraged active physical audience engagement. The power relations between actors and audience were, therefore, more fluid and interchangeable. I posit that 'mainstream' theatre primarily emphasized the role of the individual actor, the playwright and the director, as opposed to 'community' theatre's emphasis on creative collaborators. Phakama's endeavour to blur this divisive perception involved working consciously with the differences that had been constructed and perpetuated by the two, in order to realize a model that embraced both under the umbrella of performance.

In this work, artist facilitators from within and outside South Africa were engaged in projects alongside young people from diverse communities within and outside South Africa. Most of whom had no or little prior experience of theatre and performance. The artist facilitators brought with them particular performance-making skills that encompassed aesthetic underpinnings of the medium of theatre and performance. Some were versed in acting, others in design, while others were accomplished movement/dance practitioners, musicians, technicians or creative writers. The integration of art forms provided a space for conversations to take

---

[17] Typically the price of a ticket to a theatre production in a 'mainstream' theatre house in South Africa cost between 50 and 200 Rand, depending on where it fell on the graph that delineated 'mainstream' from 'community'.

[18] In South Africa, township refers to the urban living areas that, during apartheid, were reserved for non-white South Africans. They were built on the periphery of towns and cities. Townships still exist in South Africa, post-apartheid.

[19] Performances at transport hubs, leaned more towards street theatre or invisible theatre, which engaged the commuters in debates on matters of social concern, as they waited for their transport.

place between artist facilitators and young people. The young people provided the stories and lived experiences as well as performance forms derived from their specific cultural knowledge systems.[20] The artist facilitators were also given the opportunity to engage with disciplines that were not necessarily in their 'field' or 'line'. For example, my strength might have been in acting. I, however, had the opportunity in Phakama projects to be part of the design group, for instance, which was not necessarily one of my strengths. This afforded me the opportunity of learning alongside my co-facilitators and the participants. In this way, the notion of shared learning was truly realized. Lucy Richardson (2015), artist facilitator from the UK, attests to this:

> The facilitators are enriched by it as well. In other community theatre projects I have worked on, often the facilitators have the responsibility of making sure that everybody else is okay and making the work with them and enriching them … but they aren't part of that process themselves. They're just the doer of it. Whereas Phakama says, well you also can go and do the making if you want to … you don't have to do theatre if you don't want to … so you can be learning. You feel like you are part of the process fully. I think that is quite unusual in processes.

South African artist facilitator Caroline Calburn (2015a) adds to this:

> It also allows you to teach in a completely different way. I might have been in a room making something and I felt like I was still teaching, but I wasn't teaching from the front, which is what the facilitator would be doing. I was teaching from inside or behind. You were learning but you were also very much still a facilitator. It allowed the freedom to facilitate from behind and at times from the front.

The various Phakama projects I was involved in raised questions: how do professional artists balance facilitating the creative expression of others alongside their own artistic interests and impulses? How do artists mediate their individual artistic standards alongside collaborative and democratic processes typically associated with 'community' theatre? The kinds of performance-making processes I engaged in with Phakama were collaborative in nature and relied on the idea of democratic conversations. As Mbothwe (2015) notes:

> Phakama … was a reaffirmation and a reclaiming of … processes that are led by the philosophy of ubuntu,[21] that when we are the process it becomes a plural

---

[20] Many of the participants who were part of Project Phakama had grown up singing songs and dancing dances that were specific to their cultural practices. Many of these songs were shared across ethnic groups.

[21] A Southern African *Nguni* term that denotes a philosophical understanding and practice that underpins the belief in a shared humanity towards others that strives to connect all humanity.

process, it contains multiple voices, it's not a singularity, it becomes our work; we all contribute. It's painful because you need to listen to everyone in the process itself. … You have to explain yourself … You are challenged by your co-creators. … These processes are about reclaiming and affirming the voices of all involved in the process; reclaiming the identity and the dignity of the bodies that you work with.

This echoes Richardson's observation that Phakama affirms 'the idea of full participation and everybody who is in the room's creativity is equally important and that it's not the idea of a teacher or a director leading the process'. We negotiated the conversations between artist facilitators and the youth participants through identifying what each had to offer. In this way the young people were able to discover performative and theatrical expressions for their stories, rather than being told what to do and how to do it. Their personal stories and experiences in turn guided and facilitated the performance-making process and ultimately, the product. Synergy occurred through facilitated exchanges. In *Call Me Not a Woman*, prior to travelling to Genadendal and Mmabatho, participants from rather the Western Cape conducted several interviews with women members of their families and from their respective communities. These stories, coupled with their own stories and experiences of either being a young woman or being the son or brother to a woman, informed the stories they chose to make and share through performance. If the young people did not feel comfortable with the way in which their stories were being expressed, we collaboratively found new ways of expression that worked for all involved. Mbothwe reflects on the role of negotiation in Phakama projects:

A lot of time was spent negotiating and sharing how things should happen. There were times that we [as artist facilitators] spent with young people … where we transferred [skills] and allowed ourselves to be influenced by them and there were times where facilitators, at night, would come together and reflect and [plan]. So we allowed each and every day to feed [the planning for the next day]. There was a sense of allowing the process to shift and change. So it kept on being fresh.

Richardson adds to this: 'It demands you to be very engaged in what is going on; in the other people, in yourself and in the creative material.'

There has been a considerable body of 'community' theatre in South Africa that was driven by social action. This is particularly true of much of the protest theatre produced in the 1980s and early 1990s against the apartheid regime. In some instances, this legacy continues today as social issues including HIV/AIDS, gender violence and racism are debated through performance. Not much attention was paid to the aesthetic aspect of these works. This is reflective of perceptions of the division between 'community' and 'mainstream' theatre, where aesthetic proficiency and the effects of social action are seen to be in opposition. 'Community' theatre during the period this essay refers to did not, in the main, incorporate aspects of design. If present, design tended to service the text and did not invite conceptual interpretation. By design I do not necessarily mean an elaborate expensive set, but rather a non-didactic concept that enhances and provides a theatrical container for the lived experiences and the stories of the communities in which the performance takes place. Phakama intentionally engaged with the aesthetics of performance. Each project had a dedicated design team, facilitated by a professional artist/designer. The stories and concerns of the youth participants were interpreted through acting, dance/movement, music, creative writing and design. In this way each project achieved synergy between aesthetics and social action, resulting in a non-didactic product/performance. The emphasis on aesthetics of performance served to provoke thoughts related to social action/activism and notions of self-transformation, and thus the aesthetics of the performance became the agitator for social action/activism and self-transformation. The site-specificity of the projects contributed to this, in that the aesthetics of the location or site of the performances intersected with the content of the work so as to create an additional layer of meaning. Mbothwe reflects on the aesthetics of performance in Phakama creative processes: 'Theatre is all about the context, the content and the aesthetic ... If you want to transform someone, it's not about his or her story, but also *how* that story is being told.'

I maintain that Phakama's creative practice was largely about realizing the synergy between aesthetics and social action/activism and self-transformation. It embraced notions of social action, self-transformation and aesthetic achievement. By seeking to blur the divide between 'community' and 'mainstream', Phakama opened up possibilities for challenging these divisive terms. It provided a container for this synergy to be explored and realized within a frame that extended beyond the proscenium arch stage. Additionally, as Mbothwe reflects, 'Phakama was not only about the output – what the audience saw at the end of the process, but also the process that empowered the participants themselves that became important.' South African facilitator Clinton Osbourn (2015a) adds to this:

What was amazing about Phakama was that it was about both (process and performance) and ... even though so much emphasis was put on the process, the result was always so incredibly dynamic and captivating. ... I think that part of the reason was because people were committed to the performance ... because of the process. There was so much trust with the people that you were working with; there was so much comfort in what you were doing that you would do something with full commitment ... because you felt like you owned it. You did it with a dynamic special energy, which the audience could feel. And that's why Phakama performances were always so effective.

Performers and Audience: Embodied Conversations

Performance theorist Amy Lynne Steiger, reflecting on embodiment, notes:

> While globalization relies on the circulation of images and information through electronic technology, it has also been accompanied by an increased awareness of how human bodies carry out the knowledge and ideologies circulated across the globe by various media (2007: 4).

She continues to assert the urgency for performers to invest in their roles as 'public intellectuals who investigate the way human bodies perform identity, philosophy and community' (ibid.). Placing the liveness of the performer at the heart of this investigation, where they, together with audiences 'can explore the absolutely crucial possibilities of creating commonality while also tolerating and encouraging difference' (ibid.). Even though the youth participants in Phakama projects did not necessarily view themselves as public intellectuals, they did, however, invest in performing their identities, communities and, by implication, the associated philosophies. This investment extended to the audience. Often, audience members were invited to physically engage in activities that 'moved' the performance forward; for example, the clothes-washing ritual I mention earlier in the essay. In Genadendal, the audience were given stones and invited to write words they associated with women on the stones, to build a cairne. Mbothwe comments on how 'Phakama would make sure that the audience sang along with the songs, that they clapped hands, that the story at the end became their [the audiences] story.' There are many more such examples. Additionally, the audience would invariably walk from site to site to experience different performances that made up the performance event. The act of walking implies an active physical engagement with the performance. In these ways, the performers together with the audience were able to create commonality while also tolerating and encouraging difference.

This points to the role of affect in live performance and resonates with body theorist Lisa Blackman's understanding of the '*felt* body' as

> one that is never singular and never bounded so that we clearly know where we end and another begins. This is a *feeling body* that presents a challenge to the kind of Cartesian dualism that produces the body as mere physical substance. The affective body is considered permeable to the 'outside' so that the very distinction between the inside and the outside as fixed and absolute is put into question (2008: 10, italics in original).

Additionally, Blackman claims that 'the materiality of the body is presented as a potentiality that is dynamic and open to being affected and affecting ... [and that] the body's materiality ... has a generative force that is not static or fixed' (103). Both Blackman and Shannon Sullivan highlight the role of the skin in affective encounters. Sullivan views the skin 'as the site of transaction between inside and outside a body' (2001: 158), and Blackman sees the skin as an 'instrument of communication' (2008: 86). All Phakama performances I was involved in engaged the audience in close proximity with the performers. The skins of both performers and audience members often came into contact through physical touch. Additionally, the close proximity of audience to performers allowed for an energetic exchange that allowed for the permeability of skin as an instrument of communication.

The embodiedness of the live performance, where ideas are shared and exchanged through the skins of performers and audience, I argue, is what creates a sustained and shared sense of purpose and action in the world, where performers and audience are involved in processes of affective exchange.

As mentioned earlier in this essay, the young people in Phakama drew from their biographies/lived experiences in the creation of performances. This calls for a reflection on autobiographical performance and how it potentially engages a conversation with the audience. Additionally, I am interested in how autobiography can be viewed as a means to activating a shared sense of purpose and action in the world.

Emma Meehan proposes that 'autobiographical material derives from an ongoing, shifting set of relations, where individual autobiographies intersect with the wider environment to create collaborative autobiographies' (2013: 39) and that it is 'a negotiated, relational, and ongoing practice' (40). Embodied biographies also intersect in processes of meaning making in Garret Brown's (2013: 23) sense of inter-subjective bodies that are engaged in corporeal exchanges in the present moment. The permeability of these bodies is what facilitates the exchange. The sharing or interchange of sensations in corporeal exchanges is what inspires embodied reflection in both performers and audiences.

However, the concept of autobiography as agency does not necessarily provoke the kind of mass rally activism that comes to mind when one thinks of activist or protest action globally, but rather it inspires conversations/discussions/dialogues/ debates that move people to cogitate on their role in matters that are raised through the performance and how they are able to shift it from a point of personal reflection that potentially leads to personal action.

Live performance can also inspire a sense of deep reflection, perhaps what we would term embodied reflection, where the bodies of those experiencing the performance (both performers and audience) feel the need to 'do something' that will hopefully transform the situation. Here, corporeal feminist Grosz's readings of Deleuze and Gauttari's writings around the relationship between art, sensation and affect are pertinent. Grosz maintains that 'art ... produces sensations, affects, intensities as its mode of addressing problems, which sometimes align with and link to concepts, the object of philosophical production, which are how philosophy deals with or addresses problems' (2008: 1–2). Deleuze and Gauttari maintain that 'whether through words, colors, sounds, or stone, art is the language of sensations' (1994: 176), and that 'sensation is pure contemplation, for it is through contemplation that one contracts, contemplating oneself to the extent that one contemplates the elements from which one originates' (212).

I maintain that each iteration of a Phakama performance was shaped by the varied responses from audience members as well as the varied spaces in which they were performed. This resonates with Meehan's idea that the process of co-creating actively facilitates/includes the audience's own autobiographical experiences in a collaborative act of meaning making (2013: 38).

The Reverberation of Phakama's Creative Practice

In terms of my own creative practice, Phakama's influence is most notable in the work I have engaged in with the Mothertongue Project. In 2005 and 2006 the Mothertongue Project undertook two consecutive projects in Darling, a small town 75 kilometres outside of Cape Town. The projects explored women's stories in domestic spaces and were located in homes as sites of performance. The projects involved working with women from different communities around specific issues. Artist facilitators worked alongside the women to create a performance. The projects offered not only an exchange between professional actors and non-professional actors, but also the idea that performance potentially provides a framework for conversations between different communities, in other words, a means of crossing geographical divides between communities.

At the time of writing, The Mothertongue Project currently runs an ongoing project with unemployed youth in the rural farming region of Langeberg. The year 2013 saw the third iteration of a project that involves UCT Theatre and Performance students living and working alongside unemployed youth between the ages of 18 and 30 from the Langeberg region. However, 2013 was the first year that it officially formed part of the Learning through Drama and Theatre course offered by the University. In previous years students were involved in a voluntary capacity and did not receive academic credits for their participation. The model the project employs is that of peer mentorship, with a ratio of one student participant to every Langeberg participant. The students take on the role of artist facilitators, facilitating from within the process. The students and Langeberg youth spend a week in residence in the Langeberg region, working towards creating three 10-minute performance pieces where they integrate the disciplines of theatre, music, dance/movement, creative writing and design in actualizing their performances.

Mbothwe reflects on how Phakama's creative processes were not new in his life, but rather that they affirmed the African aesthetics he grew up with, 'where there is an understanding that we are here to collectively do something; to give and gain'. He, however, notes that 'one thing I took from Phakama, was how to work with masses of people. I love working with masses of people. It fascinates me. Phakama gave me that strength .... He concludes that, "because of its impact, [Phakama] became one of the nuclear moments of our [artist facilitators'] careers that we took with us [into our creative practices]."'

Osbourn (2015b), in his observation of how Phakama creative processes transform people, notes that

> the creative process brings about a greater awareness of the self and how to interact with people and all of the things you learn not only about yourself, but also the people around you that changes you in what that once you finish a process, you are not the same. You relate to people in a different way. I experienced that with Phakama. ... Getting people to contribute in a way that makes them feel affirmed. That is what Phakama did. ... It allowed people to come out of a process with an incredible boost to their self-esteem.

He goes on to reflect on how Phakama's creative practice has influenced his current practices:

> I have no doubt that participating in Phakama has been the most profound influence on my practice today as an artist as well as a social development practitioner. I first came across Phakama while I was teaching at Zonnebloem High School in 2002 and I participated in the *Spices* project where I experienced that it was possible with limited resources, over a 3 day period to make a performance. I never imagined that a performance made in this way could be as moving, nuanced and complex as it was. I was immediately sold. The project was run according to the 'leading from design' process, a process that I have used a number of times in other projects that I have been involved in. The limits of the materials invariably stimulate creative thinking and result in interesting design. The time pressure, combined with focussing on only one aspect of the performance as a response to someone else's creativity usually results in beautiful work, which is often surprising to the creators. It's a process I have also tailored and adapted for other projects, where I have used the idea of reflecting on other people's creative output (or sometimes one's own) as stimulus for further creative outputs.
>
> I had the fortune of being selected to participate in *The Child I Curry Project* in Morija, Lesotho, which to this day remains one of the most exhilarating creative processes I have ever participated in. This was my first experience of what it truly felt like to collaborate. This project further expanded my understanding of how to develop creative activities around a particular issue and not let it be solely about process or product, but rather a conversation between the two. I have continued to explore these ideas in much of my work post-Phakama.

Apart from the variety of games and exercises that I learnt from my co-facilitators on all the projects I worked on, it has been the creative process that flowed from the idea of give and gain that I have tried to bring into everything that I do. Phakama helped me realise what's possible and also gave me tools to create the possibilities.

Calburn (2015b) reflects on the impact Phakama has made on her creative trajectory:

Phakama taught me to think differently – from working in a team, to working on site, to working in a community, to working aesthetically and to working to a socio-political agenda. It has forever changed my way of working. I cannot be in a creative room that is homogenous without feeling that something is profoundly wrong. I can no longer work in a teaching context alone, but prefer to work with another – shoulder to shoulder. I find it impossible to engage in a process in which people take the lead with no real interest or input from those on the floor – whether it be a workshop or a discussion. I had always come from an improvisation and devising background, so while that was not new, working in that type of process with a hundred young people was. It taught me when to step forward and when to step back. It taught me to plan from the minute to the large. It taught me strategy, it taught me what a truly participatory process is, and when to stand up and defend it. It gave me a place to be both a dissenting voice and a constructive one. It taught me to balance time with product – that there is sometimes in a process, a need to sort things out before the art can be done – and when the art in fact sorts out the problem – and how to balance both. It gave me the opportunity to deal with racism in a profoundly healing way, to work through the tough stuff and not walk away. The same around issues of sexuality. I learnt that I could jump and that I could fall – and that I would be celebrated for the former and always caught in the latter. I learnt what inclusivity meant – at every level. It visioned for me who I wanted to become in the artistic world. It made the theatre world a much bigger place full of so much more possibility. It married my love of education with my love of making theatre beyond the limitations of a stage. It taught me humility and modelled different ideas of leadership, project after project after project. It taught me grit and determination. It taught me risk and what it meant to be courageous. It taught me when to hold on and when to let go (although the latter has been the hardest). All of these things were so profoundly intertwined in the creative process.

Today I run the Theatre Arts Admin Collective, and the organisation's objectives are simply an extension of Phakama's – to still work towards creating a culturally diverse theatre industry in South Africa, to provide opportunity and mentorship to young artists and to create a home for artists, young and old, to work in and flourish. I am still working without money. I am still working in an empty space. I am still working with the same people I met and worked with in Phakama, although we are all now running different organisations or working in different institutions. Within the creative process, Phakama put relationships at the heart of everything. It is to the people in Phakama that I still find myself drawn to for advice, for inspiration and for projects for the future.

The above reflections are testament to the indelible mark that Phakama made on the lives of the artist facilitators featured in this essay. It certainly was the 'nuclear moment' of our careers that Mbothwe speaks of. Notions of conversations, negotiations, collaboration, relationships and community are some of the common threads that we have taken with us into our creative processes since we worked with Phakama.

Conclusion

The entanglement of life stories gives occasion for a revision which is neither solitary nor introspective of its own past, but rather a mutual revision in which we are able to see the most valuable yield of the exchange of memories. (Ricoeur 1996: 9)

At the heart of all Phakama projects were notions of conversations. These conversations incorporated an exchange of experiences and memories through story, as well as exchanges of images, ideas and vision. They involved processes of talking, listening and doing together. Additionally, Phakama provided an opportunity to blur the binary between 'community' and 'mainstream'. It encouraged audience members to become active participants in the experience, thereby encouraging conversations and action. Synergy between 'community' theatre and 'mainstream' theatre involved notions of conversations prevalent in 'community' theatre traditions, as well as aesthetic forms, structures and theatrical skills prevalent in 'mainstream' theatre. I conclude with the words of Edward Little, who notes that 'as creators of ... [community] theatre, I believe, we are charged with the responsibility of discovering ways in which the ideologies, intentions and values of our projects may be expressed as an aesthetic weave and a social weft in the creation of an artistic fabric' (2004: 4). The fabric of Phakama's creative practice is realized through conversations between the 'aesthetic weave' and the 'social weft'.

References

Blackman, L. (2008), *The Body: The Key Concepts*, New York: Berg.
Brink, A. (1998), 'Stories of History: Reimagining the Past in Post-apartheid Narrative', in S. Nuttall and C. Coetzee (eds), *Negotiating the Past: The Making of Memory in South Africa*, Cape Town: Oxford University Press, 29–42.

Calburn, C. (2015a), Personal Communication, 28 September.

Calburn, C. (2015b), Personal Interview, 30 April.

Carlson, M. (2003), *The Haunted Stage: The Theatre as Memory Machine*, Ann Arbor: The University of Michigan Press.

Cohen-Cruz, J. (2001), 'The Liz Lerman Dance Exchange', in S. C. Haedicke and T. Nellhaus (eds), *Performing Democracy*, Ann Arbor: The University of Michigan Press, 213–25.

Constitutional Court of South Africa (n.d.), Available online: http://www. constitutionalcourt.org.za/site/theconstitution/history.htm (accessed 24 September 2015).

de Certeau, M. (1984), *The Practice of Everyday Life*, Berkley: University of California Press.

de Kok, I. (1998), 'Cracked Heirlooms: Memory on Exhibition', in S. Nuttall and C. Coetzee (eds), *Negotiating the Past: The Making of Memory in South Africa*, Cape Town: Oxford University Press, 29–42.

Deleuze, G. and F. Guattari (1994), *What is Philosophy?*, translated by H. Tomlinson and G. Burchell, New York: Columbia University Press.

Dunne, J. (1996), 'Beyond Sovereignty and Deconstruction: The Storied Self', in R. Kearney (ed.), *Paul Ricoeur: The Hermeneutics of Action*, London: Sage Publications, 137–157.

Garret Brown, N. (2013), 'The Inter-Subjective Body', in S. Reeve (ed.), *Bodies in Performance*, Devon: Triarchy Press, 23–36.

Grosz, E. (2008), *Chaos, Territory, Art: Deleuze and the Framing of the Earth*, New York: Columbia University Press.

Little, E. (2004), 'Towards a Poetics of Popular Theatre', *Canadian Theatre Review* 117: 29–32.

Mbembe, A. (2013), 'Between the Lines 2013 – Achille Mbembe', public lecture, University of Cape Town, 26 February. Available online: http://www.gipca.uct.ac.za/wp-content/ uploads/2013/02/Keynote-Lecture-Achille-Mbembe.mp3 (accessed 20 July 2015).

Mbothwe, M. (2015), Personal Interview, 30 April.

Meehan, E. (2013), 'The Autobiographical Body: Somatic Practice and Object Relations', in S. Reeve (ed.), *Bodies in Performance*, Devon: Triarchy Press, 37–51.

Moolla, R., N. Kotze and L. Block (2011) 'Housing Satisfaction and Quality of Life in RDP Houses in Braamfischerville, Soweto: A South African Case Study', *Urbani izziv* 22(1): 138–43.

Osbourn, C. (2015a), Personal Interview, 30 April.

Osbourn, C. (2015b), Personal Communication, 29 September.

Pallasmaa, J. (2000), 'Lived Space in Architecture and Cinema'. Available online: http:// www.ucalgary.ca/UofC/faculties/EV/designresearch/publications/insitu/copy/ volume2/imprintable_architecture/Juhani_Pallasmaa/ (accessed 12 April 2005).

Richardson, L. (2015), Personal Interview, 30 April.

Ricoeur, P. (1996), 'Reflections on a New Ethos for Europe', in R. Kearney (ed.), *Paul Ricoeur: The Hermeneutics of Action*, London: Sage Publications.

Steiger, A. L. (2007), *Actors as Embodied Public Intellectuals: Reanimating Consciousness*, Ann Arbor: Proquest Information and Learning Company.

Sullivan, S. (2001), *Living Across and Through Skins: Transactional Bodies, Pragmatism, and Feminism*, Bloomington and Indianapolis: Indiana University Press.

Turner, C. (2004), 'Palimpsest or Potential Space? Finding a Vocabulary for Site-Specific Performance', *New Theatre Quarterly* 20(4): 376–90.

CASE STUDY
THE PHAKAMA WAY (PUNE, INDIA, 2002)

Vidyanidhee Vanarase

Description: This three-week training and performance project introduced the Phakama participant-centred approach to learning to potential facilitators in India. By bringing young people together from different cross-sections of the society, we were keen to understand what this approach might reveal of the context of their lives and to support them in a growing awareness of their rights.

Place: Pune, Maharashtra State, India.

Date/Duration: 6–27 January 2002.

Partnerships: South African Airways, British Council and The Royal Netherlands Embassy funded the project. Prithvi Theatre spearheaded the idea and provided some material and resources for the performance.

Lead Facilitators: Sara Matchett, Mandla Mbothwe, Andrew Siddall, Sanjna Kapoor, Divya Bhatia, Meera Oke, Vidyanidhee Vanarase (Prasad). Tony Fegan joined at a later stage.

Participants: Twenty-four potential facilitators from theatre groups, educators and other artists across the country, and eighty-six young people from Pune city.

Audience figures: Approximately 300 people.

Beginnings

Pune is recognized as an educational hub and the cultural capital of Maharashtra. The regional language spoken in this part of the country is Marathi and Marathi theatre is considered as one of the most advanced professional theatres in India along with Bengali theatre in West Bengal. Professional theatre practice in Maharashtra has always been very much text based and follows two main strands. One is of the Ibsenian 'well-made play' structure and the other is traditional Marathi Musical Theatre (known as *Marathi Sangeet natak*). Experimentation in Marathi theatre has been mainly limited to Pune and Mumbai, the big cities in Maharashtra. Theatre practitioners from both these cities have had exposure to other theatre practices influenced by European thought.

I grew up in this scenario. My mother was a theatre practitioner so I had an interesting exposure to various genres of theatre making: storytelling, Absurd Theatre, Theatre for Social Change, socially relevant theatre, musical theatre and commercial Marathi theatre, were all around me. I had attended rehearsals of the plays in which my mother used to act. Many times her rehearsals took place at our home. So theatre was always a part of my life. There wasn't a particular moment when I realized that *this* is theatre. I was experiencing it all the time.

I started acting in plays when I was eight years old. As a child, it was a thrilling experience. Until then I had been an observer: now I was an 'actor' and it felt good. In the process of growing up, I became more inclined towards directing than acting. The directors around me become my role models. In this context, I learnt that, as a director, I must know everything. A director should complete all the paperwork before going for the rehearsals – the blocking of the stage action, developing the set and lighting design, the music, props – everything. The director has to be a 'God'.

My relationship with Phakama started in 2000. After the Prithvi International Theatre Festival, I was in Mumbai for a post-festival party. Sanjna Kapoor, the festival director spoke with me about Phakama. She told me about the *Crossing the Red Ribbon Divide* project in Seshego, which she had attended, and *The Robben Island Peace Project* that was about to happen. When I heard about Phakama for the first time, I was curious. This sounded like some kind of social activity where theatre is also used. It took me some time to figure out what this could be. In 2001 we began planning a Phakama Residency in India. The purpose of the Indian residency was manifold. The primary idea was to introduce Phakama's participant-centred approach to learning to potential facilitators in India. We also wanted to see what the Phakama process could generate in an Indian context – bringing young people together from different cross-sections of the society, learning to respect each other's work, to create together and feel safe about it. We were also keen to support young people to be aware of their rights, to understand the consequences of the choices they make and take responsibility for their decisions and actions.

Letters were sent out to approximately eighty possible facilitator participants from across the country. From these, twenty-four were chosen. One of the most important factors for selecting potential facilitators was whether they were already working with a group of young people or if they had the capacity to develop a group of young people to continue the Phakama process in their community.

The Phakama Way – Facilitator Training and Devising Process

The residency took place in Pune city as it is well connected by road and rail with the rest of the country and is a cultural hub with an aware, critical and interested audience. Sudarshan Hall offered both workshop space and accommodation for the trainee facilitators. Garware Bal Bhavan, a children's recreation centre, was chosen as a space for the workshop with young participants and final site-specific performance.

The first week was devoted to working with all twenty-four facilitators, taking them through the process and framework of Phakama introducing ideas of 'Give and Gain' and 'facilitation'. All of the trainee facilitators were already working with young people in their own regions and keen to understand this new way of working with young people. Many of them were like me, they believed in the 'godlike' director figure in theatre. It was tough for most of us to understand and accept an approach to making theatre that didn't fit this idea. Many of us found it difficult to let go of our own thoughts, beliefs and preconceived notions. Some of us also believed that 'we already do all of this'. This first week was intensive work: it was a time of anticipation, anxiety, curiosity, doubt, comfort, gauging each other's skills, building trust and faith and continuing work with simultaneous translations in Hindi, English and Marathi as and when required. This was the time to get to know each other, to acknowledge that everyone belongs, the interests and skills everyone has. To support this, each trainee facilitator conducted one exercise with the entire group. This process helped everyone to find out what one has to give and what one wants to gain. It evolved six areas of work facilitated by a lead facilitator: Acting by Sara Machett from South Africa; Music by Divya Bhatia; Movement and Dance by Mandla Mbothwe (South Africa); Creative Text by Sanjna Kapoor; Design by Andrew Siddall (UK) and Meera Oak; and Production and Administration was facilitated by me. At the same time all of us, the lead facilitators, also needed to gain and at some points we also changed our chosen areas. The trainee facilitators created improvised pieces on the themes of 'Departure', 'Journey' and 'Arrival', which created an opportunity for everyone to experience these six areas at some point during the process. The process of understanding of Give and Gain was a practical one and was achieved through this process. In the process, 'Journey' became a key theme for the first week.

In the second week, the daily schedule was divided into three parts. The mornings were spent in a workshop with facilitators for the purpose of planning the work. In the afternoons, the young participants joined the workshop. The trainee facilitators worked with the young participants in the afternoon. It was more like a laboratory scenario for the potential facilitators. The evenings were spent on reflecting upon the work done during the day. In the planning time, the trainee facilitators were designing their sessions with smaller groups in the six areas of work. The entire week with the young participants was structured to take them through the process of understanding each other. They worked in smaller groups as well as the entire group together. They explored the space of Garware Bal Bhavan. The focus of each area was 'myself' and 'my journey' and the presentations at the end of each day's work were focused on the way each participant represented himself/herself through a specific area chosen (Acting, Movement and Dance, etc.).

The third and final week focused on the creation of the final performance. The trainee facilitators and the young participants worked together from morning until evening. Late evening time was the reflection and planning time for the trainee facilitators. During the entire three weeks, the lead facilitators had their own reflection time and planning time in the post-dinner sessions.

The young participants and trainee facilitators continued to work in the five identified areas. In each of the areas the young participants were reflecting upon various aspects of self such as,

Who am I...
What makes me 'me'...
What are my dreams?
What are my aspirations?
What/Who is close to my heart?
What are my fears?
What makes me anxious/angry/sad/happy/joyful...
I enjoy doing...
I enjoy being...
I feel...
I love...
I hate...

These improvised expressions helped the young participants to identify their areas of Give and Gain. They started working in a chosen area to create a final performance. The exercises with the young participants started to evolve into a theme of 'Who Am I...' more than the 'Journey'. This was just days before the final performance so everyone started burning the midnight oil to bring these ideas to life.

Disruption – Reflections on My Experience of Phakama

When we decided to host the Phakama residency in Pune, I took on the administrative and production responsibility for the project. I belong to Pune: I was born and brought up here and my work has been primarily based in the city. Sanjna Kapoor, Divya Bhatia and Meera Oke had participated in a Phakama project earlier. My role was participant, observer, coordinator and administrator. All these words and other terms like 'residency', 'Give and Gain', 'rise up on your own feet', 'participatory process' and 'site specific' were new to me. During the residency they started becoming meaningful. I could not believe that a theatrical experience was actually being generated and making sense through this process. There was no 'godlike' director. People were talking to each other. There were lots of conversations, interactions, discussions and arguments but everything was culminating into a singular artistic expression. This was an absolutely new experience for me.

The process of 'Give and Gain' initially sounded like a very superficial, theoretical idea. I really wondered whether it was possible. I had previously thought that it was the responsibility of a 'godlike' director to 'give' and the poor actors would 'gain'. Then I realized that there is a lot more to it, that there is lot more for me to gain in the theatre-making process apart from enhancing my skills in directing a well-made play. Areas like 'Movement and Dance' and 'Creative Text' became interesting for me. I felt the need to gain in these areas. I was used to leaving elements of text or movement to a 'writer' or a 'choreographer', but never thought of challenging myself with these skills. I started liking and eventually loving the new role – 'facilitator'. Phakama really helped me and many more to think about the ideas of give and gain. Not only about what do we give and gain but also about *how* do we give and gain.

As a director, I always believed that I need a text to work with – that voice, speech and diction were important aspects of theatre making. The playwright was always at the centre, actors were expected to follow instruction and the director had the final word. The Phakama process however was compelling me to create my own text. Material that I would have previously discarded as 'just another improvisation' became meaningful. As I started exploring this, the 'improvisation' started becoming a 'performance'. And I liked it. I realized that the theatrical possibilities devising offers are enormous. It was able to help me understand the basics of dramatic moment. It helped me understand the theatricality in a different sense.

Collaborative creation was also new. There was no director. There was a facilitator. There were co-creators. So who would have the final say? I had no clue. In this process I learnt to have meaningful conversations. There was a negotiation of decision-making based upon the artistic ideas and aesthetic understanding of all individuals. Bringing everyone onto a common platform of conversation, even though everyone could be on a different level of understanding, was a tough task. But it allowed everyone to be a part of the creative process. It is a tough democratic process for artistic creation. Another realization for me was the difference between creating a theatrical piece and creating a theatrical experience. I was not sure about how to create an experience that allows the audience to feel empathy for the characters. The Phakama process makes one aware of the 'realness' of our experiences, as performers as well as an audience. It is not realistic. It is real. This realness allows us to feel empathy.

In the beginning we did 'Mapping the World'. The room became a map of India and everyone was standing at a point where they belong to. And suddenly the perspective of looking at each other in that room changed. The ways of relating with each other changed. That was the moment when I realized that this process of theatre making is different. When I was standing at 'Pune' and was looking around in the room, the map made me realize the enormity of the country and enormity of the cultural diversity we have. It also allowed me look at the kind of 'work experience' that was present in that room together. This process offered something that I had never experienced. This process made me question myself about the idea of 'work' and its 'context'. It made me ask a question about belongingness. Where do I belong? And where do 'we' belong as a community? What is the meaning of travel? Why do we travel? Is there any purpose for me to be 'here'? These were some of the questions which I had never bothered to encounter.

The process of understanding the principle of Give and Gain was quite elaborate. It took a good three-hour session to get a glimpse of it. It took a lot of time to understand that it is not just a trade off. It is about what I can contribute to the creative journey of all of us together and what I can learn in the process, what I *wish* to learn in the process. And whatever you decide to learn, in reality you learn a lot more. The 'Give and Gain' wheel/sun was created. It was astonishing. It made everyone a bit proud of being a part of this group that had so many skills. It looked like we, together, can create something that none of us had thought about.

The schedule of the residency was progressive in terms of learning. It was more like the process of the blooming of a flower. The first week was dedicated for working with the new 'potential' facilitators. The second week was a combination of working with the 'potential' facilitators, working with young participants, reflecting upon the work done during the day and planning and designing the next day. The last week was working together with the young participants and 'potential' facilitators. This gave a gradual progression to the entire process of understanding what we were getting into. The first week was more focusing on the 'gain' part of it. The second week started opening up the ideas of 'give'. And the third week was a process of culmination.

One important thing I realized in this process was that the experience created was real. And it will always remain real because of its participatory nature. It cannot be repeated exactly as it was. And this is distinctly different to what we say about shows when we say that every show is different. In the Phakama process, your interaction continually changes as every time there are new people in front of you as an audience, who are reacting to you. They are involved in the performance, not only as passive spectators. Sometimes their involvement influences the performance. Their reactions will decide your response as an actor.

As a theatre practitioner I always believed that I need to have a finished product that was 'perfect' and 'complete'. But what was happening in this process was different: the 'completeness' would evolve only when the audience entered into the space, compelled to engage. In *The Phakama Way,* the audience had to walk across a site of about an acre. This was unheard of! They watched small performances happening in different sites – real-life stories, images, metaphors – that, at the end of the production, made sense. It didn't matter what sequence the scenes were witnessed – the culmination point was common.

The theme that evolved during this residency was 'Who Am I?' It was about the dreams and aspirations of young participants. It was about trying to figure out the meaning of one's being; understanding what one is doing to fulfil one's own dreams and aspirations. It was also about looking at the hurdles we have created for ourselves and recognizing the strengths we have to reach to one's dreams and aspirations. I remember one of the stories very distinctly. One young girl decided to perform her story in a tree. She was standing on one of the branches, approximately fifteen feet above the ground. She held the tree with one hand and used the other hand for creating gesture. One of her feet was on the tree and, while speaking she was swinging her other foot around. This was creating anxiety in the audience – they were fearful that she might fall. As she spoke about her dreams, she spoke about the trust she expects from others. Suddenly she said, 'I know you are not listening to me. You are afraid that I will fall. That's what I am trying to tell you. Trust me! I will not fall...' It made a strong impact on the audience, compelling them to look inwards. It was an amazing example of how we as a society are not allowing each other to take risks and fly. It is an image that has stayed with me all these years. This entire process was an enriching experience for everyone. The young people decided to look beyond their comfort zone. They were ready to look at the harsh realities of life. Some of the group members were already experiencing those realities in their lives. But some of them were coming from very affluent backgrounds. Young people from very safe environments and from vulnerable environments were coming together to create a piece of art. I feel that this was one of the most important achievements of *The Phakama Way.*

The performance culminated in a striking image. The participants had created a huge bird. Everyone wrote their dream, aspiration or fear on a piece of paper and attaching it to the feathers of the bird. We were invited to think of something that we wanted to see flying high in the sky or something that one wanted to leave and let go. And then the bird took off. Everyone started singing a Thank You song – even the audience was singing and dancing with the actors. The bird started moving up in the sky and flew over the building of the children's recreation centre. This was the culmination of the Phakama residency and the beginning of a new journey.

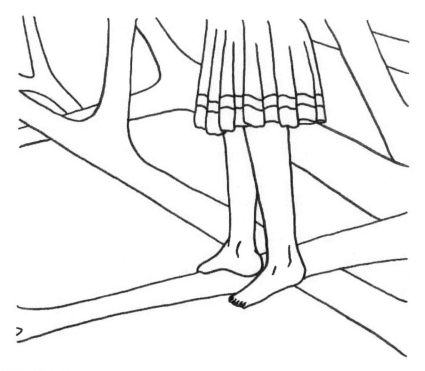

FIGURE 8 Trust.

Standing on one bare foot, the girl in the tree implores the audience to not worry about her safety, but to listen closely to her story of trust.

THE STREET IS MY BACKYARD (BUENOS AIRES, ARGENTINA, 1996)[22]

Charlotte Higgins

'We certainly make things hard for ourselves': There's no script, no set, no lights – and it's four days to curtain-up.

The sun is setting behind a cobweb of telephone wires in Chaco Chico, a barrio in the western outskirts of Buenos Aires. A drumbeat breaks out. Three teenagers are pounding away for all they are worth, cymbals yammering over the top. One of the musicians, 16-year-old Gaston Narvaez, has painted an image of Homer Simpson sporting a Cadaver (a Norwegian extreme-metal band) T-shirt on the side of his bombo, or bass drum. The drummers are joined by rows of dancers, whose slow processional steps gradually heat up into athletic floorwork and spiralling, high-kicking leaps: it's breathtaking.

This is the murga, a Uruguayan and Argentinian street-artform that combines dance, protest song, music and intricate costumes. The dance that the 35 or so people are rehearsing now will form the finale of a piece of theatre written, sung, played and performed entirely by them. Most come from Moreno, an economically hard-pressed municipality, where unemployment is at 33 per cent, and whose underachieving schools are the subject of news headlines. This is theatre on the front line: a means of self-expression in a context where few have a voice.

The British Council-funded project has brought together British, Brazilian and Argentinian directors, as well as 35 local participants (ranging in age from 13 to 57, but mostly in their mid-teens), under the auspices of Phakama, an exchange programme set up a decade ago by the LIFT. In its time Phakama has been responsible for projects in India, Africa and Britain – but this is its first incarnation in South America.

---

[22]Originally published in the *Guardian*, Monday 17 April 2006.

When I arrive at Defensores del Chaco, the youth community centre where the project is based, the strains of such an ambitious collaboration are showing. The team of local participants and international facilitators are nearing the end of a process in which every decision, exhaustingly, has been taken collectively. 'We certainly make things hard for ourselves', says Andrew Siddall (known as Sid), one of the UK facilitators. 'What I could say in three minutes takes an hour to decide'.

Linguistically, it's a nightmare: none of the British speak Spanish or Portuguese; hardly any of the Argentinians speak English; the Argentinians and Brazilians can understand each other – sort of. The only person who speaks all three languages is Brazilian-born Fabio Santos, who runs the UK arm of Phakama. As such, he is the conduit for nearly every conversation, and he looks as if he would like to retreat to a darkened room and never speak again.

Even more worryingly, there's a show to put on in four days' time, and pulling together the material that the children have devised seems a long way off. Suddenly the idea of an international bunch of theatre people turning up without a script, designs, sets, lights or any preconceived idea of what they are going to do seems something of a stretch.

There's a conflict between being true to the Phakama process – whereby the children create this show themselves – and the need to deliver a performance that's going to work. Brazilian Lulu Pugliese says: 'It's been a difficult day. We did manage to come up with something fantastic. But it was difficult not to shape everything ourselves, not to "knead the dough," and allow the participants to see what the possibilities were through their eyes, not ours'.

If sticking to the process is causing so much heartache, why do it, I ask Sid later. 'We all have something to learn', he says. 'I may have 20 years' experience of directing, but no experience of this city, this environment. I have huge amounts to gain by hearing others' voices. And for the kids, it encourages a sense of ownership in the final product. The creativity is shared equally'.

This is borne out by conversations with the young Argentinian facilitators and participants. For many of them, this is not just a few weeks' diversion, but something much more profound. Seventeen-year-old Jesica Yamila Letonai, for instance, is an extraordinary young woman who – along with friends – has set up a soup kitchen in an abandoned school in her home barrio of Santa Brigida, where, she says matter-of-factly, 'there is no electricity, light, gas, phones, transport or hospital'. Santa Brigida is an area, she says, where many cartoneros live: a frequent sight in central Buenos Aires since the 2001 economic collapse, these are people who scrape a living collecting rubbish from the streets in handcarts and selling it on to recycling companies.

Letonai and her friends found food by knocking on the doors of houses and shops, walking miles to collect enough to feed the children in her neighbourhood.

But she had always been determined that the centre should be more than a soup kitchen. 'We do murga, theatre, drawing. We have a health clinic and hold a workshop around work skills for parents'.

For her, Phakama offers strong practical benefits. 'It will bring a lot of knowledge to our centre, about how to plan and organise an event'. She's also interested in the way the project is teaching people to communicate openly. 'In my barrio, violence is an issue, not just gun violence, but verbal violence. There's a lack of education, and therefore respect'.

Over the next couple of days at Defensores, things go from bad to worse. Rain pounds down incessantly. The show was to have taken place in a garden next to the centre, but rehearsals would create a Glastonbury-esque sea of mud. It is decided to delay the performance by a day and restage it around Defensores.

There is a final burst of activity, and the show is nailed down: it will be a 'promenade' performance with six scenes set on different sites, followed by the murga finale. The environment, pollution, the gap between rich and poor, dreams and the imagination are among the subjects that the children have chosen to tackle. Costumes and scenery are finished off – including a giant pachumama (mother earth) and a huge sinister puppet made of rubbish and old drinks bottles that will rise up and threaten to engulf her.

Incredibly, the day of the performance is hot and sunny. There is a sense that everyone involved with the project has changed a little over the past weeks. According to facilitator Debora Landim, director of a children's theatre in Salvador, Brazil: 'The core of all this is the people making the art – that is the young people. If they are distant from the words, the theatre, the songs, then it doesn't work'. Today, though, it does.

PART THREE

CELEBRATION

INTRODUCTION

Part Three describes how celebration is an important tenor in Phakama, manifest in each project across a body of work over two decades. Celebration is not an arts practice itself but rather an underlying principle intrinsic to Phakama. To illustrate how this plays itself out, this, final, part builds on Preparing the Ground and Making the Performance and is divided into three sections: Connecting, Becoming and Stepping Up.

'Connecting' recognizes the value Phakama places on connecting individuals' experience with the experience of the group, as moments of celebration. Corinne Micallef's case study of *The Edible Garden* (London, 2012–16) illustrates how people's stories are acknowledged and celebrated and how new connections are forged between people from different generations living in the same city. Furthermore, it shows how food is used as the project's core artistic stimulus. 'Becoming' explores how these connections can allow those who have engaged with Phakama, (participants, facilitators, audience) to be, effectively, in the world – a heightened awareness of agency, care and relationship making. It also recognizes that this process can be painful. Lucy Neal's essay, 'Alive to the Music of What Happens', examines facets of celebration, revealing what is at play when celebratory events act as a catalyst for individual and collective change. In the subsection 'Stepping Up' we have curated a series of extracts from interviews conducted during the research for this book demonstrating how people explicitly connect their experience with Phakama in shaping and informing other areas of their lives. Lastly, in her essay 'Performing Risk', Shirley Brice Heath, a linguistic anthropologist, draws on her experience of Phakama to consider the specificity of its principles in practice and how this resonates with other organizations, such as New York Public Theater's Public Works programme, as part of a wider enquiry into how the arts support learning with youth. She situates these projects within a broader context of artwork in community settings, evidencing the value of the arts in developing critical participants in democracy.

'The evening which began at sunset ended in a fire display which illuminated a huge Xhosa wedding dance to include all the audience' (Sichel 1996). Celebration is at the heart of Phakama: staging a dance piece involving over one hundred young people and over two hundred audience members in South Africa, as described above by Adrienne Sichel; closing Tooting High Street in London to stage a large-scale carnival; dancing around a fire in the garden at the Morija Museum (Lesotho); singing at a busy London underground station; or sharing stories, recipes and food in a care home. Celebration within the Phakama context, however, and perhaps more importantly, does also take the format of more intimate and private moments where individuals are given the space to share their stories, dreams, troubles and wishes. These moments often offer opportunities for pain to be acknowledged and for transformations in understanding to take place. Thus, honouring one's personal story becomes an act of celebration in itself.

Phakama approaches celebration as both private and public, small and large, going beyond the prosaicness of everyday parties, as Julia Rowntree (2014) explains:

> Phakama's celebration isn't a party. The visible celebration is a performance that is witnessed. It's not a selfish celebration, because in order to get that celebration on the road, one has had to think from the view point of the audience. It's an exchange. It's the audience who enable a celebration of the talents, of the creativity. Celebration without the struggle to get there is a bit like instant Halloween. There's got to be a tussle to get there, a muddle in the middle.

Kelvin O'Mard (2014), a facilitator in early Phakama projects, adds: 'All Phakama projects have something chaotic and a place where things get resolved. That place of resolution is the celebration. But the celebration is not the end of it, it's the journey that Phakama takes.' Phakama's moments of public celebration are therefore informed by the more private 'muddle in the middle' moments. Moments where individuals share themselves openly and are acknowledged and celebrated, where differences are negotiated, similarities strengthened and connections are made.

Phakama's ultimate moment of celebration is the final performance itself when the doors are open and the public is invited in, but it is made from all the celebratory moments experienced during the process. Phakama's performances are made of individual stories supported by collective generosity, imagination and artistry. Real and imagined moments, factual or dreamed accounts of individuals', groups' and communities' lives are shared with audience members who, in turn, add fragments of their own personal stories creating yet another layer of connection. Although the performance ends, people (participants and audience alike) carry the experience with them, making them anew through their memory response (Hilevaara 2016). This final performance is made from the processes and practices described in this book: from the accumulation of small moments of celebration. For example, in *The Trashcatchers Carnival* (2010) a young man who thought he had nothing to contribute, was invited to support the delivery of warm-up games during the project. Later he became assistant to the facilitator making all the music for the final performance. The final performance is celebratory because the process allows people to play different versions of themselves and rehearse different possible ways of living together in the world. For example, *The Edible Garden* (2012–16) brought young children, teenagers and residents of care homes together to not just imagine but practically model a world where an explicit engagement with generational, cultural and experiential difference can be cohesive rather than divisive.

Furthermore, Phakama invites guests and members of the communities they work with to take part in and contribute to the larger and final celebration that echoes in people's memories long after it has taken place. Paul Woodmin, the Food Enterprise Manager at Stepney City Farm, a partner in *The Edible Garden*, distils this sense of being both in the audience and part of the project when he says,

It was a wonderful evening, the food and the entertainment were excellent. I enjoyed the event very much, however, what caused more enjoyment was seeing the interaction between the young people and the residents of Hawthorne Green Retirement Home. One older lady stole the show with her banter with one of the young male actors 'how's your belly off for spots?' she asked. It was very touching. If I ended my days in a place such as this, that works with the community in the way they do, I'd be quite contented.

References

Hilevaara, K. (2016), 'Orange Dogs and Memory Responses: Creativity in Spectating and Remembering', in Matthew Reason and Anja Mølle Lindelof (eds), *Experiencing Liveness in Contemporary Performance: Interdisciplinary Perspectives*, London and New York: Routledge, 34–47.
O'Mard, K. (2014), Phakama Research Meeting, QMUL, 17 December.
Rowntree, J. (2014), Phakama Research Meeting, QMUL, 17 December 2014.
Sichel, A. (1996), 'This Landmark Event', *The Star*, 5 September (LIFT Archive, LIFT/1997/CE/023/004).

CONNECTING

Introduction

We gather at the foyer of the Arts One Building at Queen Mary University of London. The group is made out of sixty young people and group leaders from across Europe meeting for the first time as part of the *Message in a Bottle* project (2011–13). Prior to leaving their homes, each individual was asked to bring an item of food that was important to them to share in our first breakfast together. We savoured delicious, at times unknown and sometimes unusual delicacies from Ireland, Poland, Portugal, The Basque Country, Turkey and the UK. Each with a story and a personal meaning attached to them. The whole session was supposed to last for two hours but as people told their stories (speaking for the first time in this group configuration) and started to reveal themselves in a way that formal introductions could never do, the whole group listened attentively as they ate the item being described. For example, a young man from Poland told the story of how he travelled to his grandmother's the night before flying to London to bake with her the cake she used to make for him when he was a child. As we ate the cake, we were transported to his grandmother's house, to his childhood and understood the connection and love between these two individuals. Stories such as this cannot be rushed and so our first breakfast together lasted for five hours.

This description by Fabio Santos reiterates the vital role that food plays in Phakama. This started as a necessity in the early projects where project leaders recognized that most of the young people they worked with were from deprived backgrounds with limited means to purchase food themselves. As the projects were residential, food was a logistical practicality that needed to be addressed. However, as with everything within Phakama, the need to provide food was turned into a creative challenge and a learning opportunity. Two decades on, Phakama continues making use of cooking, eating together and the telling of stories while doing so, as rituals to connect people. Food is now intrinsic to Phakama's processes regardless of participant resources or logistical needs. The creation of spaces through food, where people are invited to reveal aspects of themselves and their lives, be it painful or joyous, does two things: it says your story is important and creates a sense of collective care and identity.

Tea breaks, lunch and dinner times are opportunities for people to build relationships with one another. They are purposely and carefully built into the schedule in the same way as visual arts, movement or drama sessions are scheduled in. Jenny Macdonald, a facilitator who has worked with Phakama since 2004, says, 'what Phakama does so brilliantly is say the social time is as important as the working time' (2014). In a Phakama process, food, song, dance and work seamlessly blur into each other. Fabio Santos reflects on the critical place of food, of cooking and eating together during *The Child I Curry* (Lesotho, 2010):

The facilitators were housed from week two in the beautiful Mophato oa Morija Conference Centre. A group of local women employed by the centre looked after us and prepared our meals daily. For some of the team, the quality of the food was not in par with the food provided by Mme Thato Tsikona, a local chef employed by the project to feed us lunch during week one whilst we stayed at local families' homes. The desire to carry on being fed by Mme Thato Tsikona was conveyed to the cooks at the centre. Unwittingly, offence was caused and the cooks told the team straight that we had to leave the centre. The situation was quickly corrected by two of the project's facilitators realising that this food incident could represent the end of the project. And so, Lucy Richardson (UK facilitator) apologised profusely on her knees. Later Lucky Peters (Namibian Facilitator) worked closely with the cooks on a song and dance number as their offering to the final show. Their number opened the show and involved them dancing around a big cooking pot. As they sang and danced, a child emerged fully 'curried'.

This moment of near disaster was beautifully transformed into an opportunity to better understand the other, understand and celebrate the pride that these women had in their jobs and their food and, as most things in Phakama, it found its way to the final celebration shared with the audience.

In her case study, Corinne Micallef describes how *The Edible Garden*, a series of intergenerational projects working in collaboration with care homes in London and the south-west of England, celebrates the individual and the collective. It recognizes the importance of 'doing' alongside others, how that enables them to find ways of being along side. The quality of the invitation for people to meet and the equitable structures in which they spend time together, support peoples' understanding of one another and how to respond rather than react to one another: to act together and to flourish. But *The Edible Garden* also does something else: as in the incident described during *The Child I Curry* project above, it takes one of Phakama's most successful methods, the sharing of food, used during social times and places it at the centre of the creative process. Food, from planting to harvesting, from cooking to eating, becomes an artistic stimulus.

Reference

Macdonald, J. (2014), Phakama Research Meeting, QMUL, 17 December.

CASE STUDY
THE EDIBLE GARDEN
(UK, 2012–16)

Corinne Micallef

Description: *The Edible Garden* isn't a one-off project but an iteration
of Phakama's ethos. *The Edible Garden* grew out of Corinne Micallef's
relationship with both Phakama and the Women's Institute. At the time,
Corinne was working as artist facilitator with both Phakama and the Women's
Institute. From her involvement with both organizations and observing that
food played an important role in their work, Corinne proposed a project that
could bring people from different ages and backgrounds together using the
metaphor of growing a garden. The project provided a model for an inclusive
community. It was first staged in collaboration with the Women's Institute
and Mile End Children's Park in the London Borough of Tower Hamlets.
Later, Phakama partnered up with Sanctuary Housing, Newham Sixth Form
College (NewVic), Woodmansterne Primary School and Harris Academy
and delivered *The Edible Garden* in a number of care homes across London.
The Edible Garden has now been developed in a number of care homes in the
Southwest of England and continues to be adapted and tested in response to
each of these contexts.
Place: Mile End Children's Park, Residential care home in London and South
West of England, UK.
Date/Duration: September 2011 to March 2016.
Partnerships: Phakama, Women's Institute East End, Mile End Children's
Park, Sanctuary Care Housing Group, Stepney City Farm, Newham Sixth
Form College (NewVic), Woodmansterne Primary School and Harris
Academy.

Facilitators across the series of projects: Corinne Micallef, Sue Mayo, Mia Harris, Mike Knowlden, Lyndsay Officer, Thomas Kendall, Almudena Segura, Caroline Jones, Sophie Herxheimer, Juancho Gonzalez, Tom Foster, Alice Neiva, Fabio Santos, Ines Tercio, Caroline Gervay, Cedoux Kadima, Paul Brett, Alex Gichohi, Charlie Folorunsho, Valerio Oliveira, Indy Okonkwo, Sarah Quist, Sally-Ginger Brockbank, Annette Telesford.
Participants: Over 300 participants including Phakama young artists, Women's Institute East End's participants, children and their families attending activities at Mile End Children's Park, students from Newham Sixth Form College (NewVic), Woodmansterne Primary School and Harris Academy and residents of Sanctuary Care Housing Group's care homes.
Funders: Awards for All (Big Lottery Fund), National Women's Institute, Youth in Action, Sanctuary Housing (Shine!).

The word celebration conjures, for me, an image of a joyous occasion – one with people coming together, food, laughter, colour, inclusivity and noise. In this case study I reflect on *The Edible Garden* to illustrate how celebration is central to Phakama's practice. *The Edible Garden* creates shared spaces for younger and older people to consider how to grow a healthy, hardy community. Participants and artists grow food, swap recipes, share stories and together create a performed feast for an audience. The aim is to break down barriers between generations, encourage sustainable and healthy living and to use the arts as a catalyst for increasing social cohesion. The project began as a conversation between the East End Women's Institute and Phakama UK about our shared love for food, sustainability and getting people talking.

In 2012 we created the first version of *The Edible Garden* in a public space – Mile End Children's Park. We ran sessions over a period of six months, where we constructed magical dens, planted seeds, built a clay oven, told stories by the campfire, sang vegetable songs, foraged for ingredients and the project ended with a feast for over one hundred audience members and participants of all ages. The promenade performance through the different spaces in the park culminated in a feast as we sat together to eat at one long makeshift table that ran right through the raised beds in the garden: a party, with stories woven through it. People from the surrounding estate met their neighbours, sometimes for the first time, and guests from further afield were welcomed into the community.

Taking time to sit down and eat with one another is a special time. It always has been in Phakama, and there is a commonly held belief within Phakama that the greatest learning in a project happens in the meal times, lunch breaks and social spaces. It is here that common ground is found and compassion for the other is grown. We encourage these moments in a Phakama process, especially at a time when, financially, it is easier to cut these opportunities for connection. In *The Edible Garden* we created a project that put this social gathering at the heart of its process. It was a natural progression for our work.

The first *Edible Garden* made good connections within and across a community who had not come together before. We wanted to consider how interactions could go beyond the superficial, to find a structure that allowed for an impact to be made between participants at a deeper level – for relationships to be developed. In 2013 we took *The Edible Garden* into residential care homes with Sanctuary Housing Group. The project consisted of running workshops over three months with residents (some suffering from dementia) and young people from local primary and secondary schools. The workshops culminated in a transformation of the care homes – both in terms of atmosphere and in how communal spaces were arranged and dressed – and a performance party in their communal spaces.

Phakama models a position that everyone has a contribution to make to a creative process. Celebration is a time when people come together to recognize and share in a moment. In essence it's an opportunity to connect. We aim to connect people through art making and in doing so celebrate the lives of people: our very existence. Our starting point for the work is always the participants – their lives, experiences and stories. It is important to note that in any Phakama project the artist team will invite participants to share their personal stories but never force anyone to tell a story that is uncomfortable for them. The process encourages stories that celebrate human experience – in all of its complexity. In *The Edible Garden* we began with participants' stories about food: their favourite meal; a memory of a dish their parents or grandparents made; a food they hate to eat. People's stories are a rich and infinite source of material. Sharing them with each other is a recognition, it says you are important, you are valued, what you have to say is important. Because the content of the work is drawn from real-life stories, we are in a constant process of acceptance. For example, in *The Edible Garden* we met one couple, Tom and Edna, who had been married for nearly sixty years. They told us the story of how they met at a dance just before the war. Edna only went that evening because she liked Tom's friend and wanted to be with him, but she caught Tom's attention instead. They courted, and he won her heart, but no sooner had he proposed than he was sent his draft papers and called up to go and fight in the Second World War. They told us of the heartache of not knowing what would happen. The resonance of this story was felt across the group who felt that it should be included in the piece. Although not every story that is told in the process can be included in the final presentation to an audience, the overall editing process is one that is shared with the whole group in an open and democratic process. Furthermore, the acceptance of people's stories, as they are, is invaluable to the work. It means that participants aren't judged. We rarely edit or change people's stories but work with them. Each story has its own value and if it is important enough for a participant to share with us, then it will be heard and responded to as part of the process.

However, this spirit of acceptance means that things can change very quickly. Participants can share a story with us during any part of the process. Often participants are asked to respond to a stimulus in a short amount of time, for example 'tell us about a moment your heart beat faster.' And this straight away gets thrown into the mix for the final presentation. Sometimes this can unnerve participants, with the feeling 'Oh, I only said/made that up quickly, I didn't expect it to be used'. It can be unsettling for participants because they say 'It's not good enough'. It is always a negotiation but usually in those circumstances, enough trust has been developed to reassure the participants of the value of this contribution at this point in the process. All people in the process need reassurance that their ideas are valid and important enough, which is why we accept every contribution.

Another key way that participants' experiences are celebrated and accepted is that when they have shared a story it usually gets given to someone else to work on, who will recreate it, and then possibly given to someone else, who adds a new dimension and so on. In this way responsibility is shared for all the stories created. Rather than holding on to your own story you give it to someone else with a generous spirit and it is taken up by someone with a genuine care: the stories that are performed in the final presentation become everybody's. In the case of Tom and Edna in *The Edible Garden*, once they had shared their story we gave it to the young people, who used it as inspiration for the scenes they created. We made the opening of the performance a tea dance from the 1940s with the audience given dance cards from the era and cupid's circulating the party. Then two young people, Lauren and Dominic, made a scene where they played the younger Tom and Edna and the moment that he received his call up papers. Lauren was a singer and chose a song from the era to sing as she waved him goodbye never knowing if he would return. It was a moment of connection with the audience. One of the elderly residents, Kitty, who could no longer speak, began to cry and another, who was usually not engaged in any way, joined in the song with passion.

Phakama is about what you give of yourself and what you receive of others.

Nowhere is this more striking than in a care home setting. The lives of the care home residents can be isolated and they may find it hard to engage with others, particularly those not already known to them. In *The Edible Garden* workshops it took time, patience and compassion to learn about the residents and their lives. This is always the case in every Phakama process and an integral part of how we make our work but it was brought into even sharper focus working on this project with some of the participants who were suffering from dementia. For example, how can you learn that Harry was a milliner in the East End in the 1950s if he cannot remember himself? Phakama's facilitators embrace the process of discovery about people. They come from the starting point of what can be revealed of this individual and therefore what can we learn about our common humanity. The art becomes then the vehicle by which a person is revealed. During the process of *The Edible Garden*, Roger, one of the residents was asked to tell us about the favourite food he remembers from his childhood. He told us all about how he and his five siblings, Gina, Christopher, Debbie, Jackie and Carol, would come home after playing out and sit around the table and his mum would cook, but he couldn't remember what. Sophie, the artist, suggested a number of possibilities but all he would say is 'I don't know'. Sophie asked if his mum made pies and he said he thought so, but when asked what might be in the pie kept repeating 'I don't know'. So, Sophie embraced his answer and in valuing his contribution made a virtue out of the fact that he couldn't remember. We used the 'I Don't Know Pie' as the starting point for our ideas and let it take centre stage. Sophie created a giant pie, big enough for all the young participants to fit inside, so as the audience arrived to the final presentation they were met with a gigantic pie on the lawn. The young people had created a poem about 'I Don't know Pie' and with the help of our music artist Alex, had turned this into a song, which opened the show. True moments of celebration came through the acceptance of who people are and what they bring to every session, woven together and shared with an audience.

When you begin a process by listening to people's stories you start to move beyond the superficial of what we can see, beyond what we look like and the stereotypes we represent, and you start to see the whole person. In *The Edible Garden* we could move beyond seeing an older person with mobility or speech problems, beyond seeing a disease and to see the person. For example, there was a moment in a workshop where Bill, a resident whose movement and speech was severely limited, who spent most of his time in silence observing, became animated. We were making flavoured oils, with herbs grown in the garden and he wasn't allowed to taste anything because he had a restricted diet, so instead we gave him the oils and herbs to smell. When he smelt the garlic-infused oil his whole body convulsed, leapt forward and his eyes widened as he took a long deep breath in through his nose. Slowly and with great difficulty he began to tell us that he was a sailor and remembered when he first tasted garlic on one of his trips, a flavour so different from anything back home and he loved it. A revealing moment with the primary school students was when they were asked about their favourite food and one young girl said that her favourite is margarita pizza, but then went on to say it is because she ate it for the first time with her father who passed away. She went on to tell us that food reminds us of people we love who are not with us anymore and we began to see her in a new way, beyond her nine years and with an understanding of the depth of her experience. It is in these moments that people in a Phakama process connect with one another beyond the walls of the workshop space.

This process of encouraging people to see beyond outward appearance or stereotypes supports people with different experiences to find connections. In *The Edible Garden* two seemingly very different groups of people, of different generations, came together and create a shared space through their newly found common ground. In the project we did the first few workshops with the older and younger groups separately in order that we could get to know them individually first before bringing them together in the fourth week. In their first joint workshop we asked everyone to tell us the story of their first love or first crush. They were paired together and Patrick, who had lived in the East End of London since the 1950s, was partnered with João, a young man from Portugal, now living in London. These two seemingly very different people shared a life-affirming moment: João told Patrick about his first, and still current girlfriend, who he was in love with and wants to marry; Patrick, in turn, told João how he couldn't possibly remember who his first crush was as there had been so many! He went on to explain how he had arrived in London in the 1950s, a young man in the centre of town, always in the West End dancing with as many women as possible and described how he never settled down because he loved his bachelor life. Patrick went on to share his courtship advice to João and they created an affinity for one another in the most unlikely of ways. They both shared a real affection for each other, which came through the sharing of a story.

One of the moments of celebration that happens in a Phakama process is being recognized or understood by another person. In *The Edible Garden,* over and over again, younger and older participants said they didn't think others would be interested in them, that they were worried that they wouldn't want to hear what they had to say. The older participants said they were surprised by just how nice the students were and that if they saw this group of young people in the park across the road they would be afraid of them and try to avoid them. The younger people were amazed that the older people wanted to listen to them too. An example of this was when Lauren, the talented young vocalist, sang in the middle of one of the sessions. The older people shushed each other, trying to hear her. This was a revelation for the younger people, but what really surprised them was when the older people found out that another young woman, Tamana, could rap, they all wanted to listen to her and this style of music. It was a joyous exchange and confirmed a core tenet of Phakama that everyone has something to teach and everyone has something to learn.

In a Phakama process space is also celebrated. In the same spirit as accepting each person for who they are and what they offer, each space is accepted for its own inherent qualities and celebrated for what it is, rather than what it is not. Most often our work will take place outside of traditional theatre spaces and this too is approached as a virtue. Each place has its own possibilities and the work is created with that space in mind. One of the celebratory aspects of *The Edible Garden* was the way in which it made people and places look and feel the best they possibly could. The work was designed in response to the environment. The aesthetics of celebration were intrinsic to the work – thinking about the look, feel and activity of garden parties and how guests (the audience) are invited into a particular place. We opened up spaces, created communal tables, played music, gave opportunities for the audience to dress up for the event, decorated the space. Each care home presented its own challenge in relation to the size and layout of the outdoor space and because of that no two *Edible Garden* performances have been the same. We really have had to accept and embrace what was there and find a way to make it work. The first *Edible Garden* performance, in Mile End Children's Park, was set in a public and very open space, with multiple uses. We created a promenade where the audience first came into the growing space and were straight away invited to enjoy what had been grown by foraging in the raised beds. They were then led to another part of the park, to gather around the campfire and enjoy a cup of nettle tea with head gardener Lyndsay (for some of the young urban audience this was a first and revelatory experience). The audience then journeyed to another part of the park in which there was a rarely used, wooden amphitheatre, where we chose to stage a sing-a-long and the audience became the choir. Finally, the audience were led back through the park following wheelbarrows of food to the first space – the growing zone – which had been transformed into a banquet table for 100 guests laden with dishes, where they all sat down to enjoy the meal together, with the performers sitting beside them serving food and telling stories.

When *The Edible Garden* was performed at the first care home, the space was very different, with one large, private lawn and a smaller patio. The idea of travelling from space to space had to be considered in light of the older participants' restricted mobility. We decided to perform the opening on the patio, with drinks as the audience arrived, and then move through to the lawn, where we had created a large square of tables, which the audience sat around, with a playing space in the middle. Because the audience would mostly be stationary throughout the performance we focused instead on the decoration of the space. The tablecloths and napkins had been screen-printed with participants' stories. We thought carefully about the rhythm of the event so that the audience would have space to talk, eat, watch and participate equally. Some members of the audience got up spontaneously during the performance to sing or dance. It is important that the audience feel included in the making of the performance, as much as the participants felt included during the process leading to it.

We celebrate the audience, often asking them to make a contribution to the performance. In one event the audience were invited to tell one of their own food stories which was turned into a spontaneous ink painting and added to the extensive washing line of bunting which decorated the whole space. This was the same process that the participants had been through during workshops, whose paintings had formed the basis of the piece that was being shared with the audience. It is in this spirit that we aim to make connections between the audience and participants and create links that celebrate their shared process.

In order for there to be a celebration there has to be an invitation – an invitation to come, to join in, to participate and get involved, to bring something of yourselves to share with others. During a Phakama process the creative sessions can be seen as a continuous invitation. In *The Edible Garden*, as with all Phakama projects, there was a varied range of sessions that were delivered. These have included love-potion making, food storytelling, love-letter writing, hat and corsage making, aromatherapy massage, cyanotype prints, food tasting, Japanese tea ceremonies, singing, placemat and napkin making, planting. Our intention is that not everyone will enjoy every activity, but there can be one thing that sparks their interest. This was certainly true in *The Edible Garden*. In particular, I remember Grace, an older participant who was very vocal in telling us each week that she thought the activity was a waste of time and refused to join in. Her carer assured us this was normal and we continued to offer her opportunities to join in despite the fact nothing seemed to interest her. However, the week we created flowers and corsages from recycled plastic and used them to make hats, Grace suddenly became fully engaged. She smiled throughout the whole session, was vocal and animated and, after making her hat, refused to take it off. At every session after that she would ask when the party was going to be and when she could wear her hat. It was the one thing that gave her pleasure and when the day of the final performance arrived she felt connected to it. Grace's experience served as a reminder to the team to keep the invitations open and continuous.

It is these moments of connection to each other and the project that are celebrated and valued in a Phakama process. Every individual's enjoyment of what they are doing and of each other is fundamental to what we wanted to achieve with *The Edible Garden*. Yet these powerful moments of connection are also fleeting. The moments of celebrating who we are as individuals and who we can be collectively, though deeply felt, can only ever be transient. Every great party has to eventually come to an end. My abiding memory of the project was Ted's daughter telling us at that as she tucked him into bed at the end of the day of the performance he leaned in and said 'I can't quite remember what I did today but I know I had the most fantastic day'.

BECOMING

Introduction

I remember a very touching moment during an evaluation for the *Grundtvig* project (2002–2004) when a very experienced facilitator from one of our partner organisations questioned the value of the work asking 'what was this all for? We played and played but nothing of significance was achieved'. He went further to suggest that the work was a waste of time and that theatre work needed to teach 'proper' discipline and skills in order for young people to learn how to perform properly. This specific facilitator came from a traditional theatre background and struggled with what he called an unorthodox and inefficient way of making theatre. To which Faisu (a 19-year-old from Niger who has been working with Phakama UK for a couple of years) responded: 'It is like this, it may take you a while to understand yourself and become who you really are. It may take some time for you to even understand who you really want to be. So perhaps take this experience, pretend it is written in a piece of paper, fold it and put in your pocket. One day, maybe in a year's time, take that piece of paper out and read it. You will be surprised by who you have become as a result of this experience'. (Santos 2015)

The Phakama process can, at times, be challenging to some people. More often than not, the more experienced adults who are in leadership roles are the ones who struggle with the way the process works. But as demonstrated by Faisu, it seems that young people (who have fewer preconceptions about how theatre can be made) embrace the process and are open for new connections and discoveries to take place. Charlotte McCabe (2015), a former *Spotlight* participant now a Phakama UK board member, illustrates this sense of openness when she describes her first experience of working with Phakama:

Joining Phakama as a new participant with little knowledge of theatre/drama and being told by the end of the project we were going to work together to produce some sort of performance was a daunting prospect. Working together with different people who had no experience of the Phakama way of doing things, allowed us to grow in confidence together when it came to being open and creative.

During my first few days, Phakama made us feel very welcome and allowed us to embrace their way of learning in our own time. The process of 'Give and Gain' gave us the opportunity to showcase the skills we had to bring but also how much we could learn from each other.

By the end of the project, we all became extremely ambitious in what we could achieve, which in turn made us more passionate on putting on a great performance for everyone. Phakama gave me the freedom to explore, be creative and grow as an artist.

Charlotte's description illustrates how being open to try new things, revealing different aspects of oneself, embracing both the struggle and the joy can enhance a person's sense of themselves, not just who they have been but who they could be. It is an iterative, ongoing process of 'becoming'. Entering the liminal space of not knowing, as alluded by Lucy Neal in her essay below, and acknowledging feelings of grief as much as joy and hope, is an important process within Phakama's work. In 'Alive to the Music of What Happens', Lucy Neal reflects on her experience of Phakama, the sociopolitical context that shaped Phakama's early years, and considers how the model of a creative spiral, developed by environmental activist Joanna Macy's in *The Work That Reconnects*, can frame projects to productively and precisely examine facets of celebration within Phakama's work.

ALIVE TO THE MUSIC OF WHAT HAPPENS

Lucy Neal

'What is the finest music in the world?' asked the hero of the Gaels, giant Fionn MacCumhaill. 'A cuckoo calling from the hedge?' his followers replied 'a spear ringing on a shield; the sound of a child laughing?'. 'All good music', Fionn agreed, 'but the best music is the music of what happens'. (MacKillop 1986)

'The music of what happens' lies at the heart of celebration. Being alive to the moment when people's individual narratives flow into a story larger than themselves can offer a radical experience of joy: moments of transformation that carry us along as we sense connection to the wider dance of life of which we are a part. With a tangible shift, the story we have been making, ends up making us.

In its creative processes and final performances, celebration is a central characteristic of Phakama's work. Difference is celebrated, along with shared values, individual capabilities and, up against deadlines, miraculous, collective achievements. That 'something happens' once a Phakama project is underway is acknowledged by Phakama artist, Jenny Macdonald (2014):

> For *Breaking the Glass Box* (2004) we had a title and before we had even begun to make the show, someone said, great news, the show is booked out. Every time we go, that's crazy, how will we do it? And then every time, we do it. And that gives us courage for art making. For life. Imagine things and they will happen. Give it a try. There has to be a moment of nothing and allowing something to happen.

This essay gets beneath the skin of those celebratory, change-making moments and the reasons they hold such transformative energy. I describe a visit to Cape Town in 1998 when a personal Phakama narrative of celebration began for me as it exemplifies the dance of roles, common to all Phakama processes, between witness and participant; roles that switch and blur, affecting one's perception of what is being celebrated and how. Four more Phakama projects are framed by the environmental activist Joanna Macy's model of a creative spiral from *The Work*

That Reconnects to examine facets of celebration, revealing what is at play when celebratory events act as a catalyst for individual and collective change.

Met'n Sak Onner die Blad/With a Suitcase in My Hand (Cape Town, July 1998)

I'll never forget the roar as I stepped inside the Mary Atlee Sports Hall on Retreat Road, in the Cape Flats.[1] Phakama artist tutor, Pogiso Mogwera, led the drummers as one hundred young people from London, Seshego and Mmabatho sang and danced, rehearsing a show called *Met'nSak Onner die Blad/With a Suitcase in My Hand*. Their collective energy knocked me off my feet and lifted my soul to the rafters. I sensed whatever had been happening until that point had been extraordinary and whatever was going to happen, equally so.

I learnt later of the long journeys many had undertaken to get there and the mix of places people had travelled from: poor and affluent urban areas; rural districts and townships such as Lavender Hill and Khayelitsha. One group was from London. Twenty-four artist tutors from different cultural backgrounds brought arts and education skills. Visits had been made to the District Six Museum, Cape Town's castle and Robben Island: sites resonating with South Africa's long history of injustice, suffering and inequality between races. Nelson Mandela spent eighteen of his twenty-seven prison years on Robben Island, while the District Six Museum was a memorial to one of Cape Town's most vibrant, multicultural port communities, bulldozed down to create a 'whites only' area, forcibly moving 60,000 'coloured' people to the outlying Cape Flats. In contrast to lush vineyards rising up towards Table Mountain, the Cape Flats had poor soil and were subject to cold winds and flooding. Sixty years on from the forced removals they were still dotted with rows of corrugated iron shacks. The large-scale Phakama performance being rehearsed would take place at the Gilray Scout Camp in nearby Grassy Park. Focusing on memory and reconciliation, it explored responses to the Cape Town cultural visits with dance, theatre, fire and song.

I had arrived here from the Grahamstown Festival, South Africa's most prestigious arts event, in its historic twenty-fifth year. In a post-apartheid world, the festival was recognizing evident inequalities: thousands of visitors descended on the well-endowed university town surrounded by townships with 70 per cent unemployment, to enjoy theatre, film, opera and the visual arts. Children from the townships danced outside venues for twenty cents (approximately two pence in British sterling); private swimming pools were within walking distance of

---

[1] The Mary Attlee Centre was a renovated milk shed on a Jersey Barn Farm, converted into a Sports and Recreational Hall in response to the appalling living conditions – poverty, disease, malnutrition and severe winter flooding – experienced in the southern areas of the Cape Peninsula.

schools with no water. I was there as director of the LIFT Festival: adventurous, experimental performances were core to our mission of exploring theatre's role in the world for telling new stories and creating different futures. With a cultural boycott in place throughout LIFT's first fifteen years, we'd sought guidance from the African National Congress in London who supported cultural visits that gave insight into the injustices of the apartheid regime. John Kani, one of South Africa's leading actor-directors, said the plays were not protests, they are 'simply a record of what is happening to people in their everyday lives' (Fenton and Neal 2005: 53).

Few of the theatre relationships committed to by LIFT had the richness and continuity that we developed with colleagues in South Africa, many from the groundbreaking Johannesburg Market Theatre and their productions including *Starbrites* (LIFT '91), *Jozi Jozi* (LIFT '95) and *The Suit* (LIFT '95).[2] After Mandela's release from prison in 1991, South Africa's great theatre maker, Barney Simon (cofounder of the Market Theatre with Mannie Manim) advised Rose Fenton, my co-director, and I, of the pressing need to hear South Africa's untold stories. He thought storytelling and listening to stories were as organic to our survival 'as oxygen', fostering exactly the celebratory spirit of hope into which Phakama was born (SIDA 2004: 10).

Grahamstown's stage narratives of the 'new' South Africa unsettled me to my core: stories of guns, hijacking, violence, robbery and murder. Issues for a younger generation were the loss of black male youth from any socially engaged systems and the commonplace rape of young girls. There was a desperate need for an education system in which a safer, fairer future could be shaped equally by all. It was in Capetown's Grassy Park with Phakama's young theatre makers I found the stories Barney had imagined. A process of transformation was underway, carrying young people along with a shared focus on what could be achieved together.

Recovering my breath from the singing that greeted me, I studied the Give and Gain skills wheel on the sportshall wall: 'what can I give?' in yellow, 'what can I gain?' in red, mapping everyone's role in the creation of the show. I was dazzled by the self-organization going on around me. 'The bits you know we'll just do' announced Lucy Richardson, as rehearsals shifted to the Scout Camp. The rate at which young people were learning from the intensity of the process, was evident all around me: 'I've learnt' said one young person 'how to back someone up'. Phakama, had cracked a nut of how to learn through others and that included me: What could I give, what could I gain? With so much in swing, what was my role? How could I join this dance? From witness to participant, I entered a liminal space of not knowing. From swanning about as festival director, it was time to roll my own sleeves up.

---

[2] LIFT presented *Dirty Work and Gangsters* by Bahamutsi (LIFT '85) and *You Strike the Women, You Strike the Rock*, performed by Vusisizwe Players (LIFT '87). *You Strike the Women You Strike the Rock* was about the 1956 march on Pretoria by 20,000 women against the decision to impose Pass Laws on black women. This show was directed by Phyllis Klotz who issued the first invitation to LIFT in 1996 to collaborate in a series of exchanges that led to the creation of Phakama.

I was allocated the job of marketing a show in the making, to an as yet unidentified public, with four days to go. My 'office' was the Scout Master's Hut, with one small table, a landline and a telephone directory (no Google then) and an encouraging sign on the wall: 'Almighty God who has given us the Great Scout'. The Chief Scout had been Lord Baden-Powell and I was now the marketing scout, talking loudly to any television, press and radio editors I could get hold of on the telephone. Camp excitement rose as I proclaimed the project's worth to the outside world, actively recruiting new 'witnesses'.

To our delight, South African Broadcast Corporation's Cape News sent a crew on opening night. 'I was a scout here' confided the director wistfully as he peered around in the gloaming. He and the crew were called away, sadly, at the last minute to report on a shooting in Atlantis – 'seven dead'. As they pulled away, with sirens sounding, I sensed both their regret and our fortune of playing a part in a more positive story. Under a beautiful full moon, I'd entered the celebratory swing of the story.

In *Met'nSak Onner die Blad/With a Suitcase in My Hand* performers danced and sang. Hidden stories lay in each healing layer of performance. We heard the chink of prisoner rocks on Robben Island; visited moonlit graveyards and around a fire circle, warming stones were taken from the fire and handed out to be placed in the Chapel of Confessions. Reconciliations were enacted at historic, symbolic and personal levels. Olivia Barron-Beukman, a participant, reflects: 'At Gilray, we saw fire from the candles reflected in the audience's eyes and all past hatred burnt away. Years of it. We saw all the atrocities and all the hate through the work. People saw their own histories and parents' and grandparents' (2014). Moved and excited, the audiences danced, ate *koeksisters* in the scout hut and drank hot coffee. Magic was conjured beneath a full moon. I wondered how, in two weeks, people could move individually and collectively to such transformative connection. As we sang *Shosholoza,*[3] I wanted to understand how a celebratory atmosphere grew from the toughest of human experiences.

Solemn and Exuberant

The Latin word *celebrare* means 'to assemble to honour', paying attention to difficulty and loss while also affirming things of exuberant joy. As the Gilray Camp experience showed, feelings of grief and injustice as much as joy and hope gave the gathering space and meaning. Weaving solemnity and exuberance together made the journey towards celebration rich in the potential for new possibilities and change. Many

---

[3] *Shosholoza* is a call and response folk song originating in Zimbabwe and popularized in South Africa. Thought to have been sung by all-male migrant mine workers, it is often referred to as South Africa's second national anthem.

Phakama projects follow a classic pattern of a rite of passage: moments of transition in individual's lives when something happens and nothing is quite the same again. Rituals ushering us across such thresholds lie at the heart of many indigenous traditions, giving depth and form to life. These can open us to human emotions in often disorientating ways. Joyous and sad by turns, they can be testing, sometimes overwhelmingly so. Interrupting chronological time, they can carry the hidden texts of our lives, making visible our connections to each other, links between past present and future and rhythms of the natural world. They can help us begin again; a process ritual theorist Ronald Grimes calls 'transforming and renewing the real' (2002: 4). Initiation – a word common in rites of passage means a return to the beginning, a chance to recalibrate what really matters. Like life, such rituals – rather like a Phakama process – cannot be watched but must be enacted, embodied, participated in. Theatre director and long-term associate of Welfare State International, Gilly Adams, articulates this process: 'Any rite of passage is a kind of journey. It takes us over a threshold, to cross to mark change in our lives, through transitional or liminal space into the next stage of life. It has a form that can be analysed: separation – transition into change – reincorporation into the group' (2015: 152).

These patterns are recognizable in Phakama's work: individuals (especially on residential projects) leave places that are familiar to them and encounter new people. They enter a liminal space, where ordinary time is suspended. Out of one's comfort zone, there is an experience of feeling lost and confused, yet open to chance and change. Possibly, only then can something else appear. With the deadline of a show moving us forward, we scramble onto dry land with others and raise a cheer, altered, sometimes for ever.

A Creative Spiral

Such archetypal journeying can be explored further using Joanna Macy's model of a creative spiral from *The Work That Reconnects*. Macy's approach was seeded in US activist nuclear disarmament work in the 1960s and 1970s. It was further developed in Chernobyl, working with communities affected by despair after the catastrophic Soviet nuclear disaster in 1986. *The Work That Reconnects* is practised on many continents, in many languages. It includes a four-stage process, structured as a spiral, that allows people to move through personal feelings while acknowledging the deep troubles of the world to mobilize energy and commitment for action at times of uncertainty. In our current era of ecological uncertainty, Macy's work has been adopted by groups working with artists, health workers, community activists and climate scientists alike.[4]

---

[4]For more information about the *Work That Reconnects* network and reach of Joanna Macy's practice see http://workthatreconnects.org (accessed 22 May 2016).

In Macy's words the spiral 'helps us develop our inner resources and our outer community and strengthens our capacity to face disturbing information and respond with unexpected resilience' (2012: 6). Developing people's 'inner resources' and 'outer community' strikes a Phakama chord. Macy is a scholar of Buddhism, the environmental and ecological philosophy known as deep ecology, and a systems thinker (studying the parts of any system in dynamic relation to the whole). She recognizes that systemic change is not a linear process but a dynamic, iterative process with change happening on many fronts at once. The creative spiral, which supports people's capacity to act in and for the world, follows an archetypal structure with four distinct stages common to stories of facing adversity. These are detailed in *Active Hope* (2012: 37–40):

- 'Coming from Gratitude' – thankfulness and praise for what we have.
- 'Honouring Pain' – accepting difficulty, honouring the pain of the world.
- 'Seeing With New Eyes' – seeing things from a shifted perspective.
- 'Going Forth' – the point at which things are resolved and energy is mobilized.

Each stage unfolds into the next to create a strengthening journey, especially when repeated. The four elements work together, to form a whole, more than the sum of its parts. To deconstruct the Phakama process through the journeying celebration takes through adverse experiences, four Phakama projects are described following Macy's spiral. They show how celebration is key to building our capabilities, transforming ourselves and our world. In combination they make a narrative of change, building community from many people's stories and creating momentum for rethinking the future. An element of Macy's creative spiral is highlighted in each story, although all four stages of the spiral are inherent within them.

'Coming from Gratitude': *Message in a Bottle* (London, 2012)

In 'Coming from Gratitude' (2012: 38–9, 70) we are present to being alive; to gifts bestowed on us from the natural world and beauty. We turn attention from what is missing to what is already there, liberating us from a place of need and the idea that things are wrong. Gratitude puts ground under our feet, drawing on feelings of trust and empathy to bring out the best in us. In many indigenous cultures, celebrations of praise and thanksgiving mark cooperation with one another, personal well-being and appreciation of the natural world. Paying attention to what is cherished and valued, we become aware of what is violated or threatened in the world.

In *Message in a Bottle*, sixty-five 16–25-year-olds from the Basque Country, Ireland, Poland, Portugal, Turkey and the UK met for a two-week-long residency in London to investigate water's potential to create beauty and life, as well as destruction and unrest. Different ways of making art were exchanged, while exploring a potential scenario for 2025 (when participants would be in their 30s) of more than half the world's population being vulnerable to a lack of fresh drinking water. The weeks built connection and gratitude through sharing meals, traditional foods, recipes from grandmothers and accompanying cultural stories. Stories of six water-based cities emerged: from Lisbon where the Tagus meets the Atlantic; San Sebastiån, home to whale-hunting; Lublin's Vistula valley; Dublin's river Liffy; and Istanbul where the Bosporus links Asia to Europe. Fragments of London's history were dug up with archaeologist Mike Webber on the River Thames foreshore.

An environmental researcher from Essex University, Dr Zhareen Bharucha, was invited to explain the accelerated journey water is on due to global warming: warmer air changes the currents flowing around the world, melting glaciers, flooding coasts and causing heavy rain to fall, with risks to food production, ocean acidification and species loss. Science became tangible when water that participants had brought from their home cities was tested on the spot by Thames21: London's Regent's Canal was cleaner than expected while Irish hill water was contaminated by farming. Fabio Santos reflected on these findings: 'The amount of creativity and debate generated after these discoveries was astonishing. ... We glimpsed how water shapes the way we live and the socio-political dynamics within societies across Europe' (2015).

The week culminated in a performance in June 2012 at Queen Mary University of London, along the Regent's Canal as part of Phakama's *Velela!* Festival. Distant histories mixed with mythic beings and futuristic societies along with a celebration of our role as stewards of the planet. Art made a common language and water became the conduit for conversations and working partnerships. Basque anthropology students worked with artists from Dublin; rappers from Poland connected to dancers from Portugal. Lublin's Nicole taught people to make Bokashi balls – a Japanese technique mixing clay and bacteria to decontaminate rivers and oceans after ecological disasters. 'We evolved an incredible sense of being grateful for what we had', said Santos. 'Water and our growing knowledge about it as a precious resource' (2015). Water catalysed knowledge that an individual's well-being depends on the well-being of the natural world.

Gratitude builds a vital role of celebration by reversing a sense that things are wrong or missing. 'This dynamic', says Macy, 'pulls us into a cycle of regeneration' and 'our readiness to help others is influenced by the level of gratitude we experience' (2012: 45, 54). She continues, 'Gratitude feeds trust, because it helps us acknowledge the times we've been able to count on one another' (2012: 45). A new story of connection and trust becomes possible, enhancing our resilience in adversity, or what Macy calls 'Pain for our World'.

'Honoring our Pain for the World': *Strange Familiars* (London, 2003)

Facing adversity makes gratitude for life important, as the second stage of Macy's spiral, 'Honoring our Pain for the World', makes clear. The more we shy away from difficult emotions or realities, the less confident we are we can deal with them, yet they are real and matter. Macy frames 'honoring pain' as a way of valuing an awareness of difficulty, welcoming it, even when as great as 'the pain of the world' – such as ecological collapse and species extinction. We show that we notice and we care. When pain is acknowledged, emotional resource can be freed up for living.

Strange Familiars responded to London's increasing numbers of young refugees and unaccompanied asylum seekers, to explore the 'strange' and 'familiar' in the city. Collaborations with the Refugee Council and Camden, Southwark and Kensington and Chelsea local authorities engaged young people recently arrived from Africa, Eastern Europe, the Balkans and South America. Participants had experiences in common: fear and the flight from conflict; separation from family and home; and a loss of a sense of belonging.

Weekend residentials, held over a ten-month period with hundred people, culminated in a public performance at the National Children's Home (NCH), as part of the LIFT 2003 theatre season. The project sought to build confidence and life skills, while psychiatrists and social workers supported individuals who had experienced painful traumas, many from childhood.

Osman Bah was one of the young people who participated in the project. In an interview published in *Open Democracy* (Rebehn 2004), he spoke candidly about his experiences as a child soldier in Liberia and of his participation in *Strange Familiars*: 'It was very good to meet people from every part of the world. Every Saturday … We would make a drama by splitting into four groups and rehearsing, then we would perform to each other. We also do drumming, singing and dancing. We learnt a lot about acting and theatre.'

Artist tutor Tab Neal (2015), overseeing the story and design threads woven into *Strange Familiars*, recalls:

Two artists designed each workshop leading up to the week's residential at NCH. Participants were familiar with the location by the time of the final show. There were disagreements within the group, sometimes they were even at loggerheads, but there was also hilarity. I was impressed at how quickly participants grasped the right forms to use as communication, whether it was poetry, dance, large puppets, storytelling, drawing, music or song and their agility to improvise with resources to hand. They were chock full of stories to hear. We explored the common ground, for example everyone telling a story about a tree. Two boys, Mateo and Mauro, talked about climbing a tree to collect mangoes, and how they would turn upside down and dangle down over the river.

One workshop built 'dream' rooms from matchsticks to seed images and designs for the promenade performance, in and around the house and grounds. Osman says:

> We added new ideas including Good Dream and Bad Dream rooms. I designed a room with a tree made out of bamboo sticks with false fruits hanging. ... I sat alone with only one dim light hanging at the top. I was wearing African clothes and sitting in the corner with a piece of paper. I used this to tell my story. That was my first taste of performance.

As a member of the audience, Osman's story has stayed with me down the years. Born in the northern Liberia, he talked about the country's civil war and how his family took refuge in neighbouring villages. One terrible morning, he'd heard fighting and returned home to find his mother and father shot dead. His sister also died. Captured by rebel fighters, Osman was recruited as a boy soldier, subjected to the brutality of the training camps. Escaping, he came to England where he had to fend for himself. A Peckham resident, recognizing his language, took him in and contacted the Refugee Council. It was here he made contact with Phakama. Tab Neal reflects on Osman's determination to tell aspects of his personal narrative during the performance:

> He was candid. It was his story and he wanted to tell it. He performed with such dignity, reading what he had written aloud to the audience who came into his 'room' during each performance. He never wavered. He said it was his duty to tell it. There were times when he came out wretched and broken – of course it had an effect on him – but he also reached out to the others to care for them.

Osman's story was one of many shared in *Strange Familiars*. Tab continues:

> My most powerful memory of *Strange Familiars* is of going to Amsterdam with a group of three participants to collect the prestigious Anne Frank Award on behalf of Phakama. On the way back, the authorities wouldn't let one of the participants return to Britain, suggesting he should be returned to his country of origin. The young man knew that returning to his home could mean death: his father had been arrested as a political agitator, and consequently so had he and he had escaped. He had been waiting in the UK to hear from the Red Cross what he suspected – that both his parents could be dead. The support and courage the others gave to this young man, who was finally allowed to travel back to England, was incredible. They understood his pain and honoured it. As artist facilitators we make safe space for young people to create their stories with art, but the extent to which they identified with and helped each other was inspirational.

'Once anguish and despair are shared', observes Macy, 'people emerge energised and nourished by the experience. ... Feeling part of a much larger team can anchor and steady us through times of difficulty' (2012: 68, 121). In the role between witness and participant, tutors play a part in facilitating performances and holding safe space to honour pain; building trust, so that transformation and 'seeing with new eyes' becomes possible. Their emotional participation is called upon along with a shift in perspective that they're connected as participants also.

'Seeing with New Eyes': *Tripwires* (London, 2011) and *Spotlight* (London, 2013–15)

The third stage of the spiral, 'Seeing with New Eyes', is characterized by this shift of identification; a wider sense of self and knowledge things can happen through you along with a renewed sense of fellowship and community. A sense of agency emerges, along with new found capacities for action. As Osman has said:

> The projects ... I have done have changed my life. They have made me see that with art you can bring people together. You can make people feel happy. You can make people think that they are important in the world, really important. I have found myself here in London. (Rebehn 2004)

Tripwires worked with Index on Censorship to engage in debates around freedom of expression. The project seeded *Spotlight*,[5] a series of two year-long training programmes in the creative industries for 18–24-year-olds not in employment, education or training. Each year fifteen young people went 'behind the scenes' to be trained in design, budgeting, fundraising, communications, lighting, sound and front of house.

The rise in UK university tuition fees and cuts to youth provision heralded a difficult era for young people: nationally, one in five young people and 50 per cent of all black 16–24-year-olds were out of work. The Office of National Statistics reported that the Borough of Tower Hamlets, where Phakama was based, had the highest level of youth unemployment in London. Ethnic minority representation in the creative industries, already as low as 4 per cent, was in danger of dropping lower, making the sector a preserve of the privileged. Spotlight training included placements with professional arts organizations and culminated in Festival in which trainees curated and produced programmes of installation, theatre and

---

[5] *Spotlight* was funded by the CCSkills as part of its Creative Employment Programme and developed in collaboration with Queen Mary University of London, The Backstage Centre, Hackney Community College and Essex Creative Skills along with established organizations in the sector including LIFT, Free Word and Graeae among others.

film.[6] Lance Kirby, recruited via a Job Centre, who went on to become a producer of his own performances and events, describes the experience:

> With the eight-week placement, my time was jam packed. We devised a performance about food, consumerism and over indulgence. Because I came from an arts background the others said 'you do the directing'. I was shaking in my boots. I had power as director, I just didn't know what to do with it!

The collaborative process was testing but the rewards shifted Lance's sense of his own role and capabilities:

> I'd had a negative view of myself. As a child I was called 'slow' – and IT'S NOT TRUE! At school, collaboration was not glorified, it was a lot about individuality. I used to think I had to do things on my own but I like working in a group, reaching for a common goal. Two minds are better than one. I wouldn't have said that before Spotlight.

Lance expresses what Macy describes as 'seeing with new eyes': 'When people experience themselves as part of a group with a shared purpose, team spirit flows through them, and their central organising principle changes' (2012: 114). The guiding question moves from 'What can I gain?' to 'What can I give?' This is illustrated by the comments from *Spotlight* participants. Lance said, 'The best I can do for myself is in a group. It's important to me that people get an amazing experience so I can say, I did my best for those people. It made me more confident. My eyes were opened' (2015). Lora Krasteva, another participant, reiterated this, saying: '*Spotlight* showed me how many paths there are in the creative and cultural industries ... there are many people like me: lost and confused, eager to learn and create. But there are also many others; those ready to hear us, help us and teach us' (2014). One of those ready to hear, help and teach was Lucy Richardson. Acting as the trainees' artist mentor, she recognized how much she gained herself from the 'brave, imaginative and determined yet inexperienced trainees' (*Spotlight Evaluation* 2014). She notes, 'Phakama works on the basis that you don't design a show but rather a capacity, a structure from which a show can emerge' (2004: 5).

Macy draws us back to the relevance of systems:

> No one part has to have the whole answer. Rather, the intelligence of the whole emerges through the actions and interactions of many parts. ... What allows a team to gel is a shift in identification, so that people identify with, and act for, the team rather than just themselves. ... For a complex system to self-organise and function well, it requires both the integration and differentiation of its parts. (2012: 93, 100)

---

[6] Eighty per cent of Phakama recruits were from ethnic minority groups and East London.

Systems theory itself shows that the relationships in any system are strong and resilient where there are the most connections. Phakama hones a system for creating space to connect and bring different skills. Ben Victor (2014), a Spotlight trainee, details this idea and practice of the system when he says, 'You can only learn what you need to take from other people by taking a look at yourself and knowing what you don't bring to the table, and that's not a negative thing, it's an opportunity to pick things up from different people, different places.' A distributed intelligence means 'the players act freely while being guided by their intention to serve the purpose of the group' (2012: 99–100). Drawing on a diverse plurality of voices creates a more stable foundation for collective action.

'Going Forth': *The Trashcatchers' Carnival* (Tooting, London, 2010)

> This discovery that you are not alone is critical for young people in the developing world. ... The process is about thinking about 'we' not 'I'. (Banning 2005: 158)

Knowing you're not alone is a decisive factor in gaining the courage to 'go forth', the final stage of the spiral: the moment in which the many paths contributing to a shared vision, converge and connect, leading to something more ambitious than any one person could ever envisage. 'Seeing with new eyes', leads to strong onward collective action; imagining different possible futures and formulating creative responses to new challenges.

The Tooting *Trashcatchers' Carnival* drew energy from a physical and symbolic 'going forth' on a major public highway. The Carnival turned the south-west London suburb of Tooting, where I live, on its head for a day. Celebrating our relationship to Earth, it set out to make beauty from rubbish, using recycling as a metaphor for change. A year in preparation, it brought hundreds of *carnivalistas* together from Tooting's community groups, schools, streets, shops and faith houses. Produced by Transition Town Tooting, part of a global network of communities rebuilding local resilience to imagine a low carbon future and led by Phakama's Fabio Santos and Emergency Exit Arts' Deb Mullins, it was one of the first UK Tipping Point Commissions that brought together the arts and climate change.

The Carnival told the story of the Sankofa bird, a mythical creature carrying a seed of the future under its wing. Creative workshops conjured ideas for stories, music and costumes from the local community. Peak Oil and climate change workshops, adapted from Macy's own creative spiral, formed a four-stage cycle of work undertaken over the year. The Carnival, which imagined a sustainable future for the town, would be Tooting's 'Going Forth'. An abstracted sense of a possible future translated into the concrete challenge of creating a Carnival from scratch. Milk containers used by worshippers at the Sivayogam Hindu Temple were diverted to schools to be made into baby elephants. A narrative emerged as fish, elephants and octopuses took over school halls. A Giant Turtle led the water section; Share Community Garden pedalled an eight-wheeled octoped cycle and an imaginary Lady of Tooting appeared with hundreds of children and memories in her skirts. Four hundred children at one school announced they wanted to be animals, 'so that people would know that humans were not the only beings on the planet'. A space for loss as well as fun gave depth to the resulting celebration.

Transport for London declined requests to close one of London's busy 'arterial corridors', the A24, Tooting High Road. It was important, one primary head said, that the Carnival was 'visible to and significant for the local community' and at the eleventh hour the procession was registered with Scotland Yard as a public protest, albeit a highly colourful and celebratory one. The police had a legal obligation to allow such direct action on public roads.

James Hadley, Phakama's Arts Council officer at the time, recalls how the High Road was transformed:

> I sensed not just what had happened but what was about to happen. Everything held in those brilliant, still moments of sitting and waiting for the Carnival to appear. I sensed a rhythm of readiness; all the negotiations that had been going on and the fact the Carnival was needed.

As the Giant Gardener rounded the corner and *carnivalistas* drummed and danced, policemen took pictures and shops emptied to watch. In delight, people hung out of car windows and buses. Gathering on the open Fishponds Fields, nine-year-old James sang *Senzeni Na*, a South African anti-apartheid folk song from the top of the Turtle and flags fluttered in the breeze. Silence fell as people gathered in a circle to admire what they'd made. The story we had been making was beginning to make us. A good future on Earth felt possible – what one of the 800 *carnivalistas* called 'whole joy'. For one sunny afternoon, a playful, peaceful creative community came to life. The Carnival showed what was possible: 'If we can do that' people said, 'we can do anything' – a rehearsal for what could come next.

In a post-apartheid South Africa in Mmabatho, intense dialogues with police negotiated crossing a four-lane highway for *Call Me Not a Woman* in 2001. A 'going forth', said LIFT's Anna Ledgard (2015), part of Phakama's team, with 'considerable symbolic potential':

> Not only was (the road) an economic boundary between wealthier and poorer residents, between township and non-township housing, but also the main artery into the town and therefore the site of travel restrictions, road closures and blockages which had been the familiar tool of the Apartheid regime.

Audiences, escorted by performers and drummers, on foot, in donkey carts and tractors, joined police in riot uniform who danced along with everyone. Barriers came down; behaviours changed, and young people observed Julia Rowntree, laid claim 'to civic engagement, social responsibility and cultural continuity for their own communities' (2006: 94). Roles of witness and participant extended beyond immediate circles of participants to create change. Speaking of such collaborative arts practices, Sarah Woods, a playwright and associate of Emergence, an organization dedicated to arts and sustainability, says: 'Artists give communities, audiences, people involved a relationship to the idea of change. The artwork itself is about change, and has a relationship to change. It's about participation … about people being active' (Hopkins 2015). The notion of 'being active' and having a part to play is the core quality of celebration and we can all be players in action.

Energizing Capacity for Action

These stories show how celebrating helps people draw on qualities of courage, creativity and resilience to be more than the circumstances they have endured or may have to endure. Celebration energizes our capacities for action, transforming our capabilities at individual, collective and societal levels. It helps us meet the demands being made of us, keeps us going and reinvents us. Chris Johnstone, Macy's collaborator on *Active Hope*, proposed, 'I see celebration as one of those things that nourishes us psychologically, emotionally, spiritually. Without celebration, we wither away' (Hopkins 2014). Celebration reinforces values within a group, galvanizing an energy to defend and champion those values. It nourishes our enthusiasm for life, suggests Macy herself, lifting us towards an engagement with responsibility for life.

Phakama was born at a time when new stories were needed in South Africa. Its work today is made at an equally historic time, when radical change is needed to rethink the future and take responsibility for life. A new geological era called the 'anthropocene', means that everyday human activities are affecting the planet's lifesystem. At such a time, looking backward and forward, like the Sankofa bird, it is hard to imagine we are accountable for reimagining our world on behalf of ourselves and subsequent generations. At times of uncertainty, it can feel counter-intuitive to celebrate, yet the celebratory social spaces Phakama creates help us generate collective knowledge and a sense of wonder at what is possible. Assembling to honour both pain and joy, developing 'inner resources' and 'outer community' are the key to the creation of new stories about being human on Earth.

Emerging from an uncertain 'muddle in the middle', with a show materializing sometimes from a cast of one hundred and no script other than the experiences and stories each carries within them, we find we have given and gained important new knowledge of what it is to be human. We have a place to begin again from, with a part to play in the larger whole. This is the knowledge needed for survival and resilience: a place from which, together, under a full and beautiful moon, we may roar again. This is the music of what happens, and Fionn was right, it is the best.

References

Adams, G. (2015), 'Rites of Passage', in Lucy Neal (ed.), *Playing for Time – Making Art As If the World Mattered*, London: Oberon Books.

Barron-Beckman, O. (2014), Interview with Lucy Richardson and Caroline Calburn, Cape Town, 30 May.

de Wend Fenton, R. and L. Neal (2005), *The Turning World: Stories from the London International Festival of Theatre*, London: Calouste Gulbenkian Foundation.

Grimes, R. L. (2002), *Deeply into The Bone: Re-inventing Rites of Passage*, Berkeley, CA: University of California Press.

Hadley, J. (2015), Interview with Lucy Richardson, Fabio Santos and Caoimhe McAvinchey, London Metropolitan University, 20 March.

Hopkins, R. (2014), 'Chris Johnstone: "Without Celebration, we wither Away" ', *Transition Network*, 15 July. Available online: https://www.transitionnetwork.org/blogs/rob-hopkins/2014-07/chris-johnstone-without-celebration-we-wither-away (accessed 15 October 2015).

Hopkins, R. (2015), 'What Does a Successful Artist Look Like at a Time of Global Change?', *Transition Network*, 27 April. Available online: https://www.transitionnetwork.org/blogs/rob-hopkins/2015-04/what-does-successful-artist-look-time-global-change (accessed 15 October 2015).

Kirby, L. (2015), Interview with Lucy Neal, London, 3 October.

Krasteva, L. (2015), Interview with Lucy Neal, London, 3 October.

Ledgard, A. (2015), Personal Correspondence, 19 June.

Macy, J. and C. Johnstone (2012), *Active Hope: How to Face the Mess We're in Without Going Crazy*. Novato, CA: New World Library.

MacKillop, J. (1986), *Fionn MacCumhaill: Celtic Myth in English Literature*, New York: Syracuse University Press.

Macdonald, J. (2014), Phakama Research Meeting, QMUL, London, 17 December.

Neal, T. (2015), Interview with Lucy Neal, London, 15 July.

Phakama (2013), *Spotlight* Evaluation, Internal Report.

Rebehn, M. (2004), ' "I Was a Child Soldier": Interview with Osman Bah', *Open Democracy*, 22 January. https://www.opendemocracy.net/people-migrationeurope/article_1685.jsp (accessed 22 May 2016).

Richardson, L. (2004), 'Phakama: A Place of Refuge', paper delivered at On Location: women, place and representation, London Metropolitan University. https://www.projectphakama.org/wp-content/uploads/2012/08/A-Place-of-Refuge-Article.pfd (accessed 22 May 2016).

Rowntree, J. (2006), *Changing the Performance: A Companion Guide to Arts, Business and Civic Engagement*, London: Routledge.

Santos, F. (2015), Correspondence with Lucy Neal, 20 December.

SIDA (2004), *Crossing Boundaries: The Market Theatre/Stickholms Stadsteater 1994-2004*, Stockholm: Swedish International Development Cooperation Agency.

Victor, B. (2014), Interview with Lucy Richardson and Fabio Santos, London, 10 December.

STEPPING UP

During the research for this book, people spoke time and again about how their involvement with Phakama helped them step up, to take responsibility, to offer ideas, to lead a group of people through the realization of an idea, to see their individual contribution as part of a wider network of relationships and possibilities. Throughout the book there are many examples where individuals testify to this increased confidence and resilience. Jake Boston joined Phakama in 2007 and has continued to collaborate with Phakama on a number of projects since. He talks about his own personal and artistic development (2016):

> Since joining Phakama I have had the confidence to be open-minded, to be free – to Phakama – to rise up! To shout, to scream, to laugh, to cry and remember the good times; to be frustrated, to be angry. To be empowered enough to create my own company; only through Phakama has this been possible.

What people take with them and apply in the world, how the work impacted them personally and professionally, how communities and organizations changed as a result are all reasons for celebration. Sam Quinn (2015), a participant who has collaborated on Phakama projects since 2007, says:

> I think it's fair to say that a great deal of my career since leaving university has been influenced by Phakama – my acting CV is full of Phakama productions … without this experience I would not have been employable as a drama facilitator.

The Phakama process helps people understand themselves better and more accepting of the many aspects at play in other people. Juancho Gonzalez (2015) touches on this when speaking about his involvement in the *Trashcatchers* project:

> I just finished university and got to know Phakama hands-on. We were chucked into this room and we were told that we were going to do *Trashcatchers*. From the very first day I understood the whole concept behind the Phakama's Give and Gain; don't think that you're just giving stuff that you know about. It's

also about what you learn and the experiences that you gain. The mix of participants and experienced artists is important. To have experienced artists teaching you how to do things was great. But then imagine that that artist that was teaching you something then went off to tell somebody else in the group how to do something else, and you were left with another person you'd never met before, trying to work out this new thing you just learned. So it becomes all about finding that connection, learning about the other person and as a result, learning about yourself. It's that journey that you go through that makes it so special.

Stepping Up: An Act of Celebration

The following are extracts of interviews conducted during the research for this book further illustrating how people from all walks of life have taken their experience with Phakama and applied it in other areas of their lives.

Interview: Cedoux Kadima

Cedoux Kadima is a visual artist, photographer and film maker originally from the Democratic Republic of Congo. He joined Phakama in 2011 during *Message in a Bottle* and has taken part in *The Edible Garden, Velela* and *Spotlight*.

FS: The first time we met, you shared some of your amazing drawings and paintings with us. We told you about *Message in a Bottle* and said that we would love if you were involved.

Cedoux Kadima: It was November and it was cold and dark. My first winter in London. Even though I wrapped myself up well, I was shaking. When I met the Phakama team, they told me about the project and asked what I thought about it: if I would like to be involved, what I could bring. I was twenty-four years old. I said, yes I would love to be part of it because I was welcomed differently, better than I was expecting. The way the Phakama team spoke to me, helped me feel comfortable. It made me feel at ease and open up.

FS: What were you expecting?

CK: I heard from Stephanie White from The Refugee Council that Phakama was a very strict and organized company. She said they are nice people but when you work with them you have to be ready. So I felt a little bit pressured and intimidated. I had limited English and I didn't really know the system, I didn't really know how things worked. So I become a little bit anxious with a lot of questions and doubts.

Will they accept me? But when I walked in, it was completely different, I received hugs, cups of tea and biscuits.

FS: Does the organization work you hard as well as providing hugs and biscuits?

CK: Yes, and I don't think the hard work is a bad thing. It gives the organization a really good reputation in the outside world. People know that it is about hard work and being responsible and considerate. For someone who really doesn't understand the concept, it can be scary. But once you approach it, you understand that it is not there to scare people but to actually work on and with people to build their willingness and develop old or build new skills.

Phakama was pushing me to be consistent. When you start something you have to make sure you finish it. Phakama gives you the freedom to choose but when you want to work in the professional industry there are things you need to learn and try to understand and do in the way they should be done. With Phakama, the fact that you know you have a set of responsibilities, and that the whole team will be expecting something from you (and is also there to support you) is a very empowering thing. In Phakama I had the opportunity to learn things in a professional way in terms of decision-making, planning, organizing and especially production. Phakama teaches you how to be responsible, careful and considerate.

FS: Can you describe when and how you felt celebrated in Phakama?

CK: Celebration comes from giving people the opportunity to learn new things and develop their interpersonal skills, to work and connect with other people. The way Phakama works enabled me to open up, to feel comfortable, welcomed and that I belong. It offered a sense of love and care. It is about celebrating the individual and allowing time for people to develop, to grow. Phakama gives people the opportunity to be themselves, to learn, to connect, to settle within themselves and that is the big act of celebration for me. One very specific moment I felt celebrated was during *Message in a Bottle*. When I first joined the project, I did not join the whole group straight away which was a good thing as I felt it all a little daunting. I worked on my own for a while in an adjacent room to the big group. I came in first thing in the morning to join in with the warm ups and games and observe what the group was doing. Then I would go away and work by myself on the piece I was creating as an offering to the project.

I created an interactive piece which was a painting: a sort of map of the world coming out of the faces of children. Within the piece, I created space (two large bottles held by the children in the painting) for the project participants to write their messages to the rest of the world. When it was finished I brought the canvas in and explained what it was, why I came up with this idea and how they could be involved. The group's reaction was unexpected and really moving. Everyone wanting to be part of it, write something, asking me questions, talking to me. I felt overwhelmed, I felt happy, I felt accepted.

FS: Do you feel that Phakama has helped you step up? And what have you done since joining Phakama?

CK: My journey with Phakama was full of learning and helped me step up in so many aspects of my life. It enabled me to keep my art alive. Before, because of my circumstances, past experiences, coming from another country, I felt at times like giving up and stopping everything. But then I joined Phakama and I discovered something new. It gave me the motivation to push and believe in myself and my work, and try again. I took part fully in *Message in a Bottle*'s second meeting in 2012. It was great to be part of the whole group with same level of responsibility as everyone else. I also helped in *The Edible Garden* and participated in the *Spotlight* project. Phakama helped me to learn about production, how to organize, plan and make an event happen. So now I am confident I can go into the field and give a lot back. Since our first meeting in that cold winter's evening back in 2011, I have produced a number of projects on my own. I have exhibited my work in a number of spaces, I have produced film festivals, arts events and have delivered workshops for children and young people.

Interview: Liesl Hartman

Liesl Hartman is a designer and an art educator. She joined Phakama in 1997 during *Met'n Sak Onner die Blad/With a Suitcase in My Hand* when she was the principal of the Battswood Arts Centre, South Africa. Liesl went on to take part in many Phakama projects in South Africa and internationally. She is currently the director of the Frank Joubert Art Centre, Cape Town.

FS: Describe your experience with Phakama.

Liesl Hartman: My experience with Phakama really opened me up. I'm a shy person by nature, so expressing myself either physically or with voice doesn't come easily or naturally to me. I'm not a performer, so stepping into that space was a frightening experience initially. But it was an amazingly supportive space, where you could make mistakes – and I did. To look at young people who were courageous and didn't have any of those barriers or boundaries that one has as an adult, was pretty amazing.

And then Phakama's concept of design was, for me, amazing. It had to tell the story in a very direct way.

FS: Can you think of how Phakama has helped you in other areas of your work?

LH: Well, soon after my time with Phakama my children were born, so I became a mother and that was all-encompassing. I left the Battswood Arts Centre and worked at the Frank Joubert Art Centre on a part-time basis. Even though the institution was specifically for teaching visual art and design, there were always opportunities to bring in performance so I brought my experience of Phakama directly into that. When I started working there we participated in the Cape Town Festival and they said, 'why don't you do this project with your kids? You can make some sort of masquerade masks'. Because of my Phakama experience in making large-scale puppets or objects for performance, my natural tendency was to make huge things which the kids could carry. So when I said to my colleagues right, you can come and see these masks, I think they were expecting things that fitted on your face, and they were these huge structures. They loved it, it was totally not what people were envisaging.

FS: Do you think that Phakama helped you develop more effective ways of working with young people?

LH: Absolutely. I brought in my Phakama experience into the work with the children at the Frank Joubert Art Centre. I knew that it had to express something of the young people's experience of Cape Town, so I said: 'what are the issues that you want to speak about? Who are you as an individual?' I put all of that experience into the lesson and they created these amazing things and took them proudly into the Cape Town Festival. Also, at the time my husband and I were working in our local church as confirmation teachers and we decided that we were not going to teach the catechism or the religious curriculum in a way that put people to sleep or made them wonder why they were doing this process in the first place. We thought, young people need to talk about why they're doing this. Most of them were told by their parents, you have to go and do this because it's the next step in your life. We wanted to get them to think about that, to question it and understand it. This is definitely something I gained from Phakama. We worked around performance with the young people and the issues they wanted to address. I think we scared some people and I think we annoyed a lot of people in the church in the way in which we worked. There we were making this biblical story more physically real for people. And we travelled, we didn't sit in a church hall and present the show. We got people outside and made fires and walked into the church and into the very holy spaces and put slideshows on in the sanctuary. I think it enabled people to reimagine their relationship with the church and gave us a deeper insight into our own spirituality and what that meant for us on a personal level.

Interview: Jean September

Jean September is deputy director of British Council South Africa. She is the former director Cape Town and was the chair of Phakama South Africa's Board (2006–10).

FS: How do you think Phakama impacted on you and your organization?

Jean September: In 2000/2001 the British Council was a very different organization to what it is now. At the time the overall view of the British Council was that it was a funding agency. Since then it's moved more to a position of a cultural relations organization and that means working with people, creating links between them and providing opportunities worldwide. Because it's an international cultural relations organization, it's making the links between people from different countries, in this case South Africa and the UK. But in reality, it's people who make those links so now we work mainly on partnerships and collaborations. I think some of the work that we were doing with Phakama was groundbreaking because it led the way towards the British Council thinking about itself differently, that it's not a funding agency, it's an agency that works with people.

Personally, I also learnt from Phakama that those processes are really important. Now the British Council is an organization where people come if they want to work together/collaboratively and looking for partners. And the partnership does not only mean money; but also ideas, a shared understanding of what it is that you want to achieve, and bringing change within those communities in which you want to work. So it shifted almost completely, but it needed time to do that.

The process and the methodology Phakama was using was useful for me to tread that path. I come from a trade union, teaching background, which involves debates, arguments and being clear. When I started in the British Council I said, 'I'm only prepared to take the job if it's going to assist with the transformation within South Africa at all levels of society. If that's not what it is, if I've got the wrong idea of what this organisation is about and what my role is going to be, then I am out of here, I'm not interested.' I was told clearly that that's certainly what the British Council would like to do in South Africa. Being involved in projects like Phakama gave me the strength to actually continue. You are working against the tide, people don't like change, they're very comfortable where they are but you begin regardless, with faith that you will take people with you. By attending those Phakama sessions and just talking to people, you get ideas of how you can implement that kind of change within an organization that you're working in.

Interview: Alpha Thiam

Alpha Thiam is originally from Guinea. He joined Phakama in 2004 during *Strange Familiars* and went on to take part in many projects both as a participant and as a trainee facilitator. Alpha went on to study economics and politics at Brunel University, London and now works as a facilitator for Refugee Youth.

LR: How did you get involved in Phakama, how did you find out about it?

Alpha Thiam: I came through the Refugee Council. Stephanie White introduced me and said, 'I think you should go to this place, just go, you need to start somewhere'. When I first got involved in Phakama we were just newly arrived in the country, we could barely speak English. Art, theatre was never something that had come up in our vocabulary, we didn't even know what it was. We knew how to drum, we knew how to use the instruments, but art wasn't necessarily the big thing that we'd have thought of. In Phakama you're given an instrument, you're given drums to play and crayons to draw and a lot of tools for you to have an imagination and be a child again.

LR: What do you think you gained from being involved?

AT: It gave me a lot of long-term friendships and a network of people. I didn't have any family or networks when I moved here. I didn't do anything apart from waking up at six o'clock in the morning, going to college and then coming back. I didn't have anything to do at the weekends. It would have been me going back to my foster family on the Saturday and then staying indoors until the following Monday to go back to school. I didn't speak a word of English so it was very difficult for me to make friends. Still, now, one of my best friends I met in Phakama, and he just got married and had a baby. So that's what it gave me. It gave me new connections and long-term friendships.

LR: How has it impacted on you personally?

AT: Phakama messed me up! I remember once we did a workshop at Bloomberg with LIFT's Business Arts Forum. I could never imagine going to a building like this and facilitating a session to bankers. Phakama showed me how much I could do and gave me the drive to pursue any path I choose in terms of career. Most of us involved in Phakama at the time didn't have a clue about the arts. So the career choices would be to work in Burger King or to work in law, or social services, not necessarily the arts. I don't really mean Phakama messed me up, I actually mean the opposite – Phakama gave me completely a different way of seeing things. Phakama gave me an option. It gave me the opportunity to go and work in many different organizations using the arts. I pursued a career in marketing, which I never considered before. It also opened my eyes to social issues and that's something that I feel very strongly about. That's the reason why I've been always involved in Phakama and have moved now to working with Refugee Youth. Phakama inspired me to use art for change, to work with and advocate for other young people who have been through similar situations as me, to make a change.

Interview: Beverley Randall

Beverley Randall, a theatre and television producer, was one of the four practitioners that travelled to South Africa on the first project in Johannesburg in 1996. Beverley worked on *Be Yourself* in London in 1999 and now works as an English teacher in Barcelona, Spain, working with a broad range of pupils, ranging in age from two-and-a-half years old to adults.

FS: Tell me about how you first became involved with Phakama?

Beverley Randall: Lucy Neal and Rose Fenton were speaking to me about an idea for a project and whether I would want to be a participant. The project would address what kind of arts relationship could be formed between us, in Britain, and those in South Africa. It felt a bit like a think-tank. We would get together and talk about ideas. There were a lot of us around the room led by Tony Fegan. I remember lots of conversations and lots of debate, which was really good fun and when a decision was taken by Tony about who would go to South Africa, I was quite surprised that I was one of the four. I got a sense of what other people could do because they were artists or they could make things, or they pulled things together, which absolutely was what Rose and Lucy and Tony did. I just didn't have a sense of what it was that I could give. I could understand how I could take part in a conversation, a debate, but it was very difficult for me to pinpoint what my role could be. Every time I asked Tony, 'what exactly is it that you would like me to do?' he would answer and it was as if he was speaking in a foreign language I didn't understand. This was my feeling all the way up to getting on the plane and the four of us taking off and going on to South Africa. So I had a first time experience of what it really means to have a panic attack. Literally, we'd fallen asleep and then I woke up sweating and scared and just thinking, 'You should be clear! How can you not be clear? Crazy woman!' So I went to the bathroom and I tried to pull myself together. And then a wonderful airhostess came out and she said to me, 'Are you okay?' So I told her what my problem was. She was so sweet – she said to me: 'Does this project have a lot of money?' And I said: 'Not really, no'. So she said: 'So a quarter of the fees are going to you. Don't you think they must have known why they would want you if they're prepared to pay you to come and do this thing?' But I still didn't know. This is part of the beauty of Phakama, because it is about the fluidity of how you work and some of the things that you are involved in you might have an idea about, but the reality of it comes together when all the parties are in the room. I couldn't wait for that to happen, and that's why I panicked. I didn't understand how important that essence would be in this project, because I'd never done anything quite like that.

FS: Can you describe the essence of Phakama?

BR: It was just a very gentle pulling together of people's ideas. Everybody had a voice. The idea of Give and Gain as a concept is lovely, but when you're in the room and seeing how that comes into play, it is really quite beautiful. It was about what each of us had within us as well as our skill, and therefore the thing that we're worried about or concerned about would be the thing that we would gain from somebody else. That is how it works. I remember some of the process of working towards that, with the teaching and artist practitioners in South Africa. For example, the use of the boxes in which you put three things which were representative of you. Then the boxes were put in the middle of the room and because we didn't know whose box was whose, we were careful handling the objects and with what we were saying. We were telling the truth of what we felt. It instantly created a bond because people realized how easy it was to be able to see into someone else's life with just three items. It broke down the walls between us very quickly, because we all started to speak in a much more open way: that was vital.

Phakama takes away the label of choreographer, the professional director, the dancer as your sole identity. This may be what you do, but you are not it: *you* have to enter the room. That's part of the beauty of how Phakama works: this idea that there is more to you than that one aspect of yourself. Often, as artists, we can hide behind the work and in Phakama there's very little space for that. It can become messy because of that, because people are made vulnerable.

FS: How did all of this way working came about?

BR: A lot of this came from Tony Fegan, then LIFT's Director of Learning. Of course the four of us got together to talk about things but it was Tony who put the information on the table and then supported us to talk about it, look at it and then think of the best way to present it to the group. With Give and Gain, everybody had a story to tell in terms of their own life experience and we worked with that experience so that nobody in the room felt that these ideas that the UK people were talking about were being imposed on them as South Africans.

Some of the things that were being discussed were uncomfortable. Race issues came up, not just among the South African practitioners, but also within the UK team. We were four people living in an apartment together for that period of time and our own issues around race were also raised. There were no bystanders in the experience of Phakama. During those two weeks everybody ended up being open and therefore vulnerable, and that vulnerability was touched. This was very much a joint effort that could only be arrived at through openness. People felt heard and that was important. We had to be able to recognize what we could bring to the table and what we would gain from being around the table. We had to do that work before we could then allow the young people to have access to what they wanted to do. If we did not feel safe we would make them feel very unsafe. And the thing is, sometimes, no matter how much planning you do, there has to be fall out because the process is very fluid; you can't cover everything. And the young people came with so much more than they realized.

FS: What did you gain from Phakama?

BR: As artists people are used to fulfilling their specific roles. So the minute you say, that's not the role, you ask, 'Well, what do you want me to do, I don't understand.' So that thing of being used to operating in boxes was the first thing that would have to be broken down. And I grew to love it. Even the producer role was quite fluid. What was most important was the work with the young people to facilitate what they wanted to say. We'd have an overarching idea about how we would begin, but after that the process had to involve the young people. It's that funny thing about giving yourself recognition for what you can do and also being very open to the fact that this is a thing that you don't feel you have a grasp of or that you want to learn more about. The opportunity in Phakama allows you to do both those things. I think that sometimes there's a bit of a preciousness about having a particular role: I am the producer and that means I'm in charge of everything. There was something about bringing more and more people in, not necessarily for them to take responsibility for my work, but to add to it in a way that made the work more fluid and made people feel more a part of something; I think that's what Phakama does. It affected me. I remember I was producing a television show at the time and we were talking about some ideas and I included the production secretary and someone said: What's she doing here? And I said. 'What, you don't think she has any ideas?' Phakama reminded me that *how* I am is first and then *what* I do is second and that that is allowed to flow through in whatever I do. It doesn't matter what the job title is, the fact is, I could be me. It made absolute sense, once I'd stopped panicking about what I should be doing, my role was pastoral; it's me. And there was something very beautiful about having a process, an artistic process, a project, being able to give back to me. Because then I was very clear that it was also giving to other people: if you had no other artistic involvement for the rest of your life, you would be given the gift of knowing something about who you are. And if that's all that Phakama did for you, fantastic. What a beautiful thing to gain.

Interview: Clinton Osbourn and Mpotseng Shuping

Clinton Osbourn is a visual artist and joined Phakama in 2003 during the *Spices* project. He took part in other projects as coordinator, facilitator and performer including *The Child I Curry* (2004), *Move* (2009), *Mutu* (2010), *Journey To* (2011) and *Man of Men* (2013). He now works as Training Coordinator for Sex Workers Education and Advocacy Task Force (SWEAT), Cape Town, South Africa.

Mpotseng Shuping is a dancer and choreographer and took part in many Phakama projects both in South Africa and internationally. She is now a sign language interpreter and company manager for Unmute, South Africa's first integrated performing arts organization. She was professionally trained by Jazzart (1987–91) and continued working as a professional dancer there until 1997. Between 1998 and 2004 Mpotseng focused on her dance teaching career, she has taught in Africa and the United States. Since 2005 she has been teaching and performing for Remix Dance Company.

LR: What do you think you have gained from Phakama?

Mpotseng Shuping: It taught me a lot of things. If I go and watch a site-specific performance it has to be on point, because there is no excuse for it not to be. If Phakama can put a high standard performance in three days and you had a whole month to put together a site-specific performance and it is not great, then I have a problem with that. Also the fact that I can stand in front of hundreds of people and teach and talk to people and not feel that I'm getting hot flushes or I'm about to die. It has taught me to be able to teach and put things together, from nothing to something. I still have friends from other countries through Phakama. There is love that you get from people that you don't even know, that you've just met. It gave me that.

Clinton Osbourn: It really showed me how to develop a way of working which is open; something that leads on to something else, that then leads on to something else, that comes to a point where there is a performance. Phakama taught me about process, about how to work *with* process and its power to be transformative. It's something that I hadn't fully seen happen before, it was something that I just believed in because I wanted it to be true. But with Phakama I really saw how you could do that and how it worked and how this process really did change people in a short space of time.

Phakama also showed me how to make a performance in a very short space of time and with hardly any money. I think we did the Khayelitsha project, with a 100 rand budget for the whole week. That's all we had. We just found newspapers and bottles and stuff around the site, and built things and made things out of it. Because we didn't have a lot of money, we couldn't really help people with food and transport. So all the people that lived in Khayelitsha who didn't require taxi fare to go home used to bring change and then the change would be shared out among all the kids that had to take trains or taxis, so that even though we didn't have money, everyone that was involved was contributing to making sure that everyone could be there.

MS: There was always enough for everyone to get there and back every day and buy some bread that everyone could eat. It connected people, bringing them together.

LR: What have you taken from Phakama to other areas of your work?

CO: In my current job as the training coordinator for SWEAT, the Sex Workers Education and Advocacy Taskforce, I am responsible for capacity building for the entire Global Fund National Sex Work Programme, training peer educators, site coordinators and human rights defenders as well as doing sensitization about sex work. I made a Give and Gain tree with a group of sex workers last week and was thinking about Phakama and the massive influence it has had on my practice and how I work with people. Sometimes in subtle ways and sometimes in really obvious ways like last week when I used a number of exercises I learnt while working on various Phakama projects which I adapt to the new context. I used *Drawing the Body*, similar to what we did in *The Child I Curry*. I also did the free writing and *Poetry Cuts* – a longstanding exercise that we used since the very first project and they created really amazing poems about sex worker's vulnerability as well as their rights. It always creates such strongly emotional poetry.

Interview: Luvuyo Mabuto and Craig Koopman

Luvuyo Mabuto is a dancer and an actor. He joined Phakama in 1998 with *Met'n Sak Onner die Blad/With a Suitcase in My Hand*. Later, he became a Phakama trainee facilitator and took part in other Phakama projects. Luvuyo now works at Project Playground, teaching drama to children and young people.

Craig Koopman participated in Phakama from 1998 to 2000. He currently works for a company selling bicycles while studying towards a degree in theology and undertaking an Anglican Church ordinance programme from which he will, ultimately, be ordained as a priest.

LR: Tell us what you've been doing since you've finished working with Phakama, and what you're doing now.

Luyuvo Mabuto: From 2000 I joined Jazzart Dance Theatre through Mpotseng Shuping who I worked with at Phakama. I trained with them until 2005 and they employed me until 2007. Then I wanted to change career and was approached by Jennie Reznek, who was cofounder of Magnet Theatre and a lecturer at the University of Cape Town (UCT). I enrolled at UCT drama school and graduated in 2010. Currently I'm working at Project Playground, teaching drama there to kids from nine years old through to 21-year-olds.

LR: Do you see a direct connection from Phakama to the rest of your career?

LM: Definitely. We joined Phakama as dancers. We were a group from Langa who were crazy about dancing and were doing African and contemporary dance. And then as soon as we joined Phakama it was different – you could design, you could act, you could start creating images and that was wow to me. That led me to go into acting. Even the way I teach is drawn from Phakama, like the Give and Gain process. I still use that. And the name games that I learnt from Phakama. All that stuff has stayed with me.

LR: As well as the exercises, do you think the ethos of Phakama have influenced the way you teach?

LM: Yes. Punctuality was new to me and the structuring of class when I was training with Phakama to become a facilitator.

LR: And what about the relationships with the students?

LM: When I joined Phakama, it was the first time I encountered other races because I was born during the time when apartheid was still at the highest peak. For me, someone coming from Langa, I would see a coloured person as someone who was more privileged than me, and then a white person was a superior person. And then as soon as we integrated in Phakama, I started learning about other, different cultures, and I started meeting other races. There were Sotho as well from Gauteng, others from North-West and Botswana and others from Northern Cape and we integrated. And we gelled very well actually, so it opened my mind and my way of thinking. Phakama literally introduced me to travelling. When you travel and then you come back to where you live, you started thinking that there's a lot that you can change in your community. So all of this impacted on my journey from '96 to here and in the way I can interact with any of my students regardless of their races.

LR: Is there a moment that stays with you?

LM: It will be mostly socializing for my part. Coming from Langa (a township), seeing our older brothers, uncles and parents having a relationship with one another, I mean a black to black relationship, I never thought that we could date outside black. I like to believe what kept me in Phakama was the girls [laughs]. Even though we went there for girls, we managed to come out with something concrete within ourselves. So a wow moment for me was, and something that changed my mind set, was when I was attracted to a coloured girl.

LR: Because you thought that would never be possible?

LM: I didn't think that it would happen, not with me, not with anyone. I'd never seen it, because that were forbidden in South Africa. If you were caught having a cross-cultural relationship you would be prosecuted. I didn't know then, I only knew about it when I reached university and when my granny started sharing all these stories about apartheid. But for me, that was like, wow. I emigrated to another culture and I started seeing white women as attractive too.

Craig Koopman: We come from an era where apartheid was high and we were on different sides, but yet during the production we were singing freedom songs together, standing like one, like brothers and you could see here's a black, here's a coloured, here's a white, and there weren't any judgemental thoughts. We were united, we were singing, we were learning the songs from them and we were singing Afrikaans songs together. Something that was very, very different for me.

LM: In Phakama we stopped looking at people for the colour of their skin, we started looking at you for who you were. Like Mildrett was Mildrett, Lindy, who is now in New Zealand, was Lindy and we would contact each other and she invited me to her huge place. And Berger was an Afrikaner from Somerset West. I stopped looking at him as a Boer (a slightly derogatory term for an Afrikaner), I looked at him as Berger and the person that I can share anything with.

LR: So do you think that Phakama really helped build a sense of integration?

LM: Absolutely. But sadly I think that one of the things that South Africa failed to do was to address the issues of apartheid, because people are still hung up on that. I have a fiancé who's a coloured who's comes from Ocean View. She's living with me in Langa, and when they see us together, because they're not exposed to these things, they're like wow, you have a coloured girlfriend. They don't get nasty because she's a woman, but as soon as a coloured man steps into Langa, then they start being nasty to him. Cross-cultural relationships are still funny and people who live in a township are still looking at white people as tourists who just come to do research about the township, who never step foot in a township before. But it's mostly people who are in the township who've never been outside. They have never been exposed to what life is outside the township.

LR: People say that sometimes ignorance is bliss, if you expose people to other possibilities and then put them back in a situation where those possibilities aren't there any more, that's actually worse for them than never showing the opportunities at all. Do you think Phakama did a bit of that?

LM: I think it is because you're reminding them of what they wanted to forget. If you take them and show them the opportunities and what's happening outside the township, then their knowledge becomes vast and they open up. Then as soon as you take them back there, instead of trying to change the environment they live in, they start shutting down again. Then you don't have that opportunity to share and to be themselves again and they start developing this anger and being aggressive inside.

LR: But in fact that hasn't happened to either of you.

LM: Never, never.

LR: And why's that?

LM: I think it's because we stuck with Phakama longer and Phakama was consistent about the values, the beliefs and the aims.

LR: So these values and beliefs stayed with you?

LM: As soon as I started with Jazzart, I moved away from Langa and then I lived here in Obs, and then I went back to school and then I went back to Langa again and things started to change. But I realized that okay, Langa is not going to change who I am – I will influence life.

LR: Can you describe a moment in one of the productions which you still remember in detail?

CK: All the places that we went to visit were way before my generation when I was born, but through Phakama, with acting, it felt like I was really part of it all. I was part of Robben Island or I could see the slavery in District Six. It was almost like I was living in that specific time.

LR: You were stepping into somebody else's shoes...

CK: Yes. And actually realizing that long walk to freedom when we travelled over the waters to Robben Island, that distance, that's a really long walk to freedom. So I visualized that and I appreciated more what the people did for us and for our country.

LR: And did that change your relationship with your parents?

CK: Yes, because now I wouldn't challenge them when they say you're lucky, the opportunities that you have. Now I appreciate what they have been through, and when they say they moved from Wynberg to Mitchells Plain, now I understand where it comes from. I have a deeper appreciation for life.

LM: One moment that is stuck in my head now is from *Call Me Not a Woman*, in Mmabatho. We entered someone's house and changed it and made it a stage. It was a kitchen scene. We used food to create art on top of their kitchen table.

CK: It was the picture, it was the woman in her dress and she had all the pots.

LM: It was made out of beans, rice and food ingredients. I never thought that you can take organic things from the kitchen and make art out of them. As a dancer, back then, the only platform I knew that you can perform on was a formal stage. I never knew that you could do a site-specific show where you could go to other people's houses and use it as a stage, where people can just go, come in and view what you were doing.

LM: It was something new, something different. The elders, when they entered the houses and saw what we were doing, were, wow. There was a scene in someone's bedroom, but you couldn't open and enter, you could only hear voices coming from inside the bedroom. There was a lot of argument happening and then it started developing into something. You had to imagine what was happening inside.

LR: You both work with young people now, has Phakama influenced the way you relate to young people?

LM: In my time in Langa, if you're naughty you will be disciplined immediately. It's either a smack or a pinch you will endure if you're naughty, immediately. And then I came to Phakama, I'm naughty, and then I'm only told, don't do this again or else you will stop coming here. It felt different, it felt odd, really, really odd. It influences the way I work with the kids now. I just tell them that if you do this again there will be consequences. We do home visits as well. When we visit their parents and we say, 'this one sometimes misbehaves like any other kid' and the parent says, 'you must hit him or her.' Then we try to tell them that we won't and if they do it themselves we will have to take actions as they are not allowed to. So we're looking after those kids like they're our babies. It's something that I learnt from Phakama.

CK: Talking about discipline – do you remember Berger? How naughty he was, and I remember how he just used to laugh. Whenever we were doing an exercise he would just laugh, he would disrupt everything, and I remember Tony just gently taking him aside and saying to him, 'Berger, do you want to be the class clown?' And he said, 'no'. He said, 'well then, stop behaving like that.' And that was it. And he stopped after that.

FS: Being given responsibility is intrinsic to how Phakama creates opportunities for people to step up. I remember we were doing a project in a very, very challenging boys' school in south London and they were very, very naughty, but there was one boy specially who was almost impossible to work with, he wouldn't do anything at all, he would always disrupt everybody else. And I was getting so frustrated. And then Sid gave him a lot of responsibility and said you're going to be responsible for doing this and this and that. I said, 'Sid, what are you doing?' And he said to me 'this boy has been told by everybody – his parents, his colleagues, his friends at school, his teachers – that he's good for nothing, and he just keeps disrupting everybody. Give him a little bit of responsibility and change his own mind set and you'll see how he will behave'. And sure enough, he was brilliant. He was really on the ball doing and participating in everything. It was just a little bit of changing in how we related to him, which was incredible. It was really good to see. Sid is a clever, clever man.

References

Boston, J. (2016), Interview with Fabio Santos, London, 5 April.

Gonzalez, J. (2015), Interview with Caoimhe McAvinchey, Lucy Richardson and Fabio Santos, London, 5 April.

Hartman, L. (2015), Interview with Fabio Santos Cape Town, South Africa, 5 May.

Kadima, C. (2016), Interview with Fabio Santos, London, 24 April.

Mabuto, L. and C. Koopman (2015), Interview with Lucy Richardson and Fabio Santos, Cape Town, South Africa, 5 May.

Osbourn, C. and M. Shuping (2015), Interview with Lucy Richardson and Fabio Santos, Cape Town, South Africa, 5 May.

Quinn, S. (2015), Interview with Lucy Neal, London.

Randall, B. (2015), Interview with Fabio Santos, 20 August.

Santos, F. (2016), Interview with Caoimhe McAvinchey and Lucy Richardson, QMUL, London, 18 February.

September, J. (2015), Interview with Fabio Santos, Cape Town, South Africa, 5 May.

Thiam, A. (2015), Interview with Caoimhe McAvinchey, Lucy Richardson and Fabio Santos, London, UK, 5 April.

FIGURE 9 Food.

Celebrating aspects of Woman and Home with seeds, rice and pulses on a kitchen table: art made for the provider from her provisions.

In her essay 'Performing Risk' Shirley Brice Heath asserts the importance and value of learning which is engaged with voluntarily. She argues that participatory theatre, such as Phakama, allows young people to access high-quality voluntary learning. She draws upon her experience of Phakama and how its principles resonate with other organizations, such as New York Public Theater's Public Works programme. She situates these projects within her broader knowledge of artwork in community settings, to evidence the value of the arts in developing critical participants in democracy.

PERFORMING RISK

Shirley Brice Heath

Introduction

My life with Phakama began back in 1999. The timing and context could not have been better. I had just returned from several stints across two years in South Africa, and I had recently completed a documentary for Public Broadcasting Service and a book on youth arts organizations in marginalized communities of the United States (Heath and Smyth 1999). I came to Great Britain to learn from individuals and organizations working with immigrants, refugees, homeless youth and disenfranchised young people. I came with a jaded and bitter attitude about the ways in which institutions (governmental, judicial and educational) disrespected marginalized youth. When I arrived in London (a city I knew well from having worked and studied there in earlier years), I sought out colleagues who shared my positive view of what many term 'informal learning'. I was so embittered by both South African and American schools that I refused to use the term 'informal' learning, believing the dichotomy between 'formal' and 'informal' to be a false one. That 'informal' is set out as oppositional to 'formal' indicates the view that instructional learning is the norm. In fact, across societies and contexts, most deep learning comes through self-directed purposeful voluntary engagement in order to do and know more.

My introduction to Phakama came through friends working with LIFT. They set up a 'premier' showing of my documentary film, *Artshow* [Arts show how], at the LIFT offices, and there I met the leaders of Phakama as well as other individuals engaged in art-centred voluntary participatory learning. My documentary portrayed two youth arts community centres located in impoverished urban areas of the United States and two such centres located in rural areas. Each site illustrated, though in differing ways, the essence of participatory voluntary learning and ways that imagination, persistence, resourcefulness and effective communication skills made the work of learning possible for the young people involved.

After seeing the documentary and related materials, the leaders and young people of Phakama allowed me to join in their learning enterprise. What follows here draws on what I learnt in working with them. In addition, I offer also a comparative instance of participatory theatre I had the privilege of helping initiate with The Public Theater in New York City over a decade after working with Phakama in England. Both groups include in their midst individuals who have faced oppression from governmental forces, rebel groups, organized gangs, prison life, schools, family and friends, as well as severe poverty and deprivation of basic resources. Most seriously for such individuals, much of their suffering and exclusion comes from individuals or institutions that wish to exclude them in order to retain their own power and resources and to preserve their elite way of being and thinking.

Four sections follow. The first introduces 'voluntary learning' in contrast to the misnomer of 'informal learning', often applied in modern economies to participatory theatre and other art forms and sites created in large part by individuals without formal credentials. The second section explores briefly and at a general level two key points that the neurosciences help us understand about how our brains work in voluntary learning. This information certainly does not figure in the minds of those who initiate participatory theatre or other art forms. However, knowing key points about what the brain sciences tell us related to such learning can affirm intuitive processes and practices of participatory engagement with the arts. The penultimate section discusses aspects of the work of Phakama in its first decade or so. A comparative case comes from Public Works, the participatory theatre of The Public Theater in New York City. Adapted to the realities of this city, Public Works incorporated within the programme-intensive longitudinal research in order to learn the effects on both The Public Theater and its staff and the community ensemble participants over the first four years. A final section offers an appeal to readers to look around the world and to consider the strong evidence for the values of participatory theatre.

Voluntary Learning

My academic training, research and teaching (primarily at Stanford University, but also within universities in Sweden, South Africa, Germany, Italy, Australia, Mexico and England) has centred in linguistic anthropology. I often explain my core field as 'the anthropology of learning', because since 1998, I have spent much of my time working and learning within small groups of neuroscientists and neurologists whose research complements my core interest in how individuals learn. I have taken knowledge from these 'hard sciences' into my own longitudinal fieldwork in contexts of participant-centred arts around the world.

In blending my social science background in anthropology and linguistics (fields some academics refer to as 'soft' science) with the hard sciences, I have sought to understand deeply how learning goes on voluntarily and the critical contextual features that help determine sustained voluntary learning across the life span. Not surprisingly, most of such learning starts when an individual learner or a group determines that particular information and skills will be useful. Sometimes such learning takes place under crisis situations. The travels of refugees present such an example, as does the diagnosis to parents that a toddler's behaviour results from being on the autism disorder spectrum. We can think of many ways in which individuals and groups are thrown into sudden realization of the desperate need to know more and to do something different from what has been routine.

Other forms of voluntary learning come about in more peaceful ways. An individual refugee chooses to renew early memories of the tailoring skills of a deceased parent or grandparent. Learning based on memory, trial and error, and often some type of formal study often also goes on in such instances. Individuals who enjoy cooking voluntarily decide to learn to create a new type of cuisine, a new skill (such as baking bread), or immerse the family in an entirely different type of diet (e.g. vegan, raw food, or gluten free).

Many decisions to undertake voluntary learning spring from an image of having seen such learning or perhaps participated, even peripherally, in this kind of experience. Memory of that occasion, including information, ideas and emotions, provide 80 per cent of the brain's image, while only 20 per cent of what eventually becomes learned through participatory voluntary learning comes from new input or external sources of knowledge and skills (Squire 1992).

Central to voluntary learning across the spectrum from the most practical and skilled to the most abstract and esoteric is risk. Initial (and sometimes repeated) efforts at baking bread often fail for novices. Taking up a specialized skill such as tailoring may require skills and disposition (e.g. patience) in short supply on the part of the would-be learner. Risk is unavoidable when an individual or group makes the decision to participate in learning and doing something new. Voluntary learning often calls for entry into formal classes for courses that accelerate and ground the learning and practice of unfamiliar information and skills.

The power of risk-taking comes through both the neuronal structure of the brain and the chemistry of adrenaline. Knowing that one is at risk from attempting purposively to learn something stimulates adrenaline flow, which in turn powers forward thinking and planning, as well as imagining alternatives. Such mental actions amount to 'executive function', the term that neuroscientists use to describe results of aspects of the neuronal connectivity in the frontal lobe of the brain (Zuk et al. 2014). Transcranial magnetic stimulation studies allow neuroscientists to see how the prefrontal lobe works during those times when activities, such as problem-solving, managing and planning goal-directed behaviour, and maintaining information in working memory are simultaneously called for.

Such research has analysed, for example, what happens during times of participatory engagement in certain types of arts activities (such as ensemble music, theatre or dance). As individuals sustain their practice, the frontal lobe registers cognitive flexibility as well as facility in task switching (Best, Miller and

Jones 2009; Heath 2016). Through participatory learning within an ensemble of like-minded participants, individuals engage in cross-modal switches to move from one type of activity to another often rapidly and simultaneously (e.g. from *reading* musical notation to *playing* the instrument to *interpreting* the movements of a conductor (Barrett et al. 2013; Heath 2015). Joint attention provides the backbone of ensemble music or dance as well as theatre. Brain research reveals how engaging in joint attention enables participants to learn to coordinate perceptual and cognitive processes. In doing so through actions as simple as joint gaze, individuals register emotional pleasure. In colloquial or everyday terminology, joint attention indicates to parties involved that there is a 'meeting of minds' (Amodio and Frith 2006).

Theatre, in particular, forces individuals to engage the senses to interpret at a rapid pace the bodily motions and expressions of emotions from others. Observing or joining to watch the same object, person, or scene and then 'playing out' or undertaking what has been viewed involves cross-modal task switching: moving, speaking, showing emotions and portraying a sense of character. Participatory theatre that involves singing, dancing or responsive chorus brings high demands for participants to absorb cognitively and through embodiment what has been observed and heard.

Essential in any discussion of 'high risk' is the distinction between *high challenge* and *high anxiety*. When the risk of voluntary undertakings brings the latter, individuals give up hope, turn away or decide perhaps to try again in the future. Too often for marginalized and excluded populations, the fear of failure is real, and abandoning voluntary pursuits seems a sensible move. The reality is that the risk-taking called for in voluntarily undertaking new experiences in order to gain something not available in one's current state often brings real threat, even death. Refugees who leave their war-torn nation behind endure treacherous boat travel on the open sea in the hope of new opportunities to learn and a chance to begin again. At the individual level, any form of threat brings fear, desperation and a pending sense of utter failure. When these strong negative emotions produce deep stress, cognitive operations fade in the face of elemental limbic responses that lie outside the conscious control of individuals.

In participatory theatre, *high challenge* characterizes the most effective programmes. Research on the history of voluntary learning (from the medieval period forward) shows the positive power that comes when individuals can assume risk as challenge (Heath 2012). In these cases, time and relative predictability produce in the learner(s) a sense of security, a 'can-do' attitude and a foundation for laying down new concepts.

Concepts are flexible distributed representations comprising modality-specific features. For example, some individuals gain concepts almost entirely through movement in association with specific touch sensations or spatial alignment. Others gain concepts primarily through auditory means. Some musicians indicate that their individual practice takes place as they 'hear again' in their head specific interpretations created by the instructor or the ensemble's conductor in past sessions. Positive outcomes result for other individuals when the learning environment offers a combination of emotional support mixed with systematic input of information and skill demonstration. In some cases, when such support is sustained, individuals tend to speak of 'mind reading'. Research in the development of empathy (sometimes thought of as 'mind reading') stresses the impact of 'shared intentionality' as well as participation in multi-modal activities based on joint attention (Singer 2006; Tomasello and Carpenter 2007). Neuroscience research repeatedly reveals that the brain stores features of particular concepts in distinct sensory and motor brain areas linked to long-term memory. This peculiarity of storage makes it possible for learners to recall concepts in relation to specific sensory and motor experiences that occurred during concept acquisition. The particular touch sensation created by a specific quality of velvet or ripe peach conjures up memories as well as concepts related to how to handle each of these items. The same is true of abstract concepts such as integrity or beauty.

Thus it is the case that taking on roles, such as those essential to participatory arts, means that individuals act in the identity of another person, thus expanding one's own sensory and motor system into what it means to be 'within' the experiences, emotions and core of knowledge of another. Moreover, intensive practice during ongoing rehearsals as well as the reality that a final public performance is called for will accelerate and 'plant' knowledge and skills gained while in the role of the 'other'. Such identity-shifting knowledge includes vital concepts, embedded within each of the art forms, from visual arts to ensemble music to theatre. Taking on the role of another brings 'embodiment' of conceptual representations, and as practice of this embodiment goes forward, neuronal connections in the brain and throughout the body deepen learning. An actor who has played the role of Shakespeare's Hamlet many times carries in every fibre of the body memory of space, timing, smell and touch while existing in the high challenge of being within that particular role.

Researchers in anthropology, neurology and cognitive psychology have given us an evolutionary perspective on ways the human species is naturally disposed towards co-participating to find meaning as they learn (Donald 2006). Throughout the archaeological history of human development, we find evidence of participation as the central form of learning. Anthropologists suggest that such evidence (e.g. in samples of mature design in a stone axe alongside an immature sample) shows that modelling and demonstrating through apprenticeship to a master craftsman have gone on forever (Goody 1989). Contemporary cross-cultural work on child development as well as the floor of corporate offices demonstrates how 'apprenticeship in thinking' works as co-participation (Coy 1989; Pine and Gilmore 1999; Rogoff 1990). Current terms such as 'community of practice' and 'legitimate peripheral participation' capture the essence of voluntary learning that takes place within a group or within a duo team of novice and apprentice (Lave and Wenger 1991; Wenger 1998; Wenger, McDermott and Snyder 2002).

A final aspect of participatory learning takes us to a smaller level of focus than we have considered through executive function and embodiment, or engagement of the senses and motor skills in conceptual acquisition. Let's look at the hands and forearms. In the past decade or so, neurologists have given intensive attention to the role of our hands in evolutionary history and today (Wilson 1998; Pallasmaa 2009).

Of focus in this research has been the gripping action of hands, clearly important in the development of all primates. However, such actions show up most obviously with humans in tool-making, signalling with the hands to another located at some distance, and in the creation of all art forms. Learning to use our hands comes from co-participation in practice, and any use of the hands (not just the fingers) requires help from the forearms. For example, in acting as well as playing an instrument in an ensemble, individuals use their hands in a host of ways to help them interpret the structured symbol systems (whether dramatic text, group-composed text or musical notation) critical to performance. Neurologists now talk about the value of our uses of the hand as we struggle to make meaning as well as to craft objects ranging from stone axes and arrow-heads to mosaic tiles and painted images. Such 'shaping' through gripping tools and other objects refers particularly to the connectivity critical to development of both receptive and productive abilities with language or other structured symbol systems, such as mathematics, musical notation, etc. In sum, the hand and eye work together for 'embodiment' or the sensation throughout the body of aligning musculature, nerves and bones to the 'right' positioning for optimization of excellence in performance that requires absolute precision. The embodiment aided by the hands and forearms helps us 'plant' skills and also deepens entry of information into long-term memory. Thus, in recent years, neurologists have come to maintain in stronger terms than before how use of the hand shapes the brain, influences language development, and also interpretation and conceptual grasp of symbolic systems.

The Reach of Participatory Theatre: Phakama and Public Works

Phakama and other arts programmes that enlist individuals in the full process of creating a theatre, dance, or musical performance or a collaborative work of visual art bring about special effects for marginalized or disenfranchised populations. Entering into art takes individuals temporarily outside their own current sense of themselves, who they are and what they are enduring beyond the role they assume in the creation of art. This suspension into both participation within a group and a particular role within a piece of theatre, ensemble music group, or community arts project enables healthy emotions and sensations to enter the mind and body. Because of the high risk or high challenge, individuals have to focus intently on what is happening and what they must do to be appropriate parts of the action. Doing so builds healthy emotional responses.

Phakama has for several decades been a major exemplar of the kind of learning that takes place for even those who have experienced extreme trauma in their lives before they engage in theatre. Phakama's core members, often those who themselves have entered Phakama as newcomers months or years before, convene in unlikely places. For example, in 2000, in a town in northern South Africa, young people from several local regions joined with Phakama veterans from London to create a drama around women's issues, *Call Me Not a Woman*. Violence, the growing AIDS epidemic, abandonment and severe deprivation suffered by the women became the core theme of the performative work. However, Phakama members, new and old, experienced and inexperienced, joined in and decided that the production could best illustrate the harm to women through demonstrating the extreme amount of physical labour they endured. This labour was, to be sure, essential to the ongoing life of the village, but was it appreciated and did it bring respect to the women? Staged in two houses across the road from each other, the production brought 'audience' members or bystanders into the first house and its garden, and across the road to the second home. Verses of songs, poems and sayings had been hung from limbs of the trees of this garden. These messages reflected the work of the women, and the audience was invited to examine, perform and consider each message in turn. The 'spread' of performance even led the local police to stop traffic on the road and to join in (literally) the moving drama that ended in song and dance linking men and women, young and old.

Here the mix of structured symbol systems (writing, dance, music, song and police signals) is evident along with the emotional portrayals by the locals and Phakama members from London. To be sure, occasions such as this one (as well as *The Robben Island Peace Project*, the 2001 performance by Phakama at the opening of the museum on Robben Island off the shore of Cape Town) seem to be one-off or single-celebratory-experience events. However, it is essential to recognize that Phakama members do not wait for such celebratory or one-occasion-only opportunities. They have also worked in hostels for youth seeking asylum in England to produce theatre that socializes educators, social workers, philanthropists and the general public about who the participants are, where they come from and where they have hopes of going.

On one occasion, in London during *Strange Familiars* (2004), Phakama secured an unoccupied house that had a large garden leading down a steep hill. The group, including former child soldiers and other asylum seekers plus some experienced Phakama members, planned a series of events for theatregoers in London. Audience members entered the door of the house, went through to the back garden area, and there Phakama members provided aerial feats on high bars before the onlookers were led back into the house. There in each room on the two floors of the house, participants had created works of visual art, brought artefacts and installed other forms of representation of their memories of home as well as their experiences in transit. In addition, some rooms provided background music appropriate to the home sites reflected in the room. Audience members moved in the order they wished through the house and back into the foyer and garden for a pyrotechnics exhibition before talking with the young actors. Not only in the performance, but throughout the development of the piece, members of Phakama worked together to agree on primary themes, modes of illustration and activities inside and outside the house and garden. Communication flowed during this process, as did modes of demonstrating and illustrating through sketches of the various ideas proposed. Much as a staff meeting of a major corporation might work, Phakama members planned, problem-solved, negotiated, represented ideas and brought to action their very integrated arts performance(s).

Individuals who had come to England from nations run by despots and rebel groups entered into the socialization process of creating theatre together. They learnt to think, plan, communicate and interact in ways that illustrated democracy or co-citizenry in action towards an outcome on which all agreed and in which all took part. As xenophobia spreads across modern economies in the face of increased migration and movement of refugees from war zones, such socialization processes will be essential for those accepted into European nations. Learning to keep one's voice down, listen to others, wait one's turn to speak and deliberate in relation to words that have gone before become essential in the democracies to which these migrants come. Respect for property and personal space, as well as precision of timing and need for joint planning stand as core values in the receiving nations. Irreparable damage can be done when newcomers either do not know or disregard these values, so often subtly displayed and rarely directly expressed by citizens of the receiving nations.

Another instance of the values deeply integral to Phakama's life operates in New York City through The Public Theater. My experiences with Phakama in England and South Africa (as well as with similar groups in other parts of the world; see Heath and Robinson 2004) led to my collaboration with The Public Theater in 2011. The artistic director, Oskar Eustis, a former colleague in university teaching, and I set out to bring participatory theatre opportunities to marginalized populations in the five boroughs of New York City. We drew up plans, vetted these with other theatre groups in the City and set in motion initiation of Public Works. Several premises guided establishment of the programme, designed to bring together as a city disenfranchised populations from all five boroughs of the City. The Public Theater is located in Manhattan, the borough that also draws the majority of tourists, audience members for Broadway performances and individuals seeking out the numerous cultural centres located in this borough. Though the New York transit system operates in all five boroughs, many people who live in boroughs other than Manhattan never come into that borough and thus have little or no knowledge or possibility for attendance or performance in the numerous theatres or other cultural centres such as museums located in Manhattan.

The philosophy behind Public Works was to change this situation to the extent possible. In each of the five boroughs, one local community centre that included marginalized individuals partnered with The Public Theater. In 2013, the initial year of Public Works, individuals of the five community groups undertook throughout the academic year (in their own community centres with teaching artists from The Public Theater) classes in drama/acting as well as other aspects of musical theatre. They did so to prepare for auditioning in May for parts in William Shakespeare's *The Tempest* as a musical. The free performance would take place in September at the Delacorte in Central Park, New York City's largest theatre venue. Themes within the play (such as the isolation that comes from displacement to an unknown island, the poisonous effects of revenge and the power of faith in the next generation) brought a metacognitive awareness of the timeless themes of dramatic literature to community participants and audience alike.

The Public Theater initiated the community participatory programme of Public Works as renewal of the vision of founder Joseph Papp. He instituted The Public as a theatre 'of, by, and for the public'. This vision called for a public theatre open and accessible to everyone.

Lear de Bessonet, who came in 2012 to The Public Theater to direct Public Works, both amplified and intensified the commitment of Public Works to being a sustained series of partnerships with community centres in the boroughs. The Public Theater provides classes and other opportunities throughout each year in preparation for six–eight weeks of intensive rehearsal before a performance such as *The Tempest*. The initial group of community partners illustrates the inclusive agenda of The Public. Included, for example, was the Fortune Society, a community organization of formerly incarcerated individuals working and learning to find their way back into employment and civil life after years of imprisonment. These individuals often compared themselves to Prospero, once seeking revenge but transforming to move on to learn how to live forgiven and forgiving. Other community partner groups reflected similar inclusion of the marginalized: foster children (often homeless at times), elders living in a neighbourhood of deprivation, and domestic workers and nannies who served primarily wealthy families living in Manhattan. From the Bronx came young people living in communities with few public schools that offer rich in-school or after-school opportunities in arts studios or science laboratories. These young find their way to the Dream Yard, a community organization dedicated to immersion in the arts for all young people and their parents. For each of the annual performances in Central Park, one hundred of these community members joined with one hundred members of several 'cameo groups' reflecting participatory art (dance, hip hop, gospel singing, etc.) from across the entire City of New York. These groups made cameo appearances within the production. Five Equity actors (some with Broadway backgrounds) joined with the two hundred community ensemble members in each year's production. In addition to work in singing and dancing groups, some community members also played featured or support roles in some years.

From the outset of planning for Public Works, all of us involved knew research on effects of the programme for participants would be essential. Each year, a duo of linguistic anthropologists that I led became immersed within rehearsals for the annual performance in Central Park. Results of this research indicated changes in several hard-to-alter behavioural and attitudinal areas of learning. Participants across the age range reflected an increase in reading participation both in direct relation to the play and beyond. Additionally, individuals without prior experience with the public transport systems on other islands of New York City learnt to navigate new and additional portions of the transport system, predict transport times to different rehearsal venues and study ahead to learn which stations provided accessible entry and exit from the underground.

Additionally, individuals across the age groups showed a strong shift of attitude regarding their own capabilities. Initially, during joint rehearsals that brought community members from all five boroughs together, participants opened their stories to one another during the long wait times of rehearsals with litanies of 'I never thought I could ...' (do any of this, get up and perform before a crowd, be willing to speak in public, have this kind of hope, meet a real expert). As rehearsals continued over several weeks, participants ceased talking about their past fears and sense of inadequacy. Instead, in their conversations with others, they began to share and celebrate stories of their past positive individual achievements.

From the primary school participants to the elders, their conversations portrayed a meta-awareness of the importance to their learning of taking on new roles, literally and figuratively. They gained a new and different sense of responsibility for what they could and should do in the future. They began to undergo annual physicals to monitor their health, joined work-out clubs in their community centres and altered ideas about diet and exercise. 'I've got to stay fit. I've got to be ready for auditions' was often heard throughout the year. Teenagers, in particular, seemed struck by the need for them to reconsider their prior views of groups such as the formerly incarcerated, gays, 'old people', and their own parents. In several instances, parents and children together took part in each year's performance. In the majority of these cases, either the child or the parent initially agreed to audition and was chosen. Thereafter, the other decided to try out in late auditions. The shared experience of rehearsals, unique to both parent and child, led to sustained conversations between older and younger, opening, in the eyes of parents, 'a way for me to talk with my kid about something neither one of us ever imagined we would or could be doing'.

Premises of the programme from the outset insisted that the group reflect multi-generational members and all comers, regardless of how they reflected their own hesitations about participatory art or their prior experiences. Moving about the city via a transport system whose reach and schedule had never been known also gave participants a new sense of the geography of New York City. Many expressed the view that their persistent sense of 'feeling poor' lifted when they saw what the rest of city dwellers and subway riders were like. 'Getting to know this place [primarily Manhattan] tells me all the poor people like me don't live where I live. There are folks like me all over this city'.

The Critical 'So What?' Question

In a world of growing focus on capitalism and accumulation of material goods and enormous wealth, many doubters and naysayers view the arts as unnecessary for the poor and disenfranchised of such a world. In particular, views of the arts often held by elite members of modern economies centre on a passive role as spectator or audience member who critiques and reviews the levels of expertise of known performers. Participatory art rarely receives substantial reviews in the standard press, and rave reviews of such performances almost never appear. Public Works became a notable exception, garnering fulsome positive reviews in major outlets, such as the *New York Times*. In addition, just as Phakama has done, The Public Theater is spreading the concept of Public Works as participatory theatre to other locations in the United States, and by 2017, several cities were prepared to present their first performance based on community engagement and inspired by Public Works.

Yet the 'so what?' question remains. Why create such performances? How does art of any kind make a significant difference in the lives of the world's most oppressed? This question comes from those who recognize the increasing number of individuals and groups marginalized by various forces beyond the control of any single source. These situations include (a) regional or ethnic strife as well as racism and xenophobia, (b) sporadic military actions targeting a particular population or region by either their own government or military forces of neighbouring nations and (c) the continuity of wars sustained by the arsenal and weaponry of modern nations engaged in disputes and human rights abuses by leaders of other sovereign nations.

We must take heart, however, in the promise of sustained research on the participatory arts. Hard and soft sciences consistently show that performative work through the arts improves individual lives, inspires predictable thinking about the future and engenders positive social relations to democratic interaction. These outcomes need to speak to funders and governmental bodies whose sense of value-for-investment may lead them to want more participatory arts.

Another 'so what?' question asks why the marginalized and inexperienced should be brought on stage or into site performance spaces when plenty of experts, such as trained artists, lack opportunities to work. Moreover, artists garner low wages, and insecurity is a way of life for most. Both Phakama and The Public Theater keep these points in mind, bringing trained artists from different fields of art and Equity actors into programmes of community participatory art. Moreover, many of these professional artists come to value highly the direct experience they gain in seeing close-up what performance work within theatre, dance, film, or musical ensembles can bring about for marginalized populations. Professional artists begin to turn the spotlight away from the stage or the spatial location of performances and onto the communities and contexts from which performers come. Longitudinal research on Public Works shows positive developments in the mental and physical health of those who formerly lived in despair with little hope and no engagement as full citizens in their neighbourhoods. Professional artists value these outcomes for the promise they hold for new theatregoers and the spread of knowledge about the arts in communities previously unaccustomed to taking part in the life of museums, theatres and other performance spaces.

Moreover, professional artists report their own special sense of participation when they can see how audiences previously unfamiliar with the arts react to immersion experience as participants. For Public Works, the free annual performances in Manhattan's Delacorte Theater in Central Park enable family members, friends, employers, parole officers and building superintendents to see on-stage marginalized individuals they know only in contexts of despair and help-seeking. Previously either unnoticed or regarded with disdain, these same individuals perform Shakespeare in costumes, makeup and hair-dos created just for them. They excel in the show's music and dance. They speak, sing and perform while being surrounded by the words and emotions of Shakespeare's plays. The fact that those on stage are performing Shakespeare, written and presented as a musical, proves to be essential. The bard brings prestige, and audience members across levels of education, income and theatre experience linked to Shakespeare readily heap praise on their friends and family members who take up the challenge of being on stage.

The same points may be made about the many performances of Phakama in unlikely places with unlikely performers. The work stands out in these unlikely places. Moreover, clearly evident is the extent of the planning and managing talents of cast and crew. Also clear to cross-class audience members are the communication skills, strong work ethic and other values not usually assigned to marginalized and excluded populations.

In essence, the answer to the questions of doubters has to come through a deep grasp of what a democracy means. Full participation, engagement and respect define membership in democracies. Nothing builds these necessities for excluded and debased groups better than participatory theatre when done well with forthright intentions of excellence, social messaging and embrace of justice.

I can think of no better way to end this summary than to use the words of a former entrant into the Phakama community. He says it all much better than I can. Osman Bah was a child soldier in Liberia during the worst civil disturbances and rebel activities of that nation. Of his past history, he noted: 'I can't remember anything until I was five years old. Then what I noticed was war. ... I have spent all my life fleeing' (Bah 1994). Osman made his way to London in 2003, after every member of his family had been killed. He had been forced into the army to 'liberate the people of Liberia', and his own killing as a soldier began as he and other boys and girls marched, often drugged, across Liberia. 'It hardens you, makes you feel high, and cold in your mind. Some of us had soft minds, soft spirits, and sympathies. But when you take these drugs, you don't have any regrets. You kill a person like killing a small chicken'.

After months of soldiering, Osman was captured inside Guinea and then allowed to escape and flee. He managed to find his way into the back of a container ship that eventually brought him to England. There he became a refugee under consideration for asylum status. During his time of transition, the Phakama group began a year-long project working in London with asylum-seeking children and youth wanting to learn how to face the future. Juggling, singing, dancing, working with pyrotechnics and creating visual arts brought communication among the young, even when they had no language in common. What they shared was embodiment in new roles with new kinds of skills and plenty of action for executive functions. Weekly, they worked through stories, mime, drawing, drumming and dance to create a drama to be presented in May of 2003. Osman became a leader within the group and a spokesperson for the work of Phakama. In early 2004, he won approval from the Home Office to remain in England. Osman explains: 'Through the [Phakama] arts project, I met a boy called Mohammed from Sierra Leone. We found that we had fought on the same border between Sierra Leone and Guinea. We found out that we had even crossed the river at the same place. I was asked to talk to him'. He needed to find hope in a future, and Phakama leaders feared that he was so despondent he might not pull out of his depressed state of mind. Osman continues: 'I told him to think about his future. Don't think you are a nobody; give yourself a chance; keep on thinking courageously'. The work of Osman and many others from situations diverse in particulars but similar in negative outcomes for both nations and individuals, especially youth, captures the core of adaptive learning through participatory theatre. Osman and others with similar traumatic experiences see in the arts opportunity to bring the past, as painful as it was, together in their mind to give them strength and resolve for the future for themselves and their peers.

Greek history reminds us that democracy and theatre came about in the same era. Entry in the arts with full participation puts the democratic possibilities of playing roles and histories other than one's own. Stories embedded in all the art forms can and should give all citizens the opening to experience the potential of participatory art as platform and practice for democratic thinking towards social justice.

References

Amodio, D. M. and C. D. Frith (2006), 'Meeting of Minds: The Medial Frontal Cortex and Social Cognition', *Nature Review Neuroscience* 7: 268–77.

Bah, O. (2004), 'I was a Child Soldier', *Open Democracy*, https://www.opendemocracy.net/people-migrationeurope/article_1685.jsp (accessed 15 June 2004).

Barrett, K. C., R. Ashley, D. L. Strait and N. Kraus (2013), 'Art and Science: How Musical Training Shapes the Drain', *Frontiers in Psychology*. http://dx/doi.org/10.3389/fpsyg;2013.00713.

Best, J. R., P. H. Miller and L. L. Jones (2009), 'Executive Functions After Age 5: Changes and Correlates', *Developmental Review* 29: 180–200.

Coy, M. W. (ed.) (1989), *Apprenticeship: From Theory to Method and Back Again*, Albany, NY: State University of New York Press.

Donald, M. (2006), 'Art and Cognitive Evolution', in M. Turner (ed.), *The Artful Mind: Cognitive Science and the Riddle of Human Creativity*, New York: Oxford University Press, 3–20.

Goody, E. (1989), 'Learning, Apprenticeship, and the Division of Labor', in M. W. Coy (ed.), *Apprenticeship: From Theory to Method and Back Again*, Albany, NY: State University of New York Press, 223–56.

Heath, S. B. (2012), 'Informal Learning', in J. Banks (ed.), *Encyclopedia of Diversity in Education*, New York: Sage Publications.

Heath, S. B. (2015), 'Museums, Theaters, and Youth Orchestras: Advancing Creative Arts and Sciences Within Under-resourced Communities', in William G. Tierney (ed.), *The Annals of the American Academy of Political and Social Science*, Baltimore: Johns Hopkins University Press, 177–99.

Heath, S. B. (2016), 'The Benefits of Ensemble Music Experience (and why these benefits matter so much in underserved communities)', in C. Witkowski (ed.), *El Sistema: Music for Social Change*, London: Omnibus Press, 73–94.

Heath, S. B. and L. Smyth (1999), *ArtShow: Youth and Community Development*, Washington, DC: Partners for Liveable Communities.

Heath, S. B. and K. Robinson (2004), 'Making a Way: Youth Arts and Learning in International Perspective', in N. Rabkin and R. Redmond (eds), *Putting the Arts in the Picture: Reframing Education in the 21st Century*, Chicago: Center for Arts Policy, Columbia College, 107–26.

Heath, S. B., S. Lie and T. B. Hayden (2016), *Public Works: On the Stage in our New York City*, New York: The Public Theater.

Lave, J. and E. Wenger (1991), *Situated Learning: Legitimate Peripheral Participation*, London: Cambridge University Press.

Pallasmaa, J. (2009), *The Thinking Hand*, Chichester: John Wiley & Sons.

Pine, B. J. and J. H. Gilmore (1999), *The Experience Economy: Work is Theatre and Every Business a Stage*, Cambridge, MA: Harvard Business School Press.

Rogoff, B. (1990), *Apprenticeship in Thinking: Cognitive Development in Social Context*, New York: Oxford University Press.

Singer, T. (2006), 'The Neuronal Basis and Ontogeny of Empathy and Mind Reading: Review of Literature and Implications for Future Research', *Neuroscience & Biobehavioral Reviews* 30: 855–63.

Squire, L. R. (1992), 'Declarative and Nondeclarative Memory: Multiple Brain Systems Supporting Learning and Memory', *Journal of Cognitive Neuroscience* 4 (3): 232–43.

Tomasello, M. and M. Carpenter (2007), 'Shared Intentionality', *Developmental Science* 10: 121–5.

Wenger, E. (1998), *Communities of Practice: Learning, Meaning, and Identity*, London: Cambridge University Press.

Wenger, E., R. McDermott and W. M. Snyder (2002), *Cultivating Communities of Practice*, Cambridge, MA: Harvard Business School Press.

Wilson, F. (1998), *The Hand: How its Use Shapes the Brain, Language, and Human Culture*, New York: Vintage.

Zuk, J., C. Benjamin, A. Kenyon and N. Gaab (2014), 'Behavioral and Neural Correlates of Executive Functioning in Musicians and Non-musicians', *PLoS ONE* 9 (6).

EPILOGUE

The plain fact is that the planet does not need more successful people. But it does desperately need more peacemakers, healers, restorers, storytellers, and lovers of every kind. It needs people who live well in their places. It needs people of moral courage willing to join the fight to make the world habitable and humane. And these qualities have little to do with success as we have defined it

D. W. ORR IN STONE AND BARLOW 2004: 12

We finished preparing the manuscript for this book in 2017, a time of humanitarian crises. The civil war in Syria has decimated the country, killing over a quarter of a million people in the last five years and displacing over thirteen million people within and beyond the country. This humanitarian crisis has become a political crisis across Europe as ideas of borders, belonging and boundaries of care fuel xenophobia and protectionism. The implications of Brexit, Britain's exit from the European Union, the result of a narrowly-won referendum, have caused economic uncertainty, an increased reporting of hate crime and widespread concern about the rights of generations of people from across the EU who now live and work in the UK. In the United States, Donald Trump has become president despite Hilary Clinton, the Democratic Party candidate, having won the popular vote, in a campaign characterized by misogyny, racism and accusations of corruption. The process of democracy is messy, contested, contradictory and, at times, characterized by violence: it is not an easily found consensus.

In the UK we are experiencing the effects of the Conservative government's reforms on all levels of education: reduced funding, an increasingly prescribed and limited curriculum, more testing and a greater emphasis on competition and league tables. We are also reeling from the effects of austerity politics resulting in financial cuts to services that reduce the quality of life for the poorest and most vulnerable in our society. Of course these political priorities and responses mean that the arts suffer.

South Africa, meanwhile, is challenging the very existence of the proclaimed 'rainbow' nation. Inequality remains rife, xenophobia and violence are on the increase, the cost of education is rising and protests are common. The recent RhodesMustFall and FeesMustFall movements at universities throughout the country have placed the call for free, decolonized education, across all levels, firmly on the agenda. These movements evidence the urgency of challenging what is being referred to as a 'post-apartheid apartheid'.

Phakama, a practice developed in the crucible of another specific cultural moment, sustains a direct response to the current one. It offers a relational practice – educational, social, cultural – which reminds us that learning is a two-way process which can only take place in an environment where each person is valued, which demands that we give space and time to bringing people from different backgrounds together, and which celebrates creativity and humanity. It insists that interdependent practice is essential if we are to create relationships and a sustainable society.

Phakama celebrated twenty years of work in 2016.

In the UK, the practice thrives under the auspices of Project Phakama which continues to develop projects with young adults and, at times, with children and older people, focusing on collaborative projects and training. Few of the facilitators now leading the projects experienced the first international projects but the practice – particularly that of Give and Gain – remains central to the work.

In South Africa, although the Phakama organization is dormant, facilitators and participants continue to make work that is true to the Phakama ethos in many different settings: within university curriculums, schools, theatre companies, small arts centres and in major theatres establishments. Many of these have been discussed in this book.

In Lesotho, India, Ireland, Argentina, Brazil and Indonesia, Phakama has influenced the practice of leading artists and arts educators. While organizational structures may not have been feasible to maintain in these locations, the practice continues to live, disseminated through individuals' practices. In each of these places there are participants and facilitators, some working in arts and education, some in other fields including human rights and social justice, who have engaged in the Phakama process and continue to practise it in their professional and personal lives. Some, but by no means all, of their testimonies are in this book.

Theatre and performance projects committed to working in and with communities require financial support to be realized. Phakama, with its emphasis on collaborative practice and team-facilitation, may be considered to be a particularly costly approach to participatory practice. In a context where funders require that artists and organizations provide evidence of the social impacts of, often, short-term projects, we advocate for the imperative of time: time to reflect, to understand what's at stake, what's possible. This book documents the longitudinal reach, depth and range of impacts of Phakama articulated though the testimony of participants, artists and collaborators.

Some of the most potent cultural sharing has taken place in large-scale international collaborations. Realizing these projects relies on funding to support travel and communication. There are different ways to sustain projects in the host countries listed above including investment in training or in local organizational structures. This is challenging. However, the practice does not need money to be applied within programmes and projects that are already running. Phakama is about what can be found in the room, turning places into performance spaces and, most importantly, it is about connections between people. We can all apply Phakama to our work.

This book not only details work that has been done, it is a provocation for work that is yet to be done. It is about an approach to practice. By outlining it, exploring its tenets and philosophy in action, it is another way of disseminating Phakama as an approach to be considered, employed and adapted. We hope it will offer a critical challenge, however small, to the cultural moment we find ourselves in and not only lend another voice to those who are resisting, but offer a practical way forward. It sits alongside the work of many other practitioners who are developing similarly effective educational practice in both statutory and voluntary education, and in a variety of theatre and community settings. The exercises in the book are examples of ways in which the Phakama approaches of participant-centred, non-hierarchical, responsive performance have been realized. We invite you, the reader, to use your skills, competencies and imaginations to develop many more.

Take it, do what you will with it – but keep doing it.

Reference

Stone, M. K. and Z. Barlow (2004), *Ecological Literacy: Educating Our Children for a Sustainable World*, San Francisco: Sierra.

FIGURE 10 Stone Cairn.

Stone Cairn – a place of fire and forgiveness – and not forgetting.
Dedicated to those we have lost – 1996–2016 – with love.

INDEX